MEDIEVAL
BUILDING
TECHNIQUES

MEDIEVAL BUILDING TECHNIQUES

GÜNTHER BINDING

TRANSLATED BY ALEX CAMERON

TEMPUS

Originally published as Der Mittelalterliche Baubetrieb in
Zeitgenössichen Abbildungen 2001

This translation first published 2004

Tempus Publishing Limited
The Mill, Brimscombe Port,
Stroud, Gloucestershire, GL5 2QG
www.tempus-publishing.com

British Library Cataloguing in Publication Data.
A catalogue record for this book is available from the British Library.

ISBN 0 7524 2882 9

Typesetting and origination by Tempus Publishing Limited.
Printed in Great Britain by Midway Colour Print, Wiltshire.

CONTENTS

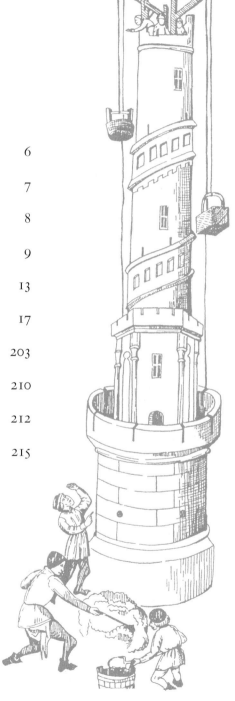

PREFACE

In 1987 we produced the *Katalog der zeitgenössischen Darstellungen des mittelalterlichen Baubetriebs Westeuropas* ('Catalogue of contemporary representations of West European building techniques'; 32nd publication of the Architecture Department of the Institute for Art History at the University of Cologne). At this time, we believed that, after the earlier editions of 1972, *Romanischer Baubetrieb in zeitgenössischen Darstellungen* ('Romanesque building techniques in contemporary representations'; 2nd publication of the Architecture Department of the Institute for Art History at the University of Cologne), and 1978, *Der mittelalterliche Baubetrieb nördlich der Alpen in zeitgenössischen Darstellungen* ('Medieval building techniques north of the Alps in contemporary representations'; by Günther Binding and Norbert Nußbaum, Wissenschaftliche Buchgesellschaft, Darmstadt), we had created a comprehensive record of 673 numbered examples. Soon afterwards, we were sent additional material by Wolfgang Schöller, published in 1987 as 'Ein Katalog mittelalterlicher Baubetriebsdarstellungen' in *Technikgeschichte* 54, 1987, pp. 77–100, with 125 examples, some of which were unknown to us. Anja Sibylle Steinmetz-Dollinger found further illustrations while preparing her dissertation, so that in 1992 Anne Schunicht-Rawe was able to prepare a supplementary volume of 193 examples (47th publication of the Architecture Department of the Institute for Art History at the University of Cologne). Angelika Steinmetz-Oppelland had already copied most of the original representations using a proven method in 1987.

The newly discovered illustrations are interpolated into the numbering of the 1987 catalogue using the suffixes a, b, c, etc. In this catalogue as in the 1987 edition, certain representations of tools in irrelevant or obscure contexts have been omitted; the tools most affected are axe, hatchet, saw, square and compasses, and all methods of transportation. As this work is concerned only with pictures of building techniques, we have selected only those representations, or parts thereof, which are relevant, and have enlarged them. However, other often complete images are given full references in the catalogue. Since 1987 we have received further information and corrections from correspondents, which have been incorporated into the present revised edition, so that some 900 representations covering the period up to 1500 are now included.

This new edition was produced by Maria Spitz, Eva Birkenstock, Akiko Bernhöft and Laura Frahm. Martina Schönenborn prepared the illustrations, including the redrawing of some of the earlier images. I would like to thank the Wissenschaftliche Buchgesellschaft, and in particular Herr Karl Freger, for the opportunity to republish after twenty-three years.

I thank the numerous libraries and museums who have provided support and generously prepared copies of works held by them.

The evaluation of pictorial representations whose forthcoming appearance was announced in the foreword to the 1987 edition has in the meantime been published together with the written sources: *Mittelalterlicher Baubetrieb in West- und Mitteleuropa bis 1460 mit Ausblicken auf England und Italien* by Günther Binding with Gabriele Annas, Bettina Jost and Anne Schunicht, Wissenschaftliche Buchgesellschaft, Darmstadt, 1993. Representations up to 1250 are examined in *Planen und Bauen im frühen und hohen Mittelalternach den Schriftquellen bis 1250* by Günther Binding and Susanne Linscheid-Burdich, Wissenschaftliche Buchgesellschaft, 2002.

With the appearance of this new edition I take my leave of the Architectural History Department of the Institute of Art History of the University of Cologne, where I have been curator of the collection of representations of medieval building techniques since 1970. I would like to thank all my keen and intelligent colleagues, particularly Norbert Nußbaum, who collaborated as my research assistant for the 1987 book and who is now to be my successor.

Günther Binding
Cologne, August 2001

FOREWORD by Dr Glyn Coppack

Those of us who study or work on medieval buildings are often only vaguely aware of how they were constructed, the tools and machinery used, or the master craftsmen who designed and built them. Today stone and timber are sawn and often dressed mechanically, raised by powered hoists, and set from tubular steel-framed scaffolding. Not so in the Middle Ages when everything was cut by hand, lifted into position by manpower with the simplest of pulleys, and put in position on the flimsiest of wooden scaffolds. Günther Binding and his researchers have done us a magnificent service, tracking down, analysing and referencing hundreds of contemporary illustrations of medieval builders at work. Some of these illustrations are well known, for instance the illustrations of building at St Alban's Abbey, though I would have been hard put to tell you where the original was before I saw this book, as well as many others hidden in European libraries that see few English scholars. All come together to give an incredibly accurate portrayal of how even our greatest medieval buildings were put together.

Stone was worked with axe and hammer. Chisels were used only for carving until the fourteenth century. It was also worked on the ground, not on a bench or banker, and was carried on stretcher-like pallets. Mortar was mixed in wooden bins, worked with mattocks or mortar-picks, and carried to the walling masons in hods. Large stones were lifted using windlass and crane, suspended from the pincer-like jaws of an external lewis, trusting only to gravity and balance. Masons worked on hurdles laid on short pieces of timber, putlogs, built into the wall as it went up. No wonder medieval accounts of building are full of stories of terrible accidents and miraculous survivals. Building work was seasonal, and here we see how masonry was protected in the winter – walls are capped with straw or rush thatching to keep out the rain and frost while the lime mortar slowly cured. What we see is an industry highly dependent on the skill of its workforce, directed by the master mason, with his badges of office, his

compasses and square. We see how he laid out complicated designs, how mouldings were cut from his templates, and the conditions in which the masons worked. All of the images are contemporary, drawn by people who actually saw the work being done. What we realise from the drawings is how much timber was needed for the masons to work – centring and scaffolding, wooden templates, the hods, their carriers and stands, the wheelbarrows and pallets. Few traces of these survive anywhere.

The carvers were the most skilled of medieval masons, and here we see them at work, their tools little changed today, but the conditions they worked in were much more rudimentary.

Every bit as skilled as the masons were the carpenters. Indeed, their trade was older in medieval Europe. Timber was prepared not by sawing but was cleft with beetle and frow (mallet and wedge), a highly skilled practice that demanded a thorough knowledge of how the grain of the timber ran. It was dressed with axes and adzes which, in skilled hands, left a flawless surface. Saws were used to cut timber to length, and in the later Middle Ages the pit saw was introduced to convert timber. The range of saws, both one- and two-handed, is incredible. They are rarely recovered in excavation, and were it not for the range displayed in contemporary illustrations we would not realise how many types there were. We do find drills, usually shell-bits used for drilling dowel and nail holes, but here we see the wooden braces needed to turn them. We also have planes and chisels, hammers and mallets, in fact the whole of the medieval carpenter's toolkit, and we can see at a glance how they were used.

Neither mason nor carpenter could work without the blacksmiths, sharpening tools, making iron cramps and nails as well as the ornate hinges for doors and shutters. Other trades are shown too, the tilers providing both roof and floor tiles, the plasterers, daubers and painters. The medieval building industry was every bit as complex as the modern building trade. This book shows us just how complex and skilled it was.

Günther Binding has done us a remarkable service, bringing together, as only a German scholar could, a remarkable collection of illustrations of medieval building in progress. It enables us to see how buildings were put together by real people in real time, with consummate skill. We will never look at surviving medieval buildings in the same way again.

Glyn Coppack

TRANSLATOR'S NOTE

For ease of reference, the numbering of the sources used here is the same as that used in the German edition. The sources are ordered according to the town or city in which they can be found today (or where they were last known, in the case of lost artefacts). These towns are generally listed alphabetically, but occasional departures from this order have been necessary where the town's usual English name is different from the German. Sources located in Wrocław, for example, appear under B (for Breslau), and those in Vienna under W (for Wien).

I would like to thank Dr Glyn Coppack for reading through a draft of the translation and suggesting apposite English equivalents for some troublesome items. His extensive knowledge of medieval architecture and building techniques was invaluable.

Alex Cameron
September 2003

INTRODUCTION

The Christian Middle Ages considered the creation of the world and the order of the cosmos within the framework of a general cosmology, and saw prestigious sacred architecture especially as a representation of the cosmos. Rationally considered, ordered and intentionally linked activity is the basis for both. Mankind's attempts at construction represent God's act of creation, which itself is referred to in Amos 9:6 as *aedificare* (to build) and *fundare* (to found). The work of the medieval architect is bound by the demands of the Book of Wisdom, 11:21: *Omnia mensura et numero et pondere disposuisti* (thou hast ordered all things by measure, number and weight). This correspondence between the work of the architect and that of Creation leads eventually to St Thomas Aquinas' definition in his commentary on Aristotle's *Metaphysics*, whereby the architect is, as it were, the all-encompassing craftsman (*architector dicitur quasi artifex principalis*). In the same mould the *Bible moralisée*, illustrated with miniatures in Paris around 1230, shows the Creator with a pair of compasses, describing the arc of the world's outline (see nos 405, 555, 621).

The medieval master mason sees himself as comparable to Solomon, who built the Temple, which serves as a prototype to the *ecclesia* of the new Christian era, which itself is the forerunner to the heavenly Jerusalem in traditional eschatology. The so-called *Mainzer Pontifikale* of 950–63 contains a chapter, *De aedificanda ecclesia*, which deals with the construction of Solomon's Temple, through which Solomon fulfilled his father David's wishes. The reference to the Temple is based on the theological concept that the *ecclesia* is an improved version of its antitype the Temple, just as the cult of the Temple is mirrored in the liturgy of the Church. The theological concept of typology is, as Friedrich Ohly has demonstrated, a Christocentric interpretation based on history, according to which the objects, people and events of the Old Testament are forerunners or prototypes which find their perfected versions in eschatology. The old version will be raised up in the time of Christ and his Church, as a glimpse of the future. The types of the Old Testament point towards the antitypes of the New Testament or of the present-day Church, which in its turn is a prefiguration of the future. In the microcosm of buildings, mankind can reflect the universal cosmos of time, space and creation: 'The bringing together of the past and the future into one whole visible at once to the eye turns the stream of history into a stationary possession through visualisation.' According to Hugo von St Viktor (*c.*1096–1141) in *De vanitate mundi*, 'you have inside you another eye, whose clarity far surpasses that of your natural eye, which can perceive simultaneously the past, the present and the future'.

Similar typological comparisons are made, with the support of the Venerable Bede (d.735), by the former Archbishop of Trier and professor at the court school in Aachen, Amalar of Metz (*c.*775/80–*c.*850), in his systematic work dedicated to Emperor Louis the Pious, *Liber officialis*, which was created in 823 and was highly esteemed throughout the Middle Ages: 'Therefore, when we … come together to pray to God, it is expedient for us to know that we must take on the work of building the walls of our churches (*opera murorum aedificandum ecclesiae nostrae*), just as He took on that of building the City of Jerusalem.... The walls of our church have as their foundation Christ; on this foundation are supported the Apostles, and those who through them have believed, believe now and will believe. At the present day we are part of the ordered structure of this wall, which will continue to be built until the end of the world. Every saint, for whom eternal life has been predestined by God, is a stone in this wall. And one stone is laid upon another, so long as the teachers of the Church attract younger disciples to the same studies, to teach, to correct and to strengthen within the holy Church. Each one has above it another stone, set in place by brotherly love.'

Medieval representations of buildings under construction are depicted as part of this concept, for the illustrations were created in monasteries or cathedral scriptoria. It is not the act of construction in itself, but the progress of current work within the framework of eternal improvement, which is worthy of representation as corresponding to theological examples of building; for, ever since its earliest days, the *ecclesia* has always been under construction, a work in progress, as stated in Ezra 5:16: '[He] laid the foundation of the house of God which is in Jerusalem: and since that time even unto now hath it been in building, and yet it is not finished' (*et ex eo tempore usque nunc aedificatur et necdum completum est*). The *structura muri*, the ordered positioning of stones upon each other, is also the means of representation, i.e. the construction 'of the present day'. Therefore medieval representations of building are a reliable source of contemporary building techniques for all skills, methods and tools.

'Contemporary depictions are often too primitive or downright wrong, because the illuminators did not fully understand their subject or because, when working at home on what were often very stylised representations, they relied more on remembering visual impressions of their subject rather than making precise draughtsman's studies on site. Consequently, without further information it is not possible to create a reliable picture of past events.' So writes Bodo W. Jaxtheimer (*Knaurs Stilkunde Gotik*, 1982, p. 55) in the chapter entitled 'Building in the High Middle Ages', thereby repeating a widely held opinion. This may be true in the case of many representations, but many others nevertheless show a truly surprising understanding of technical details. This applies both to a number of the earlier illustrations, such as those in the *Hortus deliciarum* of Herrad von Landsberg (*c*.1175–91; no. 526), and a pen-and-ink drawing from the Life of St Alban by Matthew Paris (*c*.1250; no. 168), and also to those from later periods, such as the detailed depiction of putlog scaffolding in a Flemish book of hours (see no. 254), in which the elements and their connections using knots are individually shown, and a mosaic in St Mark's Cathedral in Venice (second half of the thirteenth century, see no. 592). Similarly, the *Chroniques* of J. de Tavernier (*c*.1450, no. 103) give us an insight into carpentry techniques, and a miniature by Jean Fouquet (late fifteenth century, no. 462) gives information on stonemasonry during the construction of the base of a cathedral-like building.

Few illustrations are known from the early period, mainly through copies of late Classical versions of the *Psychomachia* of Prudentius (tenth or eleventh centuries), where Concordia or Fides are shown measuring the construction site or the building itself, but also in a manuscript from St Gallen of around 1000 (no. 541), which shows dressing, cutting and transport of stones during church construction as a prefiguration of the *ecclesia*. The same applies in the mid-ninth-century *Psalterium aureum* from St Gallen (no. 540), which shows work being carried out on an almost complete building. However, even as early as the first half of the eleventh century, a pen-and-ink drawing in the Noailles Bible in Paris (no. 431) shows a church under construction with a double arcade on pillars of a contemporary style. It depicts three people working with stone blocks using a trowel, hammer and plumbline, and the blocks are being brought to the scene by workmen and a four-wheeled ox-drawn cart. Similarly, a fresco on the central nave vaulting in the abbey church of Saint-Savin-sur-Gartempe in the Vienne department of France (no. 544) shows the construction of a tower with arcades below and dressed blocks above, and is the earliest known portrayal of a 'gallows'-style crane with rope and pulley.

In 1023 a monk at Monte Cassino illustrated Hrabanus Maurus' work *De origine rerum* as part of *De linguis gentium, aedificatio turris*, in which he shows a square tower with pole scaffolding and a ladder as well as four workmen and a master mason. Aelfric's metrical version of the Pentateuch and Joshua from the second half of the eleventh century (no. 265) also shows a church under construction but almost completed, with scaffolding, ladders and workmen, and a man overseeing the whole enterprise, namely God striking an omniscient pose on a ladder pointing heavenwards.

The Utrecht Psalter (no. 583) from the first third of the ninth century illustrates Psalm 101 verses 14-15: *Tu suscitans misereberis Sion quia tempus est ut miserearis eius quoniam venit tempus quoniam venit pactum | Quoniam placitos fecerunt servi tui lapides eius et pulverem eius miserabilem* (Ps. 102:13-14 of the Authorised Version, 'Thou shalt arise, and have mercy upon Zion: for the time to favour her, yea, the set time, is come. | For thy servants take pleasure in her stones, and favour the dust thereof.'). Inside a town wall of dressed stone with round corner towers, two gabled constructions and a central building are, three winged angels working with hammer and chisel; this view is recalled in a similar depiction on fol. 38 (no. 582) but instead of the angels there are seven men with short overalls. In these and other similar early representations, though, a clear sense of the unfinished nature of the buildings is missing.

Around 1130 or 1140 the church at Idensen, selected as the shrine to Sigward, bishop of Minden (d.1140), was decorated (no. 208). The pictures on the south side of the ceiling of Old Testament scenes offer corresponding prefigurations of the New Testament, including the building of the Tower of Babel which is assigned to the picture of the Pentecost. The construction of the Tower of Babel is found with this antithetical, prefigurative meaning in many varied representations in the following centuries, often with different interpretations. Bernard of Clairvaux (1091–1153) wanted above all to abandon the Jewish literal understanding of the Old Testament, and concentrate on its Christian, i.e. typological and allegorical, meaning. In the middle of the twelfth century, under the influence of Abelard in Paris, Petrus Helie made the decisive step towards a positive interpretation; according to him, every language is rationally constructed, since language itself is an invention of Reason: *Vocem enim format artifex in diversa linguarum genera secundum artem grammaticum*. Thus the construction of the Tower of Babel is moved into a new context, and by the late twelfth century we begin to see a growth in Babel images, which serve more as practical depictions than elaborations of a principle, almost taking the form of self-portraits of workers engaged in building cathedrals. The illustration of the reconstruction of Solomon's Temple in Mid Bavaria of around 1180 is hardly distinguishable from that of the building of the Babylonian tower. Consequently, many churches under construction, even those intended to illustrate the principle of antitypical improvement, are represented realistically, so that the achievements of founders and builders which correspond to the teachings of Bishop Bernward are represented in pictures and reveal items of real technical interest. This begins with the Remaklus altar-piece at Stavelot of around 1150 (no. 99), now known only from a drawing, and reaches its apogee around 1250

with the pen-and-ink drawing of the construction of St Albans by King Offa (no. 168) in a collection of manuscripts in Dublin, compiled and probably illustrated by Matthew Paris. In this illustration, the construction process is portrayed in detail, including all those involved – not only patrons, overseers and master masons but also bricklayers, stonemasons, carpenters and general handymen, along with all the tools which would have been available to them then. This degree of detail and precision in the portrayal of individual technical elements in illustrations of both church construction and the Tower of Babel becomes common from the end of the twelfth century and remains prominent for the rest of the medieval period. It is represented in the fourteenth and fifteenth centuries particularly in miniatures and at the end of the fifteenth century is commonly seen in woodcuts. These demonstrate the development of building techniques through numerous new details, but the meaning remains unchanged, as shown by the illustration in Steffen Arnde's Low German Bible of 1494 from Lübeck (no. 288), which can be directly compared to the 1250 Dublin image (no. 168).

From the richness of the fourteenth and fifteenth centuries we will select only a few examples. A representative of the group of portrayals of the building of the Tower of Babel in the *Weltchronik* of Rudolf von Ems is the Wolfenbüttel manuscript, illustrated in Bohemia under the influence of the Wenzel workshop around 1340, with unusually life-like, part-coloured pen-and-ink drawings freely copied from earlier works. From the same period, a Zürich manuscript (no. 651) shows two cranes on a high tower, one from Stuttgart of 1383 (no. 537) gives a great deal of technical detail, and finally one from Kassel of 1385 (no. 214) with richly detailed putlog scaffolding. These and other contemporary representations grew out of the general principle that the Creator was responsible not only for the origin of earthly existence but also for its development; that after the Fall of Man and the Babel episode, the history of the world becomes a history of God's saving grace; that between the past and the future, the present as observed at the time of the work becomes a historical reality. The representation in pictures of the ongoing construction of the Tower can express its message of truth only if it corresponds to present reality, for the tide of history can only become a fixed idea through visualisation.

The trouble taken to ensure precision in technical details grows during the fifteenth century. The Girat de Roussillon manuscript of 1447 in the Wiener Nationalbibliothek (no. 620) shows a town with seven churches, of which four are under construction. Stonemasons, mortar mixers, bricklayers and labourers are enthusiastically occupied in completing God's work: the theme is a 'church landscape', the ongoing construction of the *ecclesia*. J. de Tavernier's *Chroniques et Conquestes de Charlemaine* of 1450–60 in Brussels (no. 106) shows with particular devotion and detail each technical task involved in the construction of a church with a polygonal chancel. In *Les Chroniques de Hainaut* of *c*.1465–70 in Brussels (nos 112, 115), the progress of church construction is shown in a characteristic, albeit somewhat summary, way. The *Livre des rois, mers des histoires* in the Bibliothèque Nationale in Paris (no. 434) shows a similar scene of church construction to that in the Paris MS lat. 8846 (no. 440). Finally it is worth mentioning Jean Fouquet's miniature in the *Antiquités et Guerres des Juifs* of the late fifteenth century in the Bibliothèque Nationale, Paris (no. 462), as here a Gothic cathedral is portrayed in all its delicate splendour while in the foreground the builders prepare the material so that it can be lifted with a crane. In a corner bay of a sumptuous secular building stands the king, overseeing like Christ the progress of the work, which is Gothic cathedral and Tower of Babel rolled into one, a splendid combination of the iconographical and constructional sources of medieval imagery, and at the same time a timely endpiece.

With the advent of the Renaissance and the dissemination of the ten books on architecture by the Roman architectural theorist Vitruvius and successor volumes by Alberti and Palladio, among others, the religious portrayal of building is superseded by a more documentary presentation of building methods: in other words, building itself as an organisational, financial and professional achievement becomes worthy of illustration. This can be seen in the often large-format paintings of the Tower of Babel of the sixteenth century, which concentrate on the representation of technical and organisational achievements.

TOOLS AND EQUIPMENT

BRICKLAYING

Trowel: for spreading mortar on the upper surface of the wall; flat and triangular or hollowed and tapering.

Hammer: used for knocking stones into position.

Square/straight edge: made of wood, with one long, thin side and one short, broad side.

Plumbline: a cord with a tapering lead weight at the bottom, for checking vertical alignment of walls; to allow it to swing more freely, the cord is passed through a small block of wood, which is held in the other hand against the edge to be checked.

Level: for checking horizontal surfaces; consists of a triangle with a mark at right-angles in the middle of the base-line, which can be extended with a flat length of wood. A lead weight suspended from the top of the triangle must hang directly over the mark. A similar tool was made for checking vertical alignments.

Mortar-mixing bin: a box edged with heavy boards used for mixing mortar on the ground (for hods and baskets, see 'Transporting Materials').

Mortar-mixing pick: a wooden or metal (?) blade set at right-angles across the handle. The blade may be rectangular or pointed.

Mortar shovel

Mortar tub: for carrying small quantities of mortar to where is is needed.

STONEMASONRY, SCULPTURE

Stone hammer: a hacking tool used in both hands, with a short wooden handle and a two-pointed iron head for coarse working of newly cut slabs of stone.

Stone axe: a hacking tool used in both hands, with a 30–40cm long wooden handle and iron head with two sharp edges up to 10cm long, parallel to the handle. Used for final smoothing of stone surfaces after coarse working.

Serrated stone hammer: similar to the stone hammer but with a serrated edge (usually only on one side), for coarser working of surfaces to a point.

Pointed stone hammer: a dual-purpose hacking tool used in both hands, with one side of the iron head tapering to a point and the other ending in a flat edge.

Maul or mallet: a hemispherical head made of beech-wood with a short handle for one-handed use, for beating and working iron.

Lump hammer: an iron head with two striking surfaces and a handle designed for one-handed operation, for beating and working iron.

Punch: a roughly 20cm long iron tool with a pyramidal point, held in one hand and struck with a maul or more often a lump hammer. Used for coarse shaping of bosses down to more detailed treatment of surfaces.

Chisel: a roughly 20cm long iron tool with a 2–4cm wide cutting edge, held in one hand and hit with the maul. Used for carving profiles and borders and for finer work on surfaces (broader examples used for this purpose are also known as scrapers).

Claw chisel: a chisel with a sharp, serrated cutting edge for coarser work on flat surfaces.

Square/straight edge: a triangular wooden tool with a right-angled outside edge; also used as a straight edge for checking surfaces of stone blocks.

Compasses: two straight, pointed arms connected by a hinge by which they can be turned; made of wood with curved guides and metal points or in smaller examples without metal guides.

Precision compasses: two arms, attached at a moveable hinge, which bend inwards; used for measuring, especially on complicated profiles.

Measuring staff: a 6–8ft long staff.

Template: from which numerous identical stones can be produced; made of wood or metal.

Stool: a usually round seat with one, three or four legs.

CARPENTRY

Axe: A two-handed tool with a long wooden handle fixed through the eye of a wedge-shaped iron blade whose edge is parallel to the handle; used for felling, splitting and coarse shaping of tree trunks.

Hatchet: a one-handed tool, somewhat smaller than the axe but with a broader blade and shorter handle; it has a wedge-shaped head with a straight cutting edge for splitting and cutting smaller pieces of wood, such as pegs, tenons etc., as well as a hammer-head on the upper side of the blade for knocking nails into place.

Broad axe: a one or two-handed tool with a broad, slightly curved blade for working on beams; the single-edged blade is off-set c.6–8cm away from the handle to avoid injury to the carpenter while cutting at beams.

Roofing axe: a two-handed tool with a round, curved blade attached at right angles to the handle, used for cutting out guttering, hollow moulds etc.

Adze: a short wooden handle attached to an iron head with two cutting edges, one vertical, parallel to the handle, and the other running at right-angles, for cutting mortises in beams.

Chisel: a wooden-handled cutting tool with different shapes of cutting edge; it is struck with a mallet to cut out grooves.

Auger or long-handled drill: a long iron rod with a spoon or auger bit, with a wooden bar at the top for two-handed operation.

Long saw: a 2m-long iron saw blade with two wooden cross-pieces as handles, one fixed and the other removable, used for splitting beams.

Frame or log saw: a thin saw blade fixed in a heavy wooden frame, used for vertical cutting of planks or beams, operated by two men.

Two-handed saw: a two-man saw consisting of an iron blade 90–120cm long and 10–18cm broad, with a convex cutting edge, and vertical handles of horn at each end, for cutting even timbers.

Hand saw: an H-shaped wooden framework with a fixed thin saw blade and a cord attached to a wooden knob on the opposite side for adjusting the tension. Used for cutting smaller pieces of timber. A variant consists of a fairly stiff saw blade with medium-sized teeth and a sturdy wooden handle.

Saw: with a very thin saw blade which tapers to a point.

Underwater saw: (Villard de Honnecourt; cf. no. 469).

Guide line: consists of a coil of rope and a tub of dye. The rope is dyed and two men tie it to a beam and leave it to dry on the wood, so that it makes a straight coloured line on the wood in preparation for splitting with an axe or for sawing.

Trestle or sawing horse: a wooden device consisting of a beam fitted with four legs.

Staple or dog: a U-shaped forged iron tool with pointed ends; during cutting or fixing together it secures planks together or to the trestle.

Plane: mainly portrayed in connection with half-timbering work.

TRANSPORTING MATERIALS

Hod: for mortar or sometimes stones; an elliptical wooden dish, more or less concave, measuring *c.*60 x 35cm, sometimes with horizontal handles on the narrow edges. South of the Alps it may also have a long handle or a flat, oblong wooden chest wih sloping sides. So that it can be filled and more easily lifted onto the shoulder, the hod is sometimes placed on a stand with long braced legs.

Hawk: a portable wooden stand, made from two planks connected together in a V-shape or at right angles with open sides, kept in place with two bars laid across the shoulders.

Pannier: consisting of two parallel bars connected by braces at right-angles, or by a piece of leather hung between them; used by two labourers for carrying stones.

Wheelbarrow: consisting of two sturdy boards with an axle and wheel between them at one end, and braces at right angles behind the wheel which at the other end are reduced to handles. It may additionally be fitted with straps which fit round the neck to assist in carrying heavy loads.

Handcart: a sturdy four-wheeled transport cart (*carrus, carrum, caruca, carecta*); a special two- or four-wheeled cart for large loads (*plaustrum*); a normal four-wheeled cart (*currus*); or a two-wheeled cart for smaller loads (*carpentum*).

Sledge: for transporting large loads in winter or over wet, muddy ground.

LIFTING (mechanical lifting equipment)

Pulley: a pulley-wheel attached to a horizontal bar between two uprights.

Boom crane: made from a vertical crane shaft, often fitted with a movable foot, and a horizontal boom attached to the shaft, which is strengthened by a strut beneath, either forming a triangle or fixed close up against the shaft. The lifting rope is fed through a pulley on the end of the boom. In order to reduce the tension on the boom, it is often fitted diagonally. Booms can also be doubled up and linked together with cross-pieces.

T-shaped crane: a shaft with a T-shaped boom on top, both of whose ends carry a pulley.

Trestle crane: with boom.

Winching Equipment
windlass: either free-standing or attached to a crane, intended for use with a guide pulley and with a boom crane, fitted with a handle of radial spokes or a spoked wheel.

treadwheel: free-standing or linked to the crane, either at the foot of the crane or brought up to the working level.

Building materials are raised in large *tubs* with hand-holes, or less often in *buckets* or *baskets*, or using *pallets*, rectangular wooden lifting platforms which are attached to the hoist by four ropes, one at each corner.

Dressed stone blocks are raised on the hoist using an internal or an external lewis.

An *internal lewis* consists of a straight piece of iron and two ancillary wedge-shaped elements, which are bolted with a pin onto a metal claw in the shape of a swallow's tail. The claw is fitted into a similar-shaped depression chiselled into the upper surface of the stone block.

An *external lewis* (for lifting/gripping): consists of two iron claws connected by a turning bolt, whose upper ends receive two moveable hanging chains in an iron ring. Pulling the hoisting rope which is attached to the ring applies pressure to the arms, which grip the stone block in specially created holes on opposite sides.

SCAFFOLDING

Outrigger scaffolding (or 'flying' or 'suspended scaffolding'): used for masonry and jointing work. Scaffolding planks or hurdles lie on horizontal supports, whole, halved or quartered round or squared timbers, which are fastened into the thickness of the wall during the course of construction; they are supported from underneath by struts linked diagonally to the wall; the lower ends of the struts can be attached using the holes left by the previous row of horizontal supports after removal, or indeed to the supports themselves. The struts are generally straight but can be slightly curved. Instead of support using struts, vertical ladder-like constructions are also found, which are attached to the layer of horizontal supports beneath; in this case the wall serves as a counterweight and prevents the lower level from tipping. Outrigger scaffolding is often portrayed without supports and it is to be presumed that the horizontal supports reached right through the wall to the inside and were weighed down with a few layers of masonry from the previous working level before they could take the weight of a new platform.

Putlog scaffolding: used for bricklaying work. About 1 or 1.5m out from the wall, a row of scaffolding poles or tree-trunks are erected, either sunk singly into the ground or wedged or braced together so that they stand firm. At the required height for working (*c*.1.4–1.6m), thinner timbers are attached horizontally to the poles with cord. The space between these timbers and the wall is bridged with scaffolding rods, or putlogs (8–13cm thick whole, halved or quartered trunks or squared timbers) which carry the planks or hurdles. The ends of the putlogs laid on the top of the wall are cemented in place by the next layer of masonry and, as with the outriggers, are sawn off or pulled out when building is complete.

Trestle scaffolding: a simple construction for building at low levels, consisting of vertical end-pieces and poles running between them, stiffened by cross-pieces; the work surface of planks lies on top, overhanging on all sides.

Hanging platform: suspended from loops of rope (very seldom portrayed).

Ladder

Ramp: made of two beams with flat planks nailed at right-angles across them, or fitted with rungs like a ladder (but laid flatter); also found with lattice work.

MEDIEVAL BUILDING TECHNIQUES

1   12th century
Aachen, Suermondt Museum
So-called Dish of St Ursula
Ramp, plumbline, pannier
Tervarent, Guy de: *La légende de Sainte-Ursule dans la littérature et l'art du moyen âge*, Paris, 1931, vol.2 pl.7
▼

2   c.1400
Admont, Stiftsbibliothek,
Hs. 101, fol.35
Speculum humanae salvationis. Gesta Romanorum
ILLUMINATION (Austria or southern Germany)
Trowel
Bi/Nu 288. Compare nos 193a, 340a
▼

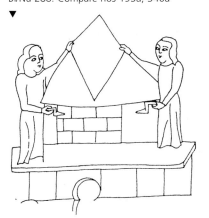

3   c.1400
Admont, Stiftsbibliothek,
MS 101, fol.35
Speculum humanae salvationis. Gesta Romanorum
ILLUMINATION (Austria or southern Germany)
Trowel, scaffolding
Bi/Nu 289
▼

3a   1332
Amersfoort, Jacob von Maerlant, *Rijmbijbel*,
10B2, 1, fol.9v
ILLUMINATION
Trowel, mortar tub, mortar-mixing pick
▶

4   1264
Amiens, Bibliothèque
municipale,
MS 23, fol.116
Bible from Corbie
ILLUMINATION
Pannier, serrated stone hammer
Bi/Nu 64
▶

5 1264
Amiens, Bibliothèque municipale,
MS 23
Bible from Corbie
ILLUMINATION
Trowel, ramp, plumbline,
pannier, serrated stone
hammer
Tyghem, fig.34

▶

7 1437
Antwerp, Koninklijk Museum voor Schone
Kunsten
Jan van Eyck, *Saint Barbara*
DRAWING
Builder's hut, mallet, crane with pallet, mortar tub,
mortar shovel, chisel, wheelbarrow, pannier
Bi/Nu 65; Tyghem fig.108; Brandt vol.1, p.302, fig.426;
de Smidt, p.6, fig.2 (detail p.7, fig.3); Recht, p.71

▶

8 end 15th century
Antwerp, Museum Mayer van den Bergh
Breviarium Mayer van den Bergh, fol.501v
ILLUMINATION
Builder's hut, broad axe, roofing axe, scaffolding,
two-wheeled carts, mallet, ladder, mortar shovel,
hod, hod-stand, chisel (or punch)
Bi/Nu 66; Tyghem, fig.174; Gaspard, Camille: *Le*
Bréviaire du Musée Mayer van den Bergh, Brussels,
1932, pl.55

◀

6 second half 15th century
Amorsbrunn, St Amor
Corbel figure
ARCHITECTURAL SCULPTURE
Mallet, chisel
Bi/Nu 227; Gerstenberg, fig.
on p.170

▶

9   c.1410
Antwerp, Museum Plantijn-Moretus,
no.180, fol.36
Bible for Emperor Wenzel
ILLUMINATION
Mixing pick, shovel, table, drying rack for tiles
Bi/Nu 286; Brandt vol.1, p.259, fig.352; Hollestelle,
Johanna: *De Steenbakkerij in de Nederlanden tot
omstreeks 1560*, Arnhem, 1976, fig.3
▼

10   1474
Augsburg, Johann Bämler, printer
Historie von der schönen Melusine, fol.20
WOODCUT
Trowel, ladder, mixing pick, mortar tub, hod
Schramm 3, no.169
For derivatives see nos 20, 205

▶

11   1475
Augsburg, Johann Bämler, printer
Jacobus de Voragine, Life of the Saints, fol.314v
WOODCUT
Schramm 3, no.430
Derivative of no.24

12 ▲   1486
Augsburg, Johann Blaubirer, printer
Hans Vintler, *Book of Virtue*, fol.200
WOODCUT
Broad axe, wooden trestle, dog or staple
Schramm 23, no.684

13   1487
Augsburg, Johann Schönsperger the elder,
printer
Bible (Germany)
WOODCUT
Eichenberger, Walter, & Wendland, Henning: *Deutsche
Bibeln vor Luther*, Hamburg, 1977, p.75, fig.169.
Derivative at reduced scale from no.225

14   1476
Augsburg, Anton Sorg, printer
Spiegel menschlicher Behaltnis, fol.73v
WOODCUT
Scaffolding, crane with lewis
Schramm 4, no.129   ▶

15   1476
Augsburg, Anton Sorg, printer
Spiegel menschlicher Behaltnis, fol.77v
WOODCUT
Stone hammer, scaffolding, trowel, crane with lewis,
ladder, mixing pick, mortar tub, four-legged stool
Bi/Nu 67; Schramm 4, no.135; Minkowski, fig.78
Compare also no.27   ▶

16   1477
Augsburg, Anton Sorg, printer
Bible, fol.195v
WOODCUT
Trowel, hod
Schramm 4, no.301   ▶

17   1479
Augsburg, Anton Sorg, printer
Boccaccio, *De claris mulieribus*, fol.57
WOODCUT
Schramm 4, no.435
Mirror-image derivative of no.576

19 ▲   1482
Augsburg, Anton Sorg, printer
Das Buch der heiligen Altväter, fo. 180v
WOODCUT
Trowel, mallet, crane with lewis, chisel
Schramm 4, no.940

20   c.1485
Augsburg, Anton Sorg, printer
Melusine, fol.23v
WOODCUT
Bi/Nu 69; Schramm 4, no.2334
Mirror-image free-drawn derivative of no.10

18   c.1476
Augsburg, Anton Sorg, printer
Duke Ernst of Bavaria, fol.49v
WOODCUT
Broad axe, wood block, auger
Schramm 4, no.268
For derivative see no.531   ▶

21   1486
Augsburg, Anton Sorg, printer
Jacobus de Voragine, *Life of the Saints*, fol.214
WOODCUT
Schramm 4, no.2489
Mirror-image derivative of no.579

22   1488
Augsburg, Anton Sorg, printer
Jacobus de Voragine, *Life of the Saints*
WOODCUT
Schramm 4, no.2710
Mirror-image derivative of the first edition of Voragine
by Anton Sorg, see no.21

23   1488

Augsburg, Anton Sorg, printer
Jacobus de Voragine, *Life of the Saints*
WOODCUT
Schramm 4, no.2567
Derivative of no.578

24   1472

Augsburg, Günther Zainer, printer   ▶
Jacobus de Voragine, *Life of the Saints*, fol.157
WOODCUT
Scaffolding, trowel, ladder, mortar tub
Schramm 2, no.204
For derivatives see nos 11, 226, 285, 397

25   before 1477

Augsburg, Günther Zainer, printer   ▶
Bible, fol.190
WOODCUT
Trowel, hod
Schramm 2, no.625; Eichberger, Walter, & Wendland,
Henning: *Deutsche Bibeln vor Luther*, Hamburg, 1977,
p.35, fig.33
The woodblock was reused in the second edition of
Zainer's Bible (1477) and by Anton Sorg at Augsburg
(1480)
For derivative see no.398.

26   c.1473

Augsburg, Günther Zainer, printer
Speculum humanae salvationis, fol.176v
WOODCUT
*Scaffolding, trowel, ladder, mortar tub, mortar-
mixing pick*
Schramm 2, no.476   ▶

27   c.1473

Augsburg, Günther Zainer, printer
Speculum humanae salvationis, fol.187
WOODCUT
Scaffolding, trowel, ladder, mortar-mixing pick, hod
Bi/Nu 68; Schramm 2, no.482; Minkowski, fig.70
Predecessor of no.15 and of later editions of
Speculum humanae salvationis   ▶

28   c.1477

Augsburg, Günther Zainer, printer
Rodericus Zamorensis, *Speculum vitae humanae*,
fol.73
WOODCUT
Square, compasses
Bi/Nu 228; Schramm 2, no.732
▼

29   c.1477

Augsburg, Günther Zainer, printer
Rodericus Zamorensis, *Speculum vitae humanae*,
fol.73
WOODCUT
Drawing board, template, square, compasses
Bi/Nu 229; Schramm 2, no.737; Hecht, p.221, fig.47
(representation of compasses, p.232, fig.55.4)
▼

30   c.1477

Augsburg, Günther Zainer, printer

Rodericus Zamorensis, *Speculum vitae humanae*, fol.139v

WOODCUT

Pointed stone hammer

Bi/Nu 70; Schramm 2, no.752; Schmidt, Leopold & Kühnel, Harry: *Alltag und Fest im Mittelalter*, exhibition catalogue, Vienna, 1970, p.24, fig.V.

▼

31   1450–60

Bad Aussee/Steiermark, chapel of St Leonhard

Panel of a winged altar, monastic foundation by St Leonhard

PANEL PAINTING (Steiermark)

Trowel, mortar tub, mortar-mixing pick, mortar shovel

▼

31a   1235–40

Auxerre, St Stephen's Cathedral

Theophilus window, Lady Chapel in the choir

STAINED GLASS

Hammer, ramp, ladder, plumbline, pannier

Schöller, p.91, no.1; Chieffo Raguin, Virginia: *Stained Glass in Thirteenth Century Burgundy*, Princeton, 1982, fig.42

▼

32   first half 14th century

Bamberg, Obere Pfarrkirche

Corbel figure at chancel crossing

ARCHITECTURAL SCULPTURE

Mallet, bolster chisel

Bi/Nu 230; Gerstenberg, fig.on p.169

▼

33   1462

Bamberg, Albrecht Pfister, printer

Four Histories, fol.5

WOODCUT

Trestle, broad axe, dog or staple

Schramm 1, no.120

▼

34   first half 15th century

Barcelona, Colección Bosquets

Francés Nicolás, *Construcción de un monasterio*

PANEL PAINTING

Two-wheeled carts, trowel, mortar bucket

Archivo Español de Arte, vol.XXXIII, no.132, Madrid, 1960, Lámina IV, p.448

▼

34a first half 15th century
Barcelona, Museum of Catalonian Art
Gonzalo Pérez, Altar to St Barbara from Puerto
Mingallo
PANEL PAINTING
Lump hammer, chisel, square, compasses
Carli, Enzo, et al.: *Die Malerei der Gotik*, Gütersloh,
1965 (= *Epochen der Kunst* 6), p.169
▼

35 1470–80
Basle, Öffentliche Kunstsammlungen,
inv. no. 1597
Master builder Jörg Ganghofer (?)
PANEL PAINTING (High Germany)
Compasses
Bi/Nu 231; Binding (1974), pl.16b;
Hecht, p.232, fig.55.1
(representation of compasses)
▶

36 1471
Basle, Universitätsbibliothek,
MS 0 I 18, fol.14
Melusine
ILLUMINATION (Basle)
*Trowel, crane with lewis, ladder, mortar tub, mortar-
mixing bin, mortar-mixing pick*
Keller, Béatrice: *Der Erker. Studie zum mittelalterlichen
Begriff nach literarischen, bildlichen und
architektonischen Quellen*, Berne & Frankfurt am Main,
1981, fig.on p.134.
▼

36a end 14th century
Basle, Unversitätsbibliothek,
MS A II 1, fol.33
Nikolaus von Lyra, endpiece to Genesis and Exodus
ILLUMINATION
*Crane with treadmill, ladder, mortar tub, mortar-mixing
tool, single-legged stool, pointed stone hammer*
Schöller, p.91, no.2; Stamm, Liselotte Esther: *Die
Rüdiger-Schopf-
Handschriften*, Aarau,
Frankfurt am
Main & Salzburg,
1981, p.79,
fig.44
▶

36b c.1400
Basle, Universitätsbibliothek,
MS A II 3, fol.98
Nikolaus von Lyra, endpiece to Joshua, Judges,
Ruth, Ezra & Job
ILLUMINATION
*Crane, mortar tub, mortar-mixing pick, single-legged
stool, stone hammer*
Schöller, p.91, no.3; Stamm, Liselotte Esther: *Die
Rüdiger-Schopf-Handschriften*, Aarau, Frankfurt am
Main & Salzburg, 1981, p.41, fig.10
▼

37 1494
Basle, Johann Bergmann, printer
Sebastian Brant, *Das Narrenschiff*
WOODCUT
Crane with lewis, measuring staff, square
Bi/Nu 279; Schramm 22, no.1126; Worringer, Wilhelm:
Die altdeutsche Buchillustration, Munich, 1912, fig.55
For derivatives see nos 399, 492, 529
▶

38   1494

Basle, Johann Bergmann, printer

Sebastian Brant, *Das Narrenschiff*

WOODCUT

Compasses

Bi/Nu 280; Schramm 22, no.1175

For derivatives see nos 400, 493

▼

39   1493

Basle, Michael Furter, printer

Columbus, *Epistola de insulis nuper inventis*, fol.7v

WOODCUT

Crane with lewis

Schramm 22, no.1047

▼

40   1496

Basle, Michael Furter, printer

Passio S. Meinradi

WOODCUT

Trestle scaffolding, trowel, mortar tub, mortar-mixing bin, mortar shovel

Schramm 22, no.537

▼

41   1496

Basle, Michael Furter, printer

Passio S. Meinradi

WOODCUT

Trestle, broad axe

Schramm 22, no.543

▼

42   1496

Basle, Michael Furter, printer

Passio S. Meinradi

WOODCUT

Scaffolding, trowel, plumbline, mortar-mixing bin, mortar-mixing pick, hod

Bi/Nu 71; Schramm 22, no.554; Hecht, p.255, fig.67

▼

43   1498

Basle, Michael Furter, printer

St. Methodius, *Revelationes divinae*

WOODCUT

Crane with treadmill, mortar tub, mortar pick, mortar-mixing bin

Schramm 22, no.567

▼

44 c.1475

Basle, Bernhard Richel, printer
Melusine
WOODCUT
Trowel, crane with lewis, ladder, mortar-mixing bin, mortar-mixing pick, hod
Schramm 21, no.387
For derivatives see nos 532, 533

45 1476

Basle, Bernhard Richel, printer
Speculum humanae salvationis
WOODCUT
Schramm 21, no.171
For mirror-image derivative see no.523

46 c.1480

Basle, Bernhard Richel, printer
Baltherus, *Die Legende des Hl. Fridolin*
WOODCUT
Scaffolding, trowel, crane, pointed stone hammer
Schramm 21, no. 294
Bi/Nu 207; Schramm 21, no.317. See p.12 also: 'The woodcuts are already illustrated in Benzinger, who ascribed them to Johann Zainer's press (Ulm, c.1480).' (C. Benzinger: *Die Fridolinlegende nach einem Druck des Johann Zainer*, Strasbourg, 1913, fig.2)

47 c.1480

Basle, Bernhard Richel, printer
Baltherus, *Die Legende des Hl. Fridolin*
WOODCUT
Crane with treadmill and external lewis
Schramm 21, no.315

48 c.1480

Basle, Bernhard Richel, printer
Baltherus, *Die Legende des Hl. Fridolin*
WOODCUT
Crane, measuring staff, mortar tub
Schramm 21, no.316

49 1481

Basle, Bernhard Richel, printer
Werner Rolevinck, *Fasciculus temporum*, fol.2
WOODCUT
Crane with lewis
Bi/Nu 73; Schramm 21, no.282; Minkowski, pl.87
Free copy of no.521

50   1066–77

Bayeux, Centre Guillaume le Conquérant
Bayeux Tapestry, scene 35
EMBROIDERY
Axe, broad axe
Tyghem, fig.8; Stenton, Frank, *et al.*: *Der Wandteppich von Bayeux.* Cologne 1957, fig.38, plate VII; Grape, Wolfgang, *Der Teppich von Bayeux. Triumphdenkmal der Normannen.* Munich & New York 1994, colour plate 6
▼

51   c.1240

Beauvais, Notre-Dame Cathedral, Lady Chapel
'Légende de Théophile' window
STAINED GLASS
Hammer, ramp, pannier, level
Bonnet-Labordie, Pierette & Philippe: *Cathédrale St Pierre de Beauvais. Un vitrail du XIIIe siècle. Le miracle de Théophile.* Beauvais 1975, nos 13, 14; Grodecki, Louis, & Brisac, Catherine: *Le vitrail gothique au XIIIe siècle.* Fribourg 1984, p.108; Gimpel (1985), figure on p.30; Cothren, Michael W.: 'The iconography of Theophilus Windows in the first half of the thirteenth century', *Speculum* 59 (1989), p.316, fig.4a
▶

52   c.1240

Beauvais, Notre-Dame Cathedral
Window detail
STAINED GLASS
Mallet, level, chisel
Gimpel (1985), figure on p.31; Schöller, p.91, no.4
▶

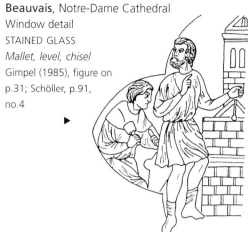

53   c.1487

Berchtesgaden, Castle
Choirstall in the Klosterkirche Weingarten, half-figure of the master mason Heinrich Yselin
WOOD CARVING
Square, compasses
Bi/Nu 233; Gerstenberg, figure on p.126; Brandt II, p.155, fig.204; Hecht, p.230, fig.54.2 (outline of compasses)
▼

54   c.1400

Bergamo, S. Maria Maggiore church
Decorative frieze at entrance to south transept
SCULPTURE
Mallet, three-legged stool, chisel (possibly a punch)

55   1440–50

Berlin, Staatsbibliothek Preußen Kulturbesitz, MS Germ. fol.245, sheet 65
Speculum humanae salvationis
ILLUMINATION (Middle Rhine)
Ramp, hod, stone hammer
Bi/Nu 291
▼

56   1210–20

Berlin, Staatsbibliothek Preußen Kulturbesitz, MS Germ. fol.282, sheet 29
Henric van Veldeken, *Aeneid*
PEN-AND-INK DRAWING (northern Bavaria or Thuringia)
Trowel, pannier, square
Bi/Nu 1; Keller, Béatrice: *Der Erker. Studie zum mittelalterlichen Begriff nach literarischen, bildlichen und architectonischen Quellen.* Bern & Frankfurt am Main 1981, figure on p.120; Warnke, Martin: *Bau und Überbau. Soziologie der mittelalerlichen Architektur nach den Schriftquellen.* Frankfurt am Main 1976, p.199, fig.3
▼

57 1210–20
Berlin, Staatsbibliothek Preußen Kulturbesitz,
MS Germ. fol.282, sheet 53v
Henric van Veldeken, *Aeneid*
PEN-AND-INK DRAWING (northern Bavaria or
Thuringia)
Axe, broad axe
Philippi, pl.26; Zimelien, Exhibition catalogue, Stiftung
Preußen Kulturbesitz, Berlin 1975, no.89
▼

58 c.1460
Berlin, Staatsbibliothek Preußen Kulturbesitz,
MS Germ. fol.565, sheet 25
Tales from the Old Testament
ILLUMINATION (Franken)
*Tub, crane with lewis and windlass, ladder, mortar-
mixing bin, mortar-mixing
pick, pointed stone
hammer*
Bi/Nu 292
▶

59 c.1460
Berlin, Staatsbibliothek Preußen Kulturbesitz,
MS Germ. fol.565, sheet 385v
Tales from the Old Testament
ILLUMINATION (Franken)
Mortar-mixing tool, carpenter's hammer
Bi/Nu 293
▼

60 c.1460
Berlin, Staatsbibliothek Preußen Kulturbesitz,
MS Germ. fol.565, sheet 395
Tales from the Old Testament
ILLUMINATION (Franken)
Broad axe
Bi/Nu 294
▼

61 c.1460
Berlin, Staatsbibliothek Preußen Kulturbesitz,
MS Germ. fol.565, sheet 396
Tales from the Old Testament
ILLUMINATION (Franken)
*Trestle, broad axe, mortar tub, mortar-mixing bin,
mortar-mixing pick*
Bi/Nu 296
▼

62 c.1460
Berlin, Staatsbibliothek Preußen Kulturbesitz,
MS Germ. fol.565, sheet 400v
Tales from the Old Testament
ILLUMINATION (Franken)
*Crane with windlass and external lewis, one-legged
stool, pointed stone
hammer*
Bi/Nu 297
▶

63   1472
Berlin, Staatsbibliothek Preußen Kulturbesitz,
MS Germ. fol.1108, sheet 16v
Tales from the Bible
ILLUMINATION (Austria)
Scaffolding, trowel, crane with pallet, hod, pointed stone hammer
Bi/Nu 299   ▶

64   c.1400
Berlin, Staatsbibliothek Preußen Kulturbesitz,
MS Germ. fol.1343, sheet 51v
Speculum humanae salvationis
ILLUMINATION (Rhineland)
Trowel, mortar tub, mortar-mixing pick, hod
Bi/Nu 300   ▶

65   first half 14th century
Berlin, Staatsbibliothek Preußen Kulturbesitz,
MS Germ. fol.1416, sheet 27
Heinrich of Munich, *Weltchronik*
ILLUMINATION (Bavaria)
Crane with lewis
Bi/Nu 301; Zimelien, Exhibition catalogue, Stiftung
Preußen Kulturbesitz, Berlin 1975, no.105
▼

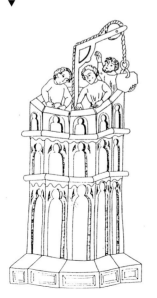

66   end 11th century
Berlin, Staatsbibliothek Preußen Kulturbesitz,
MS theol. lat. fol.323, sheet 17
Vita secunda S. Liudgeri
ILLUMINATION (Werden)
Beams, side axe
Bi/Nu 29; Binding (1972), figure on p.69 (outline);
Binding (Rhine & Maas), p.95, fig 15 (outline); Schrade,
Hubert: *Die Vita des hl. Liudger und ihre Bilder.*
Münster 1960, p.29, fig.14; Zimelien, Exhibition
catalogue, Stiftung Preußen Kulturbesitz, Berlin 1975,
no.39
▼

67   1411
Berlin, Staatlichen Museen zu Berlin, Preußischer
Kulturbesitz, copper engravings cabinet
MS 78 E 1, fol.11
Rudolf von Ems, *Weltchronik* (Toggenburg Bible)
ILLUMINATION (Wenzel workshop, Lake Constance
area)
*Scaffolding, trowel, crane with lewis, ladder, mortar
tub, mortar-mixing tool, stone hammer, square*
Bi/Nu 75; Tyghem, ig. 97; Minkowski, pic. 6
▼

68   1411

Berlin, Staatlichen Museen zu Berlin, Preußischer
Kulturbesitz, copper engravings cabinet
MS 78 E 1, fol.66v
Rudolf von Ems, *Weltchronik* (Toggenburg Bible)
ILLUMINATION (Wenzel workshop, Lake Constance area)
Trestle, broad axe, trowel, ladder, hod, shovel
Bi/Nu 75a; Zimelien, Exhibition catalogue, Stiftung
Preußischer Kulturbesitz, Berlin 1975, no.104, figure on
p.174; Stamm, Liselotte Esther, *Die Rüdiger-Schopf-
Handschriften*, Aarau, Frankfurt am Main & Salzburg
1981, p.34, fig.4
▼

69   c.1350–60

Berlin, Staatlichen Museen zu Berlin, Preußischer
Kulturbesitz, copper engravings cabinet
MS 78 E 3, fol.4
Latin (Hamilton) Bible
ILLUMINATION
Crane with windlass
Wescher, Paul: *Beschreibendes Verzeichnis der
Miniaturen des Kupferstichkabinetts der staatlichen
Museen Berlin*. Leipzig 1931, p.55, fig.44
▼

70   c.1350-60

Berlin, Staatlichen Museen zu Berlin, Preußischer
Kulturbesitz, copper engravings cabinet
MS 78 E 3, fol.4
Latin (Hamilton) Bible
ILLUMINATION
Hammer
Wescher, Paul: *Beschreibendes Verzeichnis der
Miniaturen des Kupferstichkabinetts der staatlichen
Museen Berlin*. Leipzig 1931, p.55, fig.44
▼

71   c.1470

Berlin, Staatlichen Museen zu Berlin, Preußischer
Kulturbesitz, copper engravings cabinet no. 632,
single sheet
Augustin manuscript
ILLUMINATION (northern France or Flanders)
*Scaffolding, trowel, basket, crane, ladder, plumbline,
hod, pointed stone hammer, square*
Bi/Nu 76; Tyghem, fig.155; Du Colombier, p.25, fig.9;
Minkowski, pic. 62; Recht, p.340; Coldstream (1991),
p.30, fig.53
▶

72   after 1490

Berlin, Staatlichen Museen zu Berlin, Preußischer Kulturbesitz,
copper engravings cabinet, no. 4645
(Sheet from MS n. acqu. fr. 24920, Bibliothèque Nationale, Paris)
Histoire de la destruction de Troye, illustrated by Jean Colombe,
Bourges School
ILLUMINATION (northern France)
Carpenter's chisel, scaffolding, four-wheeled carts, mallet, crane with
pulley, crane with treadwheel, ruler, measuring staff, mortar bucket,
masonry chisel, pointed stone hammer, square, stone hammer
Bi/Nu 77; Tyghem, fig.172; Du Colombier, plate on p.27, p.26, fig.11
(extract with crane), Zimelien, Exhibition catalogue, Stiftung Preußischer
Kulturbesitz, Berlin 1975, no.131, figure on p.210
                                                                   ▶

72a   second half 15th century

Berlin, Staatlichen Museen zu Berlin, Preußischer Kulturbesitz,
picture gallery, inventory no. 1642
Simon Marmion, St Bertin, *Altar von Saint-Omer*
PANEL PAINTING
Trowel, crane, mortar tub, hawk
Catalogue of the Gemäldegalerie, Berlin, Staatliche Museen Preußischer
Kulturbesitz, *Katalog der ausgestellten Gemälde des 13.–18.*
Jahrhunderts. Berlin 1975, p.252, inv. 1645
▼

73   1368

Berlin, Staatsbibliothek zu Berlin, Preußischer
Kulturbesitz, Haus 1
MS Phill. 1906, fol. 10
Bible histoire des Guiart Desmoulins
ILLUMINATION (Paris school)
Compasses
Bi/Nu 302

▶

75   1368

Berlin, Staatsbibliothek zu Berlin, Preußischer
Kulturbesitz, Haus 1
MS Phill. 1906, fol. 144
Bible histoire des Guiart Desmoulins
ILLUMINATION (Paris school)
Trowel, ladder, hod
Bi/Nu 74; Kirchner, p.81,
fig.93

▶

76   1478

Berne, Stadtbibliothek
MSS hist. helv. I, 1, 11
Diebold Schilling, *Amtliche Berner Chronik*
ILLUMINATION
*Scaffolding, crane with lewis, chisel, pointed stone
hammer*
Bi/Nu 81; Muschg & Gessler, fig.8; Recht, p.102

▶

74   1368

Berlin, Staatsbibliothek zu Berlin, Preußischer
Kulturbesitz, Haus 1
MS Phill. 1906, fol. 45v
Bible histoire des Guiart Desmoulins
ILLUMINATION (Paris school), illustrating tile-making
*Roof-tile mould, float,
shovel*
Bi/Nu 303

▶

77   1478

Berne, Stadtbibliothek
MSS hist. helv. I, 1, 145
Diebold Schilling, *Amtliche Berner Chronik*
ILLUMINATION
*Four-wheeled carts, two-wheeled carts,
mortar tub, mortar-mixing pick, mortar
shovel*
Bi/Nu 82; Tyghem, fig.154; Muschg & Gessler,
fig.10; Recht, p.30

▶

78   1478

Berne, Stadtbibliothek
MSS hist. helv. I, 1, 225
Diebold Schilling, *Amtliche Berner
Chronik*
ILLUMINATION
*Mallet, crane with windlass and external
lewis, mortar tub, chisel, punch, pointed
stone hammer, square*
Bi/Nu 83; Tyghem, fig.156; Muschg &
Gessler, fig.11; Recht, p.30
◄

79   1478

Berne, Stadtbibliothek
MSS hist. helv. I, 1, 11
Diebold Schilling, *Amtliche Berner
Chronik*
ILLUMINATION
*Trestle, broad axe, axe, mallet, crane
with lewis, guide line*
Bi/Nu 80; Muschg & Gessler, fig.9
◄

80   1484

Berne, Stadtbibliothek
MSS hist. helv. I, 16, 55
Diebold Schilling, *Spiezer Bilder-Chronik*
ILLUMINATION
*Axe, mallet, measuring staff, mortar-
mixing bin, mortar-mixing pick, mortar
shovel, hod, one-legged stool, chisel,
wheelbarrow, pointed stone hammer,
square, compasses, stone axe*
Bi/Nu 86; Tyghem, fig.164; Du Colombier,
p.30, fig.15; Boesch, pl.13; Muschg &
Gessler, fig.65; Recht, p.30
►

81   1484

Berne, Stadtbibliothek
MSS hist. helv. I, 16, 57
Diebold Schilling, *Spiezer Bilder-Chronik*
ILLUMINATION
Crane with lewis
Boesch, pl.12
▼

82   1484
Berne, Stadtbibliothek
MSS hist. helv. I, 16, 81
Diebold Schilling, *Spiezer Bilder-Chronik*
ILLUMINATION
*Crane with treadwheel and external lewis, pointed
stone hammer*
Bi/Nu 85; Boesch, pl.22; Muschg & Gessler, fig.66;
Coldstream (1991), p.43, fig.43
▼

83   1484
Berne, Stadtbibliothek
MSS hist. helv. I, 16, 89
Diebold Schilling, *Spiezer Bilder-Chronik*
ILLUMINATION
Crane with treadwheel and lewis
Bi/Nu 84; Boesch, pl.26

1484

▶

83a   1484
Berne, Stadtbibliothek
MSS hist. helv. I, 16, 100
Diebold Schilling, *Spiezer Bilder-Chronik*
WASHED PEN-AND-INK DRAWING
*Tub, stand for tub, crane with lewis, mortar shovel,
shoulder-basket, shoulder-pole*
Haeberli, Hans, & Steiger, Christoph (eds): *Die Schweiz
im Mittelalter in Diebold Schillings Spiezer
Bilderchronik. Studienausgabe zur Faksimile-Edition der
Handschrift Mss. hist helv. I, 16 der Burgerbibliothek.*
Lucerne 1991   ▼

84   1484
Berne, Stadtbibliothek
MSS hist. helv. I, 16, 545
Diebold Schilling, *Spiezer Bilder-Chronik*
ILLUMINATION
Wheelbarrow, shoulder-pole, chisel, cart
Bi/Nu 87; Boesch, pl.244; Muschg & Gessler, fig.88
▼

85   1484
Berne, Stadtbibliothek
MSS hist. helv. I, 16, 755
Diebold Schilling, *Spiezer Bilder-Chronik*
ILLUMINATION
Mallet, crane with windlass and external lewis, chisel,
pointed stone hammer, compasses, stone axe
Bi/Nu 88; Boesch, pl.326; Recht, p.30
►

86 ▲   1248
Bologna, Archivio di Stato
Italian statute book, *Matricola dei*
Falegnami
ILLUMINATION
Axe, trestle, broad axe
Tyghem, fig.26

86a   15th century
Bologna, Pinacoteca Nazionale
Tarot card (Germany)
ETCHING
Hatchet, trestle, roofing axe, frame saw,
rope windlass, pointed stone hammer,
square, compasses
Gatherings in honor of Dorothy E. Miner.
Baltimore 1974, p.69, fig.28
►

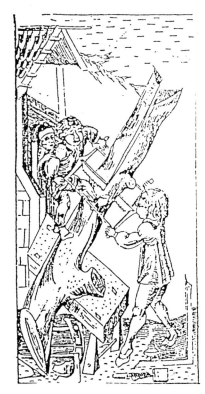

87   14th century
Bologna, University library,
cod. 346, fol.112
ILLUMINATION
Trowel, ramp, mortar-mixing bin, mortar-mixing tool,
hod
Tyghem, fig.67
▼

88, 89   c.1400
Boulogne-sur-Mer, Bibliothèque municipale,
MS 55
French Augustinian manuscript
ILLUMINATION
Stone hammer, scaffolding, pointed stone hammer,
hawk, square
Bi/Nu 305, 306; Minkowski, no.57, or figure
▼   ▼

87a   beginning 13th century
Bonn, Rheinland Landesmuseum, Depot
Half of a block of four capitals from the cloister at
St Gereon in Cologne
ARCHITECTURAL SCULPTURE
Mallet

87b   second half 15th century
Boston, Public Library,
MS 1483
Vita S. Augustini
ILLUMINATION (Schwabia)
Scaffolding, trowel, mortar-mixing pick
Schöller, p.91, no.5; Courcelle-Ladmirant: *Vita Sancti*
Augustini imaginibus adornata. Paris 1964, p.155

90   1210–15
Bourges, Cathedral of Saint-Etienne, north side
of the outer chancel ambulatory
Window, 'Lazare et le mauvais riche'
STAINED GLASS
Trowel, mallet, chisel, plumbline
Bi/Nu 90; Binding (*Ornamenta ecclesiae*), p.177, fig.16;
Aubert, Marcel, & Goubet, Simone: *Gotische*
Kathedralen und Kunstschätze in Frankreich.
Wiesbaden n.d., fig.23; Du Colombier, p.44, fig.24
(incomplete drawing); Schlink, Wilhelm: *Die*
Kathedralen Frankreichs. Munich 1978, figure on
p.152; Swaan, Wim: *Die großen Kathedralen*. Cologne
1969, figure on p.30   ▶

91   1210-15

Bourges, Cathedral of Saint-Etienne, north side
of the outer chancel ambulatory
Window, 'Lazare et le mauvais riche'
STAINED GLASS
*Bucket, basket, mortar-mixing bin, mortar-mixing
pick, hod, water tub*
Bi/Nu 90; Aubert, figure on p.301; Aubert, Marcel, &
Goubet, Simone: *Gotische Kathedralen und
Kunstschätze in Frankreich.* Wiesbaden n.d., fig.23;
Swaan, Wim: *Die großen Kathedralen.* Cologne 1969,
figure on p.31

▶

92   1210–15

Bourges, Cathedral of Saint-Etienne, north side
of the outer chancel ambulatory
Window, 'Lazare et le mauvais riche'
STAINED GLASS
Pannier
Bi/Nu 90; Aubert, Marcel, & Goubet, Simone: *Gotische
Kathedralen und Kunstschätze in Frankreich.*
Wiesbaden n.d., fig.23; Du Colombier, p.44, fig.24;
Swaan, Wim: *Die großen Kathedralen.* Cologne 1969,
figure on p.30; Swartling, Ingrid: *Bilder ur en medeltida
byggnadshytta. Bild 3.* Special edition by Gotländskt
arkiv 1966, pp.29–34

▶

93   between 1377 and mid-15th century
Brandenburg, Cathedral of SS Peter and Paul
Impost relief on west doorway
ARCHITECTURAL SCULPTURE
Crane with treadwheel and pallet
Die Kunstdenkmäler der Provinz Brandenburg II, 3.
Berlin 1912, pl.42b

▶

94   1447

Wrocław, museum of arts and crafts
Altar to St Barbara
PANEL PAINTING
Crane with treadwheel, trowel, mallet, chisel
Die Kunst in Schlesien. Berlin 1927, figure on p.233

▼

95   1451

Wrocław, university library,
MS IV F 192, fol.35v
Freytagsche Hedwigslegende
Buchmalerei
ILLUMINATION
Scaffolding, trowel, crane with treadwheel and
external lewis
Bi/Nu 91; Griesebach, August, *et al.*: *Die Kunst in*
Schlesien. Berlin 1927, p.251, fig.169; Kloss, pl.221.
Compare nos 312, 602a   ▶

96   12th century

Brioude (Haute-Loire), Basilica of Saint-Julien,
nave pillar
MURAL
Pointed stone hammer, square
Bi/Nu 30; Tyghem, fig.20; Binding (1972), figure on
p.54; Brandt II, p.148, fig.182; Ainaud, Juan: *Die*
Malerei der Romanik. Gütersloh 1967, fig.94
(= *Epochen der Kunst* 5); Focillon, Henry: *Peintures*
Romanes des églises de France. Paris 1950, fig.102

▼

97   1470–1500

Bruges, Noble Confrérie du Saint-Sang
Left wing of a triptych by the master of the St Barbara
legend, construction of the tower for St Barbara
PANEL PAINTING
Scaffolding, trowel, ladder, mortar tub, hod
Bi/Nu 92; Tyghem, fig.170; Friedländer, Max J.: 'Der
Meister der Barbara-Legende', *Jahrbuch für*
Kunstwissenschaft, 1924/25, pp.20–5, fig.1; Schöller,
p.91, no.6; *Le siècle des primitifs flamands.* Exhibition
catalogue, Bruges 1960

▼

98   1484

Bruges, Colard Mansion, printer
Ovid moralisé
WOODCUT
Trowel, crane, hod
Bi/Nu 93; Brandt II, p.42, fig.38; Henkel, M.D.:
De Houtsneden van Mansion's Ovid moralisé.
Amsterdam 1922, pl.XVII

▼

98a c.1480
Bruges, Groot Seminarie, 158/189
Valerius Maximus, *Facta et dicta memorabilia*,
vol.4, fol.1, by the Dresden Prayerbook master
ILLUMINATION (Flanders)
Crowbar, scaffolding, stone hammer
Vlaamse Kunst op perkament. Handschriften en
miniaturen te Brugge van de 12de tot de 16de eeuw.
Exhibition catalogue, Gruuthusemuseum, Bruges
1981, fig.17, cat. 97; Brinkmann, Bodo: *Die*
flämische Buchmalerei am Ende des Burgunderreichs.
Turnhout 1997, p.383, fig.86

▼

98b end 15th century
Bruges, Saint-Sang
ARCHITECTURAL SCULPTURE
Trowel, square (?), chisel
Sosson, Jean-Pierre: *Les travaux publics de la Ville de*
Bruges XIVe–XVe siècle. 1977, p.283, pl.XII & XIV

99
Brussels, now no. 295b

100 1410–15
Brussels, Bibliothèque Royale,
MS 3, fol.3
Les grandes chroniques de France
ILLUMINATION (Paris)
Trowel, shoulder carrier, pointed stone hammer
La Librairie de Bourgogne. Cinquante miniatures.
Brussels, n.d. (= *L'art en Belgique/Fondation Cultura*),
fig.9; Schöller, p.91, no.7

▼

101 1448–65
Brussels, Bibliothèque Royale, MS 6, fol.554v
L'Histoire de Charles Martel
ILLUMINATION
Masons' lodge, hammer, trowel, mallet, mortar
shovel, hod, wheelbarrow with belt, pannier,
square, claw chisel, temporary shelter
Bi/Nu 94; Tyghem, fig.147; Du Colombier, p.55,
fig.31; Recht, p.342; Coldstream (1991), p.10, fig.8

▼

102 1448–65
Brussels, Bibliothèque Royale,
MS 6, fol.558v
L'Histoire de Charles Martel
ILLUMINATION
Pick, basket, wheelbarrow
Bi/Nu 95; Tyghem, fig.140

102a   c.1410

Brussels, Bibliothèque Royale,
MS 9001, fol.45v
Guiart des Moulins, *Bible historiale*
ILLUMINATION (Paris)
Scaffolding, trowel, pointed stone hammer,
square, compasses
Schöller, p.91, no.8he LA 2025/29

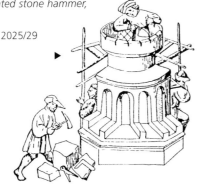

102b   c.1415–20

Brussels, Bibliothèque Royale,
MS 9004
Guiart des Moulins, *Bible historiale*
ILLUMINATION (Paris)
Compasses
Debae, Marguerite: *La librairie de Marguerite d'Autriche*. Exhibition catalogue,
Brussels 1987, fig.cat. 34

102c   1431

Brussels, Bibliothèque Royale,
MS 9018 (Cat.108), fol.80v
Utrecht Bible
ILLUMINATION (Netherlands)
Drill, broad axe
Byvanck, Alexander Willem, & Hoogewerf, Godefridus Joannes: *La miniature*
hollandaise. The Hague 1922, pl.224

▼

103   c.1450–60

Brussels, Bibliothèque Royale,
MS 9066, fol.85
J. de Tavernier, *Chroniques et Conquêtes de Charlemagne*
ILLUMINATION
Chisel, broad axe, mallet, spoon-bit, measuring staff, auger, saw
Bi/Nu 96; Tyghem, fig.123; Brandt II, p.44, fig.40
▼

103a   15th century
Brussels, Bibliothèque Royale,
MS 9024
Guiart des Moulins, *Bible historiale*
ILLUMINATION
Compare 496a
▶

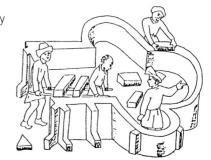

104   c.1450–60

Brussels, Bibliothèque Royale,
MS 9067, fol.110
J. de Tavernier, *Chroniques et Conquêtes de
Charlemagne*
ILLUMINATION
*Bucket, trowel, mallet, crane, ladder, mortar shovel,
hod, stand for hod, punch*
Bi/Nu 97; Tyghem, fig.120

▶

105   c.1450–60

Brussels, Bibliothèque Royale,
MS 9068, fol.203
J. de Tavernier, *Chroniques et Conquêtes de
Charlemagne*
ILLUMINATION
*Trestle, broad axe, bucket, hammer, mallet, pincers,
spoon-bit, mortar tub, mortar shovel, hod, frame
saw, various saws, square*
Bi/Nu 98; Tyghem, fig.122; Brandt II, p.44, fig.41

▶

116   c.1468

Brussels, Bibliothèque Royale,
MS 9243, fol.176
Chroniques de Hainaut II
ILLUMINATION (Bruges)
*Broad axe, scaffolding, hammer, trowel,
ladder, mortar shovel, hod*
Cockshaw, Pierre: *Les miniatures des
Chroniques de Hainaut*. Hainaut 1979,
figure on p.160f; Schöller, p.92, no.13

▶

117   c.1468

Brussels, Bibliothèque Royale,
MS 9243, fol.210
Chroniques de Hainaut II
ILLUMINATION (Bruges)
*Broad axe, scaffolding, trowel, ladder, mortar shovel,
hod, stand for hod, saw*
Cockshaw, Pierre: *Les miniatures des Chroniques de
Hainaut*. Hainaut 1979, figure on p.160f; Schöller, p.92,
no.14

▼

118   c.1390

Brussels, Bibliothèque Royale,
MS 9295, fol.122
French Augustinian manuscript
ILLUMINATION
Scaffolding, crane, mortar bucket, stone hammer
Bi/Nu 104; Tyghem, fig.83; Minkowski, pic. 52

118a   c.1405

Brussels, Bibliothèque Royale,
MS 9393, fol.3
Christine de Pisan, *La cité des dames*
ILLUMINATION
Trowel, hod
Schöller, p.92, no.15; Meiss (1974), fig.37.
Compare nos 273a, 464, 464c

▶

118b   c.1405

Brussels, Bibliothèque Royale,

MS 9393, fol.35v

Christine de Pisan, *La cité des dames*

ILLUMINATION

Crane with windlass

Schöller, p.92, no.16; Meiss (1974), fig.40.

Compare nos 464a, 464b

▼

118c   1470–80

Brussels, Bibliothèque Royale,

MS 9503–04, fol.2

Jean de Courcy, *La Bouquechardière* II

ILLUMINATION (Lyon)

Basket, crane, mortar tub, mortar-mixing pick, mortar shovel, water tub

Debae, Marguerite: *La librairie de Marguerite d'Autriche*. Exhibition catalogue, Brussels 1987, fig.cat. 6

▶

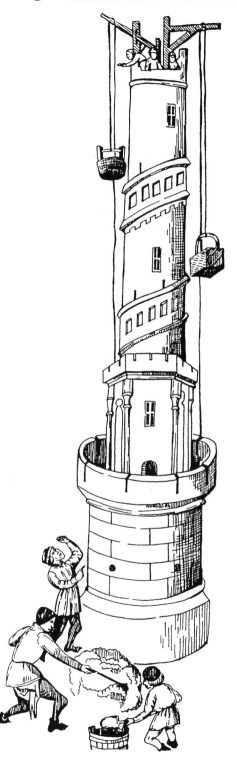

118d   1470–80

Brussels, Bibliothèque Royale,

MS 9503–04, fol.75

Jean de Courcy, *La Bouquechardière* II

ILLUMINATION (Lyon)

Debae, Marguerite: *La librairie de Marguerite d'Autriche*. Exhibition catalogue, Brussels 1987, p.19, no illus.

118e   1380–1430

Brussels, Bibliothèque Royale,

MS 9541, fol.65v

Guyart des Moulins, *Bible historiale*

ILLUMINATION

Trowel, ladder, measuring staff, hod

Cockshaw, Pierre: *Miniatures en grisaille*. Exhibition catalogue, Brussels 1986, p.5, no.2

▼

118f   c.1460–70

Brussels, Bibliothèque Royale,

MS 9571–2, fol.4v

Le livre des chroniques de Troye

ILLUMINATION

Axe, scaffolding, crane, ladder, mortar tub, mortar-mixing pick, mortar shovel, hod, stand for hod, pointed stone hammer, hawk

Cockshaw, Pierre: *Miniatures en grisaille*. Exhibition catalogue, Brussels 1986, p.37, no.18

▶

119   before 1000

Brussels, Bibliothèque Royale,

MS 9987–91

Prudentius, *Psychomachia*

PEN-AND-INK DRAWING (Lower Rhine)

Stettiner, Richard: *Die illustrierten Prudentiushandschriften*. Berlin 1905, pl.72

Copy from Leiden, compare no.237

120   1376

Brussels, Bibliothèque Royale,

MS 11201–02, fol.36

Aristotle, *Politiques et Economiques* (French translation by Nicole Oresme)

ILLUMINATION (Raoulet d'Orléans, active at the court of Charles V)

Measuring staff, plumbline, square

Manuscrits datés conservés en Belgique. Tome I: 819–1400. Brussels & Ghent 1968, p.44, pl.184 ▶

121   1461

Brussels, Bibliothèque Royale,

MS IV 106, fol.49v

Ludolphe de Saxe, *Vitae Christi* (French translation by Jean Aubert)

ILLUMINATION (Brussels, Loyset Liedet)

Trestle, broad axe, bow saw, hand saw

La librairie de Bourgogne. Cinquante miniatures. Brussels, n.d. (= L'art en Belgique/Fondation cultura), fig.9

▼

121a   15th century

Burgos, Museo Arqueológico de Burgos

PANEL PAINTING

Trowel

Guías de los museos de España III. Museo Arqueológico de Burgos. Madrid 1955

122   1040–50

Cambridge, Corpus Christi College,

MS 23

Mixed volume with a *Psychomachia* manuscript

PEN-AND-INK DRAWING (Malmesbury Abbey, Wessex; following an Anglo-Saxon forerunner of the 9th or 10th century)

Measuring staff

Stettiner, Richard: *Die illustrierten Prudentiushandschriften*. Berlin 1905, pl.65.7

Compare no.266

122a   c.1445

Cambridge, Massachusetts, Fogg Art Museum, no. 1924.0495

Francesco Pesellino (Francesco di Stefano)

PANEL PAINTING

Trowel, mortarboard or hawk

▼

123   mid-12th century
Cambridge, Trinity College,
MS R. 17.1, fol.100
Eadwin Psalter
PEN-AND-INK DRAWING (Canterbury, copy of the
Utrecht Psalter, fol. 38)
*Axe, stone hammer, trowel, chisel, pointed stone
hammer*
Millar, E.G.: *La miniature anglaise du Xe au XIIIe siècle.*
Paris & Brussels 1926, plan 42

123a   beginning 14th century
Cambridge, Trinity College,
MS B. 11.22, fol.192
Book of hours
ILLUMINATION (Flanders)
Mallet, chisel
Randall, fig.C, 483
▼

124   after 1241
Cambridge, University Library, Sign.
E.e 359, fol.33
La Estoire de Seint Aedward le Rei
PEN-AND-INK DRAWING (Matthew Paris school)
Axe, hammer, level
James, M.R.: *La Estoire de Seint Aedward le Rei. The
Life of St Edward the Confessor.* Oxford 1920, plate on
p.50f
                                           ▶

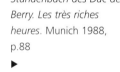

125   after 1241
Cambridge, University Library, Sign.
E.e 359, fol.41
La Estoire de Seint Aedward le Rei
PEN-AND-INK DRAWING (Matthew Paris school)
Axe
James, M.R.: *La Estoire de Seint Aedward le Rei. The
Life of St Edward the Confessor.* Oxford 1920, plate on
p.53
                                           ▶

126   c.1413
Chantilly, Musée Condé,
MS 65, fol.49v
Limburg brothers, *Très Riches Heures* of Jean, Duke
of Berry
ILLUMINATION
Crane with windlass, plumbline
Bi/Nu 105; Meiss, fig.47; Cazelles, Raymond, &
Rathofer, Johannes: *Das
Stundenbuch des Duc de
Berry. Les très riches
heures.* Munich 1988,
p.88
▶

126a   c.1413

Chantilly, Musée Condé,
MS 65, fol.35v
Limburg brothers, *Très Riches Heures* of Jean,
Duke of Berry
ILLUMINATION
Bucket, scaffolding, crane
Cazelles, Raymond, & Rathofer, Johannes: *Das
Stundenbuch des Duc de Berry. Les très riches heures.*
Munich 1988, p.78

127   c.1413

Chantilly, Musée Condé,
MS 65, fol.55v
Limburg brothers, *Très Riches Heures* of Jean,
Duke of Berry
ILLUMINATION
Trowel, ramp
Bi/Nu 106; Meiss, fig.54; Cazelles, Raymond, &
Rathofer, Johannes: *Das Stundenbuch des Duc de
Berry. Les très riches heures.* Munich 1988, p.98

128   end 13th century

Chantilly, Musée Condé,
MS fr. 590, fol.13
French manuscript (Cicero, *Rhetorica*)
ILLUMINATION
Trowel, hod, rope, pointed stone hammer
Bi/Nu 107; Tyghem, fig.51; Delort, Robert: *Life in the
Middle Ages*. London 1974, figure on p.186; *Meyers
illustrierte Weltgeschichte vol.12*. Mannheim 1980,
p.69; Folda, Jaroslav: *Crusader Illumination at St Jean
d'Acre 1275–1291*. Princeton 1976, fig.27

129   15th century

Chantilly, Musée Condée,
MS 728
Jean de Courcy, *La Bouquechardière*
ILLUMINATION
Scaffolding, trowel, crane, ladder, mortar shovel, hod
Bi/Nu 109; Du Colombier, p.25, fig.10

130   15th century

Chantilly, Musée Condée,
MS 728
Jean de Courcy, *La Bouquechardière*
ILLUMINATION
*Trowel, mallet, measuring staff, chisel, pointed stone
hammer*
Bi/Nu 108; Aubert, figure on p.315; Du Colombier,
p.106

131   15th century

Chantilly, Musée Condé,
MS 722 ex. 1196
Vinzenz von Beauvais, *Speculum Historiale*
ILLUMINATION
Broad axe, basket, pointed stone hammer, square
Dammertz, Victor, et al.: *Benedictus. Eine*
Kulturgeschichte des Abendlandes. Geneva 1980,
p.386, fig.354
▼

131a   c.1450

Chantilly
Jean Fouquet, Book of Hours of Etienne Chevalier
ILLUMINATION
Axe, drill
König, Eberhard: *Französische Buchmalerei um 1450.*
Berlin 1982, pl.163, fig.322
▼

132–136   c.1220–30

Chartres, Notre-Dame Cathedral
Eastern window in south aisle, 'Les miracles de
Notre-Dame', lower four leads
STAINED GLASS
Ladder, mortar tub, square
Binding 1985 (*Ornamenta ecclesiae*), p.174, no.10
▼

137   c.1220–25

Chartres, Notre-Dame Cathedral
Window in the south-eastern ambulatory, 'Histoire
de Saint-Silvestre'
STAINED GLASS
Hammer, ladder, scoring chisel, pointed stone
hammer
Bi/Nu 110; Tyghem, fig.45; Du Colombier, p.17, fig.5a;
Delaporte, Yves, & Houvet, Etienne: *Les vitraux de la*
cathédrale de Chartres. Chartres 1926, vol.4, pl.81;
Schöller (1998), fig.9, p.112
▼

138   c.1220–25

Chartres, Notre-Dame Cathedral
Window in the south-eastern ambulatory, 'Histoire
de Saint-Silvestre'
STAINED GLASS
Pannier
Bi/Nu 114; Tyghem, fig.49; Delaporte, Yves, & Houvet,
Etienne: *Les vitraux de la cathédrale de Chartres*.
Chartres 1926, vol.4, pl.81
▼

139   c.1220–25

Chartres, Notre-Dame Cathedral
Window in the south-eastern ambulatory, 'Histoire
de Saint-Silvestre'
STAINED GLASS
Hammer, trowel, level, template, pointed stone
hammer, square
Tyghem, fig.48; Du Colombier, p.30, fig.16; Delaporte,
Yves, & Houvet, Etienne: *Les vitraux de la cathédrale de*
Chartres. Chartres 1926, vol.4, pl.81
▼

140   c.1225

Chartres, Notre-Dame Cathedral

Window in the north-eastern ambulatory, 'Histoire de Charlemagne'

STAINED GLASS

Ramp, level, pannier

Bi/Nu 111; Delaporte, Yves, & Houvet, Etienne: *Les vitraux de la cathédrale de Chartres*. Chartres 1926, vol.4, pl.107; Frodl-Kraft, Eva: *Die Glasmalerei*. Vienna 1970, figure on p.10 (after R. de Lasteyrie, *L'architecture réligieuse en France à l'époque gothique*. Paris 1926); Grimme, Ernst Günther: 'Das Karlfenster in der Kathedrale von Chartres', figure on p.17, in *Aachener Kunstblätter* 19/20, 1960/61

▶

141   c.1220–25

Chartres, Notre-Dame Cathedral

Window in northern choir chapel, 'Histoire de Saint-Chéron'

STAINED GLASS

Mallet, plumbline, level, template, punch, pointed stone hammer, square, serrated stone axe, compasses

Bi/Nu 112; Tyghem, fig.46; Andrews, pl.II, fig.2; Aubert, figure on p.34; Du Colombier, p.17, fig.5b; Delaporte, Yves, & Houvet, Etienne: *Les vitraux de la cathédrale de Chartres*. Chartres 1926, vol.4, pl.123; Friederich, fig.110; Grodecki, Louis, & Brisac, Catherine: *Le vitrail gothique au XIIIe siècle*. Fribourg 1984, fi. 58; Schlink, Wilhelm: *Die Kathedralen Frankreichs*. Munich 1978, figure on p.161 (back to front); Schöller (1998), fig.9, p.112; Gimpel (1980), lower figure on p.31

▶

142   c.1205–15

Chartres, Notre-Dame Cathedral

Window in northern aisle of nave, 'Histoire de Noé'

STAINED GLASS

Trestle, axe

Bi/Nu 114; Brandt I, fig.439; Delaporte, Yves, & Houvet, Etienne: *Les vitraux de la cathédrale de Chartres*. Chartres 1926, vol.4, pl.179, 182

▶

143   c.1220–25

Chartres, Notre-Dame Cathedral

Window in northern ambulatory, 'Saint-Julien l'hospitalier'

STAINED GLASS

Axe, trestle, broad axe

Bi/Nu 114; Delaporte, Yves, & Houvet, Etienne: *Les vitraux de la cathédrale de Chartres*. Chartres 1926, vol.4, pl.132; Hauglid, Roar: *Norske Stavkirker*. Oslo 1976, fig.258

▼

144   c.1220–25
Chartres, Notre-Dame Cathedral
Window in northern ambulatory, 'Histoire de Saint-Thomas'
STAINED GLASS
Hammer, ramp, pannier
Bi/Nu 114; Delaporte, Yves, & Houvet, Etienne: *Les vitraux de la cathédrale de Chartres.* Chartres 1926, vol.4, pl.137

▼

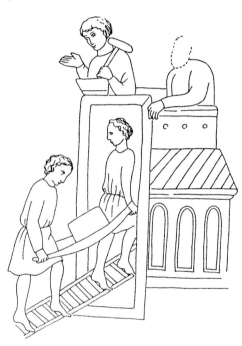

145   second quarter 13th century
Chartres, Notre-Dame Cathedral
Window
STAINED GLASS
Serrated stone hammer
Bi/Nu 307; Violett-le-Duc in *Annales archéologiques* 15, 1846

▶

145a   second half 15th century
Cherbourg, Bibliothèque de Cherbourg, MS 50, fol.60v
Heures du Saint-Esprit, Livres d'heures rouennais, Speculum humanae salvationis
ILLUMINATION
Scaffolding, basket, crane with treadwheel and pallet, ladder, mortar shovel, hod
Lafond, Jean: *Livre d'heures rouennais.* Rouen 1929, pl.XIII
Compare no.456

146   before 1217
Cividale, Museo Archeologico Nazionale
St Elizabeth's Psalter, fol. 239
ILLUMINATION
Trestle, broad axe, mallet, chisel, pointed stone hammer, square
Bi/Nu 32; Brandt I, p.266, fig.367; Haseloff, Arthur: *Eine thüringische-sächsische Malerschule des 13. Jahrhunderts.* Strasbourg 1897, pl.XXV, no.56; Philippi, pl.28

▼

146a   second half 13th century
Clermont-Ferrand, Notre-Dame Cathedral
Medallion in the middle window of St Austremoine Chapel in the ambulatory, 'Life of St Austremoine'
STAINED GLASS
Schöller, p.92, no.18; Craplet, Bernard: *La cathédrale de Clermont.* Lyon 1976, pl.22

146b   1275–85
Clermont-Ferrand, Notre-Dame Cathedral
Right-hand window of St John Chapel in the ambulatory, 'Legend of Theophilus'
STAINED GLASS
Schöller, p.92, no.19; Cothren, Michael W.: 'The iconography of Theophilus Windows in the first half of the thirteenth century' in *Speculum* 59 (1984), p.337f; Craplet, Bernard: 'Cathédrale de Clermont' in *Dossier du visiteur.* Le Puy 1977, p.23, no illus.

147   end 13th century
Colmar, St Martin
St Nicholas doorway, vaulting figure
ARCHITECTURAL SCULPTURE
Drawing board, square
Bi/Nu 235; Anstett, Peter: *Das Martinsmünster zu Colmar.* Berlin 1966, fig.18; Brandt II, p.148, fig.185;Du Colomier, p.104, fig.65; Gerstenberg, figure on p.144

▼

148   first half 14th century
Colmar, St Martin
South-eastern window in ambulatory
STAINED GLASS
Trowel, crane with lewis, hod
Bi/Nu 115; Tyghem, fig.66; Du Colombier, p.26, fig.12;
Friederich, fig.114;
Minkowski, pic. 38

▶

149   end 11th century
Conques, Sainte-Foy
Figured capital in transept
ARCHITECTURAL SCULPTURE
Stone hammer, square
Gimpel (1985), figure on p.65

▶

150   1427
Crowland, Lincolnshire, Abbey church
Memorial slab of master mason William Warrington
STONE CARVING
Square, compasses
Bi/Ni 236; Du Colombier, p.103,
fig.64; Andrews, figure on p.27;
Binding (1974), p.108, fig.11

▶

151   1433
Darmstadt, Hessisches Landesmuseum
Segment of gravestone for Hantz von Bacharach, rear view (Friedberg)
Pointed stone hammer, square, compasses
Azzola, Friedrich Karl: 'Handwerkszeichen auf der Grabplatte eines Steinmetzen und Werkmeisters', *Steinmetz und Bildhauer* year 99, Munich 1983, 5, p.375, fig.12

▼

152   1480
The Hague, Mauritshuis,
cat. no.784
Hubert van Eyck (?), Building the Tower of Babel
PANEL PAINTING
*Axe, builder's hut, bucket, scaffolding, trowel, basket,
basket for beast of burden, crane with windlass, crane
with treadwheel, mortar tub, mortar-mixing pick,
mortar shovel, stand for hod, four-legged stool, chisel,
sledge, wheelbarrow, shoulder pole with water bucket,
water jug, square*
Bi/Nu 117; Tyghem, fig.161; Minkowski, pic. 138;
Pächt, Otto: *Van Eyck. Die Begründer der
altniederländischen Malerei* (ed. Maria Schmidt-
Dengler). Munich 1989, p.207, fig.124

▶

153   c.1400
The Hague, Rijksmuseum
Meermann-Westreenianum,
MS 10 A 12, fol. 93v
Augustine manuscript
ILLUMINATION (Flanders or northern France)
Serrated stone hammer

▼

154   c.1460
The Hague, Rijksmuseum
Meermanno-Westreenianum,
MS 10 A 17, fol. 133v
Jean de Courcy, *La Bouquechardière*
ILLUMINATION
Trowel, mallet, crane with treadwheel and pallet,
mortar-mixing pick, mortar shovel, chisel, shoulder
pannier, pointed stone hammer, pannier
Bi/Nu 116; Tyghem, fig.146

▼

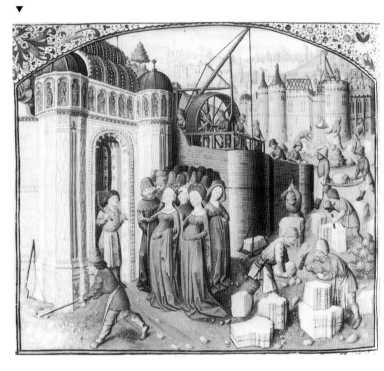

156   c.1468
The Hague, Koninklijk Bibliothek,
MS 78 D 39, fol.287v
Dutch Bible
ILLUMINATION
Broad axe, crane, mortar shovel, hod, stand for hod
Bi/Nu 119; Du Colombier, p.29, fig.14

▶

156a   c.1478
The Hague, Koninklijk Bibliothek,
MS 133 H 30, fol.107
Book of Hours
ILLUMINATION (Netherlands)
Scaffolding, ladder
Schöller, p.92, no.20; Bycanck, Alexander Willem, &
Hoogewerf, Godefridus Johannes: *La miniature*
hollandaise. The Hague 1922, pl.178

157   1111
Dijon, Bibliothèque municipale,
MS 170, fol.19
Sancti Gregorii magni Moralia in Job, Citeaux
PEN-AND-INK DRAWING
Axe, wooden mallet or beetle
Bi/Nu 34; Binding (1972), figure on p.58 (outline);
Binding (Rhein und Maas), p.95, fig.14 (outline);
Gutbrod, Jürgen: *Die Initiale in Handschriften des 8.–13.*
Jahrhunderts. Stuttgart 1965, fig.IV, p.121

▼

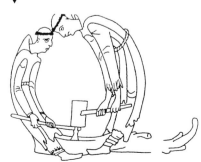

155   c.1380
The Hague, Koninklijk Bibliothek,
MS 71 A 16, fol.9
Livy, History of Rome
ILLUMINATION
Scaffolding, trowel, ladder, hod, pointed stone
hammer
Bi/Nu 118; Tyghem, fig.76

▶

158   1111
Dijon, Bibliothèque municipale,
MS 170, fol.41
Sancti Gregorii magni
Moralia in Job, Citeaux
PEN-AND-INK DRAWING
Axe, bill
Bi/Nu 33; Binding (1972),
figure on p.57 (outline);
Binding (Rhein und Maas),
p.95, fig.14 (outline);
Tyghem, fig.19; Gutbrod,
Jürgen: *Die Initiale in*
Handschriften des 8.–13.
Jahrhunderts. Stuttgart
1965, fig.VII, p.161
▶

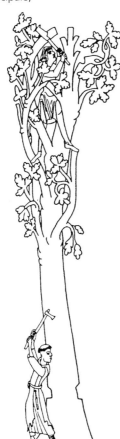

159   second half 13th century
Dijon, Bibliothèque municipale,
MS 562, fol.9
Histoire universelle
ILLUMINATION
Scaffolding, basket (?), crane with treadwheel,
mortar-mixing bin, pointed stone hammer
Bi/Nu 120; Tyghem, fig.30
▼

160   second half 13th century
Dijon, Bibliothèque municipale,
MS 562, fol.130v
Histoire universelle
ILLUMINATION
Trowel, basket, ramp, pointed stone hammer,
carrying loop
Bi/Nu 121; Tyghem, fig.31
◀

161   15th century
Dijon, Town hall
ARCHITECTURAL CARVING IN WOOD
Compasses
▼

162   c.1460
Dijon, Palais des Ducs
Tour ducale Jean Poncelet
STONE RELIEF
Square, compasses
Du Colombier, Pierre: *Les chantiers des cathédrales.*
Paris 1953, p.82, fig.17
▼

163   third quarter 15th century
Dijon, Musée des Beaux-Arts
Charlemagne as overseer
EMBROIDERY (Arras or Tournai)
Measuring staff
Bi/Nu310; *Karl der Große – Werk und Wirkung.*
Exhibition catalogue, Aachen 1965, p.550, no.758, no
illus.

164   1365

Donaueschingen, Fürstliche Fürstenberg, Hofbibliothek,
MS 79, fol.11
Rudolf von Ems, *Weltchronik*
ILLUMINATION (Pfalz, with French influence)
Scaffolding, trowel, crane with treadwheel and external lewis, mortar-mixing bin, mortar-mixing pick, hod, stool, pointed stone hammer, square
Bi/Nu 122; Tyghem, fig.77; Minkowski, pic. 23; Kratzert, Christine: *Die illustrierten Handschriften der Weltchronik des Rudolf von Ems*. Berlin 1974; Stamm, Liselotte Esther: *Die Rüdiger-Schopf-Handschriften*. Arnau, Frankfurt am Main & Salzburg 1981, p.35, fig.6
▶

166   third quarter 11th century

Dresden, Sächsische Landesbibliothek,
Hs. M 32
Eike von Repgow, *Sachsenspiegel*
ILLUMINATION (Meißen)
Bi/Nu 124; Brandt II, p.47, fig.44
Compare nos 199, 200, which are derived from the same precursor but are independent of the Dresden MS
▼

167   13th century

Dresden, Landesbibliothek
Manuscript (lost since the Second World War)
PEN-AND-INK DRAWING
Axe, broad axe
Bi/Nu 36; Binding (1972), p.12, fig.g (outline); Binding (Rhein und Maas), p.95, fig.15 (outline)
▼

165   c.1440

Dresden, Sächsische Landesbibliothek,
A 50, sheet 21b
Bible stories from the workshop of Dibolt Lauber in Hagenau
PEN-AND-INK DRAWING
Scaffolding, trowel, mortar-mixing bin, mortar-mixing pick, hod, four-legged stool
Bi/Nu 124a
▶

168   c.1250

Dublin, Trinity College Library (TCD 177),
Sign. E.i. 40, fol.59v, 60
Matthew Paris, Lives of SS Alban and Amphibalus
PEN-AND-INK DRAWING
Trestle, drill, broad axe, stone hammer, mallet, crane with windlass and hook, ladder, plumbline, level, wheelbarrow, pannier, square, compasses
Bi/Nu 3; Tyghem, fig.27; Binding (1972), figure on p.43 (outline); Binding 1985 (*Ornamenta ecclesiae*), p.171, fig.1 (outline); Neher, F.L.: 'Alles hing einmal am Haken', *Heraklith-Rundschau* 31, 1961, p.18, fig.49; Recht 1989, pp.25, 109; Coldstream (1991), p.11, fig.9.
Compare no.267

◄

169   c.1390–1410

Kloster Ebstorf, Protestant nunnery
Window in transept
STAINED GLASS (probably from the Lüneburg workshop)
Scaffolding, trowel
Legner, Anton (ed.):*Die Parler und der Schöne Stil*. Exhibition catalogue, Cologne 1978, vol.1, p.227, conclusion volume 1980, pl.90

▼

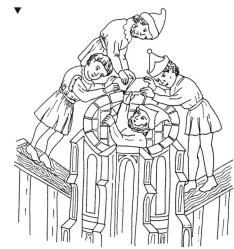

170   1497
Eichstätt, Cathedral
Console figure in mortuarium
ARCHITECTURAL SCULPTURE
Compasses
Bi/Nu 239; Gerstenberg, figure on p.187; Brandt II,
p.149, fig.186; Hecht, p.232, fig.55.5 (outline of
compasses)
▼

171   c.1500
Eichstätt, Marktplatz, inner courtyard of a house
Console figure from the former collegiate church of
Our Lady
ARCHITECTURAL SCULPTURE
Mallet, chisel
Bi/Nu 238; Gerstenberg, figure on p.171
▼

172   c.820
Epernay, Bibliothèque municipale,
MS 1, fol.12, 13v
Ebo-Evangeliar from Hautvillers
ILLUMINATION
Hatchet, mallet, chisel
Bi/Nu 37; Binding (1972), figure on p.64 (outline)
Compare nos 344a, 344b
▼

173   c.1180
Erlangen, University Library,
cod. 121, fol.288v
Gumpertsbibel
ILLUMINATION (mid-Bavaria)
Tub, crane, ramp, pointed stone hammer, pannier
Swarzenski, Georg: *Die Salzburger Malerei von den
ersten Anfängen bis zur Blütezeit des romanischen Stils.*
Leipzig 1908, plate volume, fig.131
▼

174   13th century
Eton, Eton College Library,
MS 177, fol.1v
Collected manuscript
ILLUMINATION (England)
Zahlten, Johannes: *Creatio mundi. Darstellungen der
sechs Schöpfungstage und naturwissenschaftliches
Weltbild im Mittelalter.* Stuttgart 1979, fig.286
(= *Stuttgarter Beiträge zur Geschichte und Politik,*
vol.13)

175   c.1415

Florence, San Michele
Niche of the stonemasons' guild,
Nanni di Banco, Quattro Coronati
ARCHITECTURAL SCULPTURE
Trestle, drill, mallet, plumbline,
level, square, compasses
Tyghem, fig.129; Kauffmann, Georg:
Florenz. Stuttgart 1962, figure
opposite p.320 (= *Reclams*
Kunstführer Italien, vol.III)
▶

176   after 1250–60

Florence, Baptistery of San Giovanni
Cupola mosaic
Hammer, frame saw
Brandt I, p.236, fig.309; *I mosaici del battistero di*
Firenze a cura della Cassa di Risparmio di Firenze
(Introduzione di Antony de Witt), 5 vols. Florence
1954–9, vol.IV, fig.XII
▼

176a   c.1460

Florence
Mercury
WOODCUT
Beaker, scaffolding, four-legged stool
Hind, Arthur M.: *Early Italian Engravings*. London 1938,
part I, vol.II, pl.124, A.III.6, a I
▼

176b   c.1390

Florence, Biblioteca Nazionale Rinata,
BR 367, fol.122v
Visconti Book of Hours
ILLUMINATION (Italy)
Bucket, scaffolding, trowel, crane, ladder, mortar-
mixing pick, hod
Meiss, Millard, & Kirsch, Edith W.: *The Visconti Hours,*
National Library, Florence. New York 1972
▼

177 1337–48
Florence, Museo dell'Opera del Duomo
Andrea Pisano, hexagonal reliefs from the Duomo
campanile
ARCHITECTURAL SCULPTURE
Scaffolding, hammer, ladder
Brandt II, p.70f
▼

178 1150–60
Florence, Museo Nazionale del Bargello,
Collezione Carrand no. 643
Fragment of a portable altar from Stavelot
ENAMEL
Ramp, mortar-mixing pick
Haussherr, Reiner (ed.): *Die Zeit der Staufer*. Exhibition
catalogue, Stuttgart 1977, vol.I, no.545, vol.II, fig.338;
Schöller, p.92, no.21

179 1316
Florence, Uffizi
Pietro Lorenzetti, S. Umiltà building a monastery
PAINTING
Trowel, basket, plumbline
Tyghem, fig.54
▼

180 15th century
Florence, Biblioteca Laurenziana,
cod. Ashb. 956, fol.177
Libro di Aritmetica
ILLUMINATION (Calabria)
*Scaffolding, ladder, mortar tub, mortar-mixing pick,
mortar shovel*
Disegni nei manoscritti laurenziani, secoli X–XVII.
Exhibition catalogue, Florence 1979, p.133, fig.92
▶

180a c.1450–60
Florence, Biblioteca Riccordiana,
MS 492, fol.69
Virgil manuscript
ILLUMINATION
*Scaffolding, pick, trowel, ladder, mortarboard,
mortar-mixing pick, pegs, shovel, cord*
Virgil: *Opera. Bucolica, Georgica, Aeneis. MS 492 della
Biblioteca Riccordiana di Firenze*. Facsimile edition,
Florence 1969

180b c.1450–60
Florence, Biblioteca Riccordiana,
MS 492, fol.69v
Virgil manuscript
ILLUMINATION
Ladder, mortarboard, mortar-mixing pick
Virgil: *Opera. Bucolica, Georgica, Aeneis. MS 492 della
Biblioteca Riccordiana di Firenze*. Facsimile edition,
Florence 1969

180c   c.1450–60

Florence, Biblioteca Riccordiana, MS 492, fol.72

Virgil manuscript

ILLUMINATION

Lump hammer, crane with windlass, ladder, mortarboard, chisel

Romby, Giuseppina Carla: *Per costruire ai tempi di Brunelleschi.* Florence 1979, p.61, fig.5; Virgil: *Opera. Bucolica, Georgica, Aeneis. MS 492 della Biblioteca Riccordiana di Firenze.* Facsimile edition, Florence 1969

▼

180d   c.1450–60

Florence, Biblioteca Riccordiana,

MS 492, fol.72v

Virgil manuscript

ILLUMINATION

Scaffolding, trowel, mortarboard, mortar-mixing pick, mortar shovel

Romby, Giuseppina Carla: *Per costruire ai tempi di Brunelleschi.* Florence 1979, p.60, fig.4; Virgil: *Opera. Bucolica, Georgica, Aeneis. MS 492 della Biblioteca Riccordiana di Firenze.* Facsimile edition, Florence 1969

▼

181   third quarter 12th century

Forshem, Västergötland (Sweden), church

West end tympanum

ARCHITECTURAL SCULPTURE

Pointed stone hammer, bolster

Bi/Nu 38; Andersson, Aron: *L'art scandinave* vol.II, Zodiaque 1968, p.121, fig.42; *Romanischer Baubetrieb*, figure on p.53 (outline); Tuulse, Armin: *Scandinavia Romanica.* Vienna & Munich 1968, p.267, fig.245

▶

182   1455–65
Friesach, Kärnten (Austria), Stadtmuseum
Panel from a winged altar by Konrad von Friesach,
'Foundation of Abbey by St Leonard'
PANEL PAINTING (Kärnten)
Trowel, mortar-mixing pick, compasses
Source: Institut für mittelalterliche Realienkunde
Österreichs, Krems an der Donau
▼

184   end 15th century
Geneva, Bibliothèque de Genève,
MS fr. 79, fol.204v
Compendium Historiale
ILLUMINATION
*Lump hammer, scaffolding, hammer, trowel, basket,
hod, chisel, shoulder pole with buckets, pointed
stone hammer*
Bi/Nu 127; Du Colombier, p.24, fig.8
◀

184a   1230–1300
Geneva, Bibliothèque public et universitaire,
MS lat. 76, fol.88v
Initial in Aristotle's *Liber physicorum*
ILLUMINATION (Paris)
Pannier
Beer, Ellen J.: 'Pariser Buchmalerei in der Zeit Ludwigs
des Heiligen und im letzten Viertel des 13.
Jahrhunderts', *Zeitschrift für Kunstgeschichte* 44, 1981,
p.75, fig.4a
◀

183   c.1360
Fulda, Hessische Landesbibliothek,
cod. Aa 88, fol.16
Rudolf von Ems, *Weltchronik*
ILLUMINATION (Bohemia)
*Scaffolding, trowel, basket, crane, ladder,
mortar tub, mortar-mixing pick*
Bi/Nu 125; Tyghem, fig.78; Minkowski, pic.
20; Kratzert, Christine: *Die illustrierten
Handschriften der Weltchronik des Rudolf von
Ems*. Berlin 1974
▶

185   beginning 12th century
Gerona, Santa Maria Cathedral
Frieze in south wing of transept
ARCHITECTURAL SCULPTURE
Trestle, broad axe
Buisman, Hans: *Spanien*. Darmstadt 1972, figure on
p.47; Lessing, Ernst: *Die Arche Noah in Bildern*, n.p.,
n.d., figures on pp.17, 110; de Palol, Pedro, & Hirmer,
Max: *Spanien*. Munich 1965, lower figure on p.147
▼

186   mid-12th century
Gerona, Santa Maria Cathedral
Frieze in west wing of transept
ARCHITECTURAL SCULPTURE
Stool, square, stone hammer
Durliat, Marcel: *Hispania Romanica*. Vienna & Munich
1962, p.278, fig.53
▼

187   third quarter 14th century
Gerona, Santa Maria Cathedral
Church treasure
Bible of Charles V of France
ILLUMINATION (Italy)
Lump hammer, trowel, basket, ramp, mortar-mixing
pick, hod, stand for hod, chisel
Alberti, Mariano Oliver: *La catedral de Gerona*. León
1973, figure on p.53
▼

188   c.1320–30
Göß, Steiermark (Austria), St Erhard
Central nave
FRESCO
Trestle, broad axe, trowel, pointed stone hammer
Bi/Nu 127; Kühnel, fig.12; *Österreichische Zeitschrift für*
Kunst und Denkmalpflege 32, 1978, vol.3/4, cover
illustration   ▶

189   last third 10th century
Göttingen, Staats- und Hochschulbibliothek,
MS 231
Göttinger Sakramentar
PEN-AND-INK DRAWING
Broad axe
Bi/Nu 39; Binding (1972), figure on p.62 (outline);
Elbern, Viktor Heinrich: *Das erste Jahrtausend*.
Düsseldorf 1962, plate vol., no.439
◄

190   1339–43
Gurk (Austria), Mariä Himmelfahrt Cathedral
North wall of the vestibule
FRESCO
Scaffolding, hammer
Frodl, Walter: *Die gotische Wandmalerei in Kärnten*.
Klagenfurt 1944, p.145, fig.3; Schöller, p.92, no.28

190a   1458
Gurk (Austria), Mariä Himmelfahrt Cathedral
Konrad von Friesach, Lent cloth, row 2, panel 5
EMBROIDERY
Builder's hut, scaffolding, trowel, ramp, mortar-mixing pick, hod

190b   1458
Gurk (Austria), Mariä Himmelfahrt Cathedral
Konrad von Friesach, Lent cloth, row 7, panel 4
EMBROIDERY
Trowel

190c   c.1410–20
Hakendover, Saint-Sauveur
High altar
WOOD CARVING
Trowel, ramp, mortar tub, mortar shovel, hod, lifting rope and pallet
Möbius, Friedrich, & Schubert, Ernst: *Skulptur des Mittelalters. Funktion und Gestalt.* Weimar 1987, p.373, fig.18; Müller, Theodor: *Sculpture in the Netherlands, Germany, France and Spain 1400 to 1500.* Harmondsworth 1966, p.18; Sosson, Jean-Pierre: *Les travaux publics de la Ville e Bruges XIV–XV siècles.* 1977, p.283, pl.XIII   ▶

191   c.1400
Hal, Wallfahrtskirche
Console on south-west doorway
ARCHITECTURAL SCULPTURE
Mallet, chisel
Bi/Nu 240; Brandt II, p.149, fig.190
▼

192   c.1500
Hamburg, Kunsthalle,
no. 462
Hamburg (?) master, *Crucifixion*
Scaffolding
Busch, Harald: *Meister des Nordens. Die Altniederdeutsche Malerei 1450–1550.* Hamburg 1940, fig.336 (detail), p.261; Schöller, p.92, no.24

193   c.1428
Hamburg, Staats- und Universitätsbibliothek,
cod. hebr. 37, fol.27v
Hebrew manuscript
ILLUMINATION (Rhineland)
Crane with external lewis and windlass, mortar-mixing bin, mortar-mixing pick, hod, pointed stone hammer
Metzger, Thérèse & Mendel: *Jüdisches Leben im Mittelalter nach illuminierten hebräischen Handschriften vom13.–16. Jahrhundert.* Fribourg & Würzburg 1983, p.85, fig.117
▼

193a   mid-14th century

Harburg, Oettingen Wallersteinische Bibliothek,

MS 1.2, fol.23

Speculum humanae salvationis

PEN-AND-INK DRAWING (St Mang zu Füssen)

Hammer, trowel

Schöller, p.92, no.25; Marburger Index, fiche 800/c10

Compare nos 2, 340a

▼

▼

194   c.1477

Heidelberg, Universitätsbibliothek,

cod. pal. germ. 16, fol.20

Old Testament

ILLUMINATION (workshop of Ludwig Heunfflin)

Crane with lewis, mortar tub, mortar-mixing bin,

mortar-mixing pick, one-legged stool, pointed stone

hammer

195   c.1477

Heidelberg, Universitätsbibliothek,

cod. pal. germ. 17, fol.79

Old Testament

ILLUMINATION (workshop of Ludwig Heunfflin)

Crane with treadwheel and external lewis, template,

one-legged stool, pointed stone hammer

▶

196   c.1477
Heidelberg, Universitätsbibliothek,
cod. pal. germ. 17, fol.198v
Old Testament
ILLUMINATION (workshop of Ludwig Heunfflin)
Crane with external lewis
▼

197   c.1450
Heidelberg, Universitätsbibliothek,
cod. pal. germ. 149, fol.118
*Sieben weise Meister und die Chronik des Martin
von Polen*
ILLUMINATION (workshop of Diebold Lauber in
Hagenau)
Crane
◄

198   c.1460
Heidelberg, Universitätsbibliothek,
cod. pal. germ. 60, fol.6
Bible
ILLUMINATION (High Germany)
*Two-wheeled cart, trowel, crane with pallet, mortar
tub, mortar-mixing pick, mortar shovel*
►

199   1300–15
Heidelberg, Universitätsbibliothek,
cod. pal. germ. 164
Eike von Repgow, *Sachsenspiegel*
ILLUMINATION
Hammer, ladder
Koschorreck, Walter: *Die Heidelberger Bilderhandschrift
des Sachsenspiegels*, facsimile edition. Frankfurt 1970
Compare no.166, which is derived from the same
precursor but is independent of the Heidelberg MS
►

200   1300–15
Heidelberg, Universitätsbibliothek,
cod. pal. germ. 164
Eike von Repgow, *Sachsenspiegel*
ILLUMINATION
Axe, adze
Brandt II, p.48, fig.45; Koschorreck, Walter: *Die Heidelberger Bilderhandschrift des Sachsenspiegels*, facsimile edition. Frankfurt 1970
Compare no.166, which is derived from the same precursor but is independent of the Heidelberg MS
▼

202   1420–30
Heidelberg, Universitätsbibliothek,
cod. pal. germ. 432, fol.40v
Speculum humanae salvationis
ILLUMINATION
Trowel, pointed stone hammer
Bartsch, Karl: *Die altdeutschen Handschriften der Universitätsbibliothek in Heidelberg*. Heidelberg 1887, p.136, no.237
▶

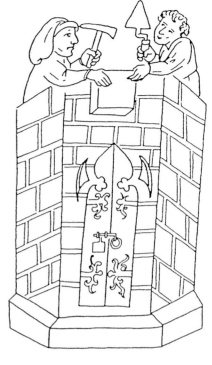

201   c.1410
Heidelberg, Universitätsbibliothek,
cod. pal. germ. 336, fol.49
Jansen Eninkel, *Weltchronik*
ILLUMINATION (Bavaria)
Builder's hut, ramp, hod, three-legged stool, square
▶

203   14th century
Heidelberg,
Universitätsbibliothek,
cod. sal. VII 31, fol.C 88
Vulgate Bible
ILLUMINATION
Trowel, ramp, hod
Bi/Nu 311; Oechselhäuser, p.76, no illus.
▶

204   13th century
Heidelberg, Universitätsbibliothek,
cod. sal. IX 5, fol.130v
Vulgate Bible
ILLUMINATION
Ramp, measuring staff, pannier
Bi/Nu 312; Oechselhäuser, p.16, no
illus.

205   1491
Heidelberg, Heinrich
Knoblochtzer, printer
Melusine
WOODCUT
Schramm 19, no.563
Free copy of no.10

206   first half 13th century
Heiligenkreuz, Stiftsbibliothek,
cod. 66
Initial in Cistercian psalter
PEN-AND-INK DRAWING
Axe, broad axe, hammer
Kloster Maulbronn 1178–1978. Exhibition catalogue,
Maulbronn 1978, figure on p.23; Gsell, Benedict: *Xenia
Bernardina* II/1. Vienna 1891, p.142; Schneider,
Ambrosius (ed.): *Die Cistercienser. Geschichte, Geist,
Kunst*. Cologne 1974, figure on p.57; Schneider,
Ambrosius, & Wienand, Adam: *Und sie folgten der
Regel St Benedicts*. Cologne 1981, figure on p.147

207   1280–1312
's-Hertogenbosch, Sint Janskathedraal
South transept, west gable, flying buttress
ARCHITECTURAL SCULPTURE
Trowel, mallet, chisel, level
Peeters, C.: *De Sint Janskathedraal te 's-Hertogenbosch*.
's-Gravenhage 1985, p.285, fig.256; de Tolnay, Charles:
Hieronymus Bosch. Baden-Baden 1965 (German
edition, Eltville 1984), figures on pp.446–8

207a   c.1500
Holkam Hall, Library of Viscount Coke,
MS 311, fol.122v
Virgil, *Aeneid*
ILLUMINATION
*Scaffolding, hammer, trowel, crane with treadwheel,
ladder, hod, shoulder basket*
Kren, Thomas: *Renaissance Paintings in Manuscripts.
Treasure from the British Library*. New York 1984, fig.6e

208   c.1130–40
Idensen, Old Church
Eastern vault span, southern half
DRY PAINTING
Hammer, ramp
Bi/Nu 4; Ehmke, Ruth: *Der Freskenzyklus in Idensen*.
Bremen & Horn 1958, figs 23–5 (= *Schriften des
Niedersächsischen Heimatbundes* NF 34); Neumann,
Eberhard, & Schwartz, Ernst: *Idensen*. Idensen 1964, fig.22

208a c.1473
Indianapolis, Museum of Arts
School of Dirk Bouts, Legend of St James
PANEL PAINTING
Scaffolding
Herwaarden, Jan van: 'Der mittelalterliche Jakobskult in
den Niederlanden', in Sauchen, Paolo Cancci von (ed.):
Santiago de Compostela. Augsburg 1995, figure on
p.336

◄

209 third quarter 12th century
Jena, Universitätsbibliothek,
cod. Bose q 6, fol.10b
Otto von Freising, *Chronica*
PEN-AND-INK DRAWING
*Trowel, hod, four-legged stool, pointed stone
hammer*
Bi/Nu 5; Binding (1972), figure on p.49 (outline);
Binding (Rhein und Maas), p.94, fig.7; Binding (1995),
p.172, fig.5 (outline); Scheidig, fig.13; Hofmeister,
Adolf, & Lammers, Walter (eds): *Ottonis episcopi
Frisigensis chronica sive historia de duabus civitatibus*.
Darmstadt 1961 (= *Ausgewählte Quellen zur deutschen
Geschichte des Mittelalters*, vol.16, ed. R. Buchner),
p.lxix, pl.2; Polaczek, Ernst: 'Die Bilder im Cod. Jenensis
Bose q 6', in Bloch, Hermann: *Die elsässischen Annalen
der Stauferzeit*. Innsbruck 1908 (= *Reg. der Bischöfe
von Straßburg*, vol.I), p.202, pl.II.
Compare no.302

►

210 third quarter 12th century
Jena, Universitätsbibliothek,
cod. Bose q 6, fol.10b
Otto von Freising, *Chronica*
PEN-AND-INK DRAWING
Pointed stone hammer
Bi/Nu 6; Binding (1972), figure on p.50 (outline);
Binding (1985), p.172, fig.5; Scheidig, fig.17;
Hofmeister, Adolf, & Lammers, Walter (eds): *Ottonis*

*episcopi Frisigensis chronica sive historia de duabus
civitatibus*. Darmstadt 1961 (= *Ausgewählte Quellen zur
deutschen Geschichte des Mittelalters*, vol.16, ed. R.
Buchner), p.lxix, pl.2; Polaczek, Ernst: 'Die Bilder im
Cod. Jenensis Bose q 6', in Bloch, Hermann: *Die
elsässischen Annalen der Stauferzeit*. Innsbruck 1908 (=
Reg. der Bischöfe von Straßburg, vol.I), p.202, pl.II.
Compare no.301

▼

211   1460–70
Jerusalem, Schocken Institute,
MS 24087, fo. 11
Haggada Nürnberg II
ILLUMINATION (Germany)
Hammer
Metzger, Thérèse & Mendel: *Jüdisches Leben im*
Mittelalter nach illuminierten hebräischen Handschriften
vom 13.–16. Jahrhundert. Fribourg & Würzburg 1983,
p.55, fig.85
▼

212   c.1360
Burg Karlstein, Great Tower
Staircase of St Cross chapel
MURAL
Scaffolding, trowel, crane with treadwheel, mortar
tub
Bi/Nu 129
▶

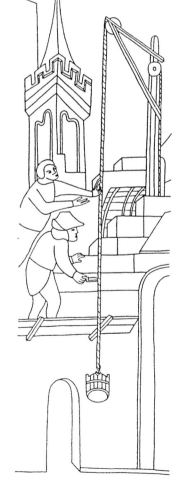

213   13th century
Källunge, Götland (Sweden),
south doorway of church
ARCHITECTURAL SCULPTURE
Mortar tub, mortar-mixing pick, pannier
Bi/Nu 128a; Swartling, Ingrid: 'Bilder ur en medeltida
byggnadshytta', *Götländskt arkiv* 1966, pp.29–34,
figs 2, 4
▶

213a   1435
Karlsruhe, Landsebibliothek,
cod. Aug. perg. 27
Bible
ILLUMINATION
Trowel, crane with pallet, ladder, plumbline, mortar
tub, mortar-mixing pick
Schöller, p.93, no.26, & p.81, fig.3; Marburger Index,
fiche 882/E1
▼

214   1385

Kassel, Landesbiliothek,

MS theol. 4, fol.28

Rudolf von Ems, *Weltchronik*

ILLUMINATION (Italy or South Tyrol)

Lump hammer, stone hammer, scaffolding, trowel,
crane with windlass, ramp, mortar tub, mortar
shovel, hod, stand for hod, punch

Bi/Nu 130; Tyghem, fig.80; Brandt I, p.247, fig.333
(outline); Minkowski, figure on p.32f, and pic. 28;
Schultz I, fig.80 (outline); Kratzert, Christine: *Die*
illustrierten Handschriften der Weltchronik des Rudolf
von Ems. Berlin 1974; Recht, p.337

◢

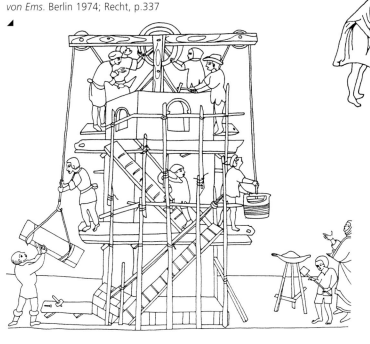

215   1180–1210

Klagenfurt, Landesmuseum für Kärnten

Millstätt Genesis, fol. 24

ILLUMINATION (Regensburg, Kärnten)

Crane, plumbline, chisel

Diener, Josef: *Genesis und Exodus nach der Millstätter*
Handschrift. Vienna 1862, vol.1, p.32; Green, Rosalie,
et al.: *Herrad of Hohenbourg. Hortus Deliciarum*.
London & Leiden 1979, fig.28; Schöller, p.93, no.27

▶

216   12th century

Klagenfurt, Landesmuseum für Kärnten

Millstätt Genesis, fol.120v

ILLUMINATION (Regensburg, Kärnten)

Trestle, broad axe

Diener, Josef: *Genesis und Exodus nach der Millstätter*
Handschrift. Vienna 1862, vol.1, p.32; Green, Rosalie,
et al.: *Herrad of Hohenbourg. Hortus Deliciarum*.
London & Leiden 1979, fig.28

◢

216a   15th century

Klagenfurt, Bibliothek des Kapuzinerkonvents

Illustrated Bible stories, fol. 31v

ILLUMINATION (Germany)

Schöller, p.93, no.28; Wickhoff, Franz (ed.):
Bescheibendes Verzeichnis der illuminierten
Handschriften in Österreich 3; Eisler, Robert: *Die*
illuminierten Handschriften in Kärnten. Leipzig 1907,
p.58

217   1501

Klosterneuburg

Rueland Frueauf the younger, *Erbauung von Stift*
Klosterneuburg

PANEL PAINTING

Mallet, measuring staff, template, chisel,
pointed stone hammer, square

Dworschak, Fritz, & Kühnel, Harry:
Die Gotik in Niederösterreich.
Vienna 1963, fig.13

◢

218 1489–92

Klosterneuburg, Stiftsgalerie

13th *Rundbild des Babenberger Stammbaums* (detail)

PANEL PAINTING (Klosterneuburg)

Crane with treadwheel

219 1310–15

Klosterneuburg, Stiftsbibliothek, CCI 2, fol.222v

Klosterneuburg Bible

Trowel, crane with pallet, pointed stone hammer

Kühnel, fig.11

220 mid-15th century

Cologne, Erzbischöfliches Diözesanmuseum

Gravestone of Cathedral master mason Nicolas von Bueren (1445)

SANDSTONE SCULPTURE

Mallet, level, chisel, square

Bi/Nu 241; Hecht, p.251, fig.64.2 (outline of level); *Das Erzbischöfliche Diözesanmuseum Köln*. Catalogue, Cologne 1936, nos 268–71, figs 66f; Clemen, Paul, Neu, Heinrich, & Witte, Fritz: *Der Dom zu Köln*. Düsseldorf 1938, p.288, fig.224 (= *Die Kunstdenkmäler der Rheinprovinz*. VI, 3, 1)

Details on individual figures are partly missing (drawing prepared from Clemen 1938)

▶

221 11th century

Cologne, Kunstgewerbemuseum

Remains of a gravestone from St Severin's church

Axe

Clemen, Paul: *Die Kunstdenkmäler der Stadt Köln* (= *Die Kunstdenkmäler der Rheinprovinz* VII, 2, 1). Düsseldorf 1929, p.237, fig.141

▼

222 *c.*1470–1500

Cologne, Wallraf-Richartz-Museum, no. 410

Masters of the St Katharine Legend and of the St Barbara Legend, *Heimsuchung* and the legend of the foundation of S. Maria Maggiore in Rome

PANEL PAINTING

Scaffolding, crane, ladder

Hiller, Irmgard, & Vey, Horst: *Katalog der deutschen und niederländischen Gemälde bis 1550 im Wallraf-Richartz-Museum und im Kunstgewerbemuseum der Stadt Köln*. Cologne 1969, pp.82–6, fig.92 (= WRM Catalogue 5); Kühnel, fig.91

223 1474

Cologne, Nicolaus Goetz, printer

Werner Rovelinck, *Fasciculus temporum*

WOODCUT

Crane with external lewis

Bi/Nu 314; Minkowski, no.71, no illus.

For derivatives see nos 49, 227, 521

224 1499

Cologne, Johannes Koelhoff the younger, printer

Cronica van der hilligen Stat Coellen, fol.16

WOODCUT

Mallet, crane with treadwheel and external lewis, mortar tub, mortar-mixing bin, mortar-mixing pick, one-legged stool, chisel, wheelbarrow, square, compasses

Bi/Nu 132; Schramm 8, no.753; Tyghem, fig.169; Andrews, frontispiece; Foerster, Rolf Hellmut: *Das Leben in der Gotik*. Munich, Vienna & Basle 1969, p.351; Klemm, fig.1; Minkowski, no.74, no illus.; de Smidt, p.13, fig.6

The same woodblock was reused several times in this book – compare fol. 17v and 62v

◀

225   c.1479

Cologne, Heinrich Quentell, printer
Low German Bible
WOODCUT
*Scaffolding, trowel, mallet, crane with treadwheel
and external lewis, ramp, mortar-mixing bin, mortar-
mixing tool, hod*
Bi/Nu 131; Schramm 8, no.363; Tyghem, fig.157;
Eichenberger, Walter, & Wendland, Henning: *Deutsche
Bibeln vor Luther*. Hamburg 1977, p.75, fig.169;
Minkowski, vol.81
For re-use of this woodblock see no.386; for
derivatives, see nos 13, 528

226   1485

Cologne, Ludwig von Renchen, printer
Jacobus de Voragine, *Life of the Saints*
WOODCUT
Schramm 8, no.664
Reversed derivative of no.11

227   1476

Cologne, Konrad Winters von Homborch,
printer
Werner Rovelinck, *Fasciculus temporum*
WOODCUT
Bi/Nu 313; Schramm 8, no.346; Minkowski, no.73,
no illus.
Copy of no.223; compare also no.521
This woodcut was used as a frontispiece for the
Chronicles of England (a) printed c.1485 in St Albans
(Bi/Nu 335; Minkowski, no. 97, no illus.) and (b) printed
c.1497–8 in Westminster by Wynkyn de Worde (Bi/Nu
336; Minkowski, no. 98, no illus.). Compare Baer, Leo:
Die illustrierten Historienbücher des 15. Jahrhunderts.
Strasbourg 1903, p. 83

228   c.1160–70

Cologne (Deutz), St Heribert church
Medallion on the sloping roof of the Shrine of
St Heribert
ENAMEL (Rhein/Maas area)
Hammer
Bi/Nu 7; Binding (1972), figure on p.47 (outline);
Binding (*Rhein und Maas*), p.93, fig.1 (outline); Legner,
Anton (ed.): *Ornamenta ecclesiae*. Exhibition catalogue,
Cologne 1985, vol.2, pp.314–23, figure on p.322;
Oediger, Friedrich W.: *Geschichte des Erzbistums Köln*
vol.1. Cologne 1972, plate after p.104

229   c.1160–70

Cologne (Deutz), St Heribert church
Medallion on the sloping roof of the Shrine of
St Heribert
ENAMEL (Rhein/Maas area)
Axe
Bi/Nu 40; Binding (1972), figure on p.59 (outline);
Legner, Anton (ed.): *Ornamenta ecclesiae*. Exhibition
catalogue, Cologne 1985, vol.2, pp.314–323, figures
on pp.314, 320

229a   after 1458
Copenhagen, Kongelige Bibliothek,
MS Thott 430, 2°, fol.98
School of Tours, *Les chroniques Martiniennes*
ILLUMINATION
Scaffolding, levering pole, crane with treadwheel,
ladder, mortar-mixing pick, pointedstone hammer,
hawk
Svanberg, Jan: *Master Masons*. Sweden 1983, p.90,
fig.44
▼

230   15th century
Copenhagen, Kongelige Bibliothek,
MS Thott 568, fol.1
French manuscript
ILLUMINATION
Crane with windlass and pallet, ladder, hod,
pointed stone hammer
Bi/Nu 133; Tyghem, fig.131; Du Colombier, p.110,
fig.73
▶

230a   first quarter 14th century
Copenhagen, Kongelige Bibliothek,
MS G.K.S. 3384.8, fol.36
Psalter
ILLUMINATION (Flanders)
Schöller, p.93, no.29; Randall, p.162, no illus.

230b   first quarter 14th century
Copenhagen, Kongelige Bibliothek,
MS G.K.S. 3384.80, fol.111
Psalter
ILLUMINATION (Flanders)
Compasses
Randall, fig. xcix, 479

229b   15th century
Copenhagen, Kongelige Bibliothek,
MS Thott 413, fol.178
ILLUMINATION
Lump hammer, scaffolding, ladder, mortar-mixing
pick, hod, chisel
Small, Graeme: 'Les origines de la ville de Tournai dans
les chroniques légendaires du bas moyen âge', in
Dumoulin, Chanoine Jean, & Pycke, Jacques, (eds): *Les*
grands siècles de Tournai (12e–15e siècles). Tournai
1993, p.109, fig.39
▶

231   first quarter 15th century
Kraków, Biblioteka Jagiellonska,
MS germ. quart. 574, fol.1
Speculum humanae salvationis
PEN-AND-INK DRAWING (Middle Germany)
Bi/Nu 298
▼

232   1325–30
Kremsmünster, Benedictine abbey
Stiftsbibliothek, Codex Cremifarnensis 243, fol. 38
Speculum humanae salvationis
Trowel, ramp, mortar tub, stone hammer with
serrated blade
Speculum humanae salvationis. Vollständige Faksimile-
Ausgabe des Codex Cremifarnensis 243 des
Benediktinerstiftes Kremsmünster. Graz 1972
▼

233   1325–30
Kremsmünster, Benedictine abbey
Stiftsbibliothek, Codex Cremifarnensis 243, fol.39v
Speculum humanae salvationis
Trowel, ramp, mortar tub, mortar-mixing pick, stone
hammer
Speculum humanae salvationis. Vollständige Faksimile-
Ausgabe des Codex Cremifarnensis 243 des
Benediktinerstiftes Kremsmünster. Graz 1972
▼

234   c.1210–15
Laon, Notre-Dame Cathedral
Choir window 'Légende de Théophile'
STAINED GLASS
Hammer, ramp, level, pointed stone hammer
Deuchler, Florenz: *Die Chorfenster der Kathedrale in*
Laon. Berlin 1956; Grodecki, Louis, & Brisac, Catherine:
Le vitrail gothique au XIIIe siècle. Fribourg 1984, p.34,
fig.23
▼

235   c.1200
Laon, Notre-Dame Cathedral
West façade, vaulting of the window to the left of
the rose window
ARCHITECTURAL SCULPTURE
Drawing board, drawing pins
Bi/Nu 315; Aubert, Marcel, & Goubet, Simone: *Gotische*
Kathedralen und Kunstschätze in Frankreich.
Wiesbaden, n.d., p.74, no.illus.

236   c.1200
Larrelt (Friesland)
Parish church, tympanum,
'artifex Ludbrud'
ARCHITECTURAL SCULPTURE
Broad axe
Bi/Nu 41; Gerstenberg, figure on
p.7; Binding (1972), figure on
p.63 (outline)
▼

237   mid-10th century
Leiden, Bibliotheek der Rijksuniversiteit,
co. Burm. Q3, fol.144v
Prudentius, *Psychomachia*
PEN-AND-INK DRAWING (Lower Rhine, Kloster
Egmond)
Stone hammer, punch
Stettiner, Richard: *Die illustrierten*
Prudentiushandschriften. Berlin 1905, pl.71
Compare no.437
▼

238   first quarter 11th century
Leiden, Bibliotheek der Rijksuniversiteit,
cod. Voss. lat. oct. 15, fol.43v
Prudentius, *Psychomachia*, collected manuscript,
so-called Specimen Book of Adémar de Chabannes
PEN-AND-INK DRAWING (Limoges, Saint-Martial; after
late Classical examples)
Measuring staff
Legner, Anton (ed.): *Ornamenta ecclesiae.* Exhibition
catalogue, Cologne 1985, vol.1, p.315; Stettiner,
Richard: *Die illustrierten Prudentiushandschriften.* Berlin
1905, pl.26
Compare no.497
▼

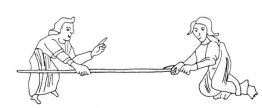

239   first half 14th century
Leipzig, Universitätsbibliothek,
Rep. I, 1, fol.1v
Livy manuscript
ILLUMINATION (northern Italy)
Axe, wood chisel, drill, broad axe, lump hammer,
scaffolding, trowel, ramp, mortar-mixing pick, hod,
stand for hod, frame saw, crowbar
Tyghem, fig.59; Brandt II, p.42, fig.37
◀ ▼

240   14th century
Lincoln, Cathedral
Gravestone of master mason Richard of
Gainsborough (d. 1300), in the crossing
STONE CARVING
Square
Bi/Nu 242; Du Colombier, p.103, fig.63 (outline);
Binding (1974), p.108, fig.11
▼

241   c.1400
Linz, Studienbibliothek, MS 472
Weltchronik
ILLUMINATION
Crane with external lewis, mortar tub, pointed stone hammer, square
Bi/Nu 134; Tyghem, fig.90; Du Colombier, p.50, fig.29; Minkowski, p.116a, after 24
Compare nos 335, 490
▼

241a   1410–15
Lisbon, Gulbenkian Foundation,
MS LA 143, fol.47
Cité-des-Dames workshop: Bocaccio, *Des cleres et nobles femmes*
ILLUMINATION
Pointed stone hammer, stone hammer, compasses
Schöller, p.93, no.31; Meiss, Millard: *French Painting in the time of Jean de Berry. The Boucicaut Masters*. London & New York 1968, plate volume, fig.371

242   1411
Litoměřice (Czech Republic), State Archive
So-called Leitmeritz Bible, fol. 114
ILLUMINATION
Scaffolding, hammer, crane with treadwheel and external lewis, hod
Bi/Nu 135; Husa, fig.95
▶

243   beginning 14th century
London, British Museum
Floor tile from church of SS Peter and Paul, Tring, Hertfordshire
Axe, broad axe
Eames, Elizabeth: *English Medieval Tiles*, British Museum, London 1985, cover and p.23
▼

243a first quarter 14th century
London, British Museum,
Add. MS 10292, fol.55v
ILLUMINATION
Lump hammer, chisel
Barral i Altet, Xavier (ed.): *Artistes, artisans et
productions artistiques au moyen âge.
Kolloquium Rennes 1983.* Paris 1990,
vol.3, title page
▼

244 1350–60
London, British Museum,
Add. MS 14761, fol.30v
Hebrew manuscript
ILLUMINATION (Barcelona)
Hammer, trowel, crane, ladder, stone hammer
▼

244a 1350–60
London, British Museum,
Add. MS 14761, fol.43
Hebrew manuscript
ILLUMINATION (Barcelona)
Trowel, crane, ladder
▼

245 c.1460
London, British Museum,
Add. MS 14762, fol.7
Joel Ben Simon Haggadah
ILLUMINATION (southern Germany)
*Scaffolding, trowel, crane with external lewis, ladder,
mortar tub, mortar-mixing bin, mortar-mixing pick*
Metzger, Thérèse & Mendel: *Jüdisches Leben im
Mittelalter nach illuminierten hebräischen Handschriften.*
Fribourg & Würzburg 1983, p.166, fig.221
▼

246 beginning 15th century
London, British Museum,
Add. MS 15245, fol.3v
St Augustine, *De civitate Dei*
ILLUMINATION
Compasses
Block Friedman, John: 'The architect's compass in
creation miniatures of the later middle ages' in *Traditio*
30, 1974, fig.XI
◀

247 c.1285
London, British Museum,
Add. MS 15268, fol.1v
Histoire universelle
ILLUMINATION (Akkon, with English influence)
Compasses
Zahlten, Johannes: *Creatio mundi. Darstellungen der
sechs Schöpfungstage und naturwissenschaftliches
Weltbild im Mittelalter.* Stuttgart 1979, fig.284
(= *Stuttgarter Beiträge zur Geschichte und Politik,*
vol.13)
◀

247a   end 14th century
London, British Museum,
Add. MS 15277, fol.15v–16
Old Testament
COLOUR-WASHED PEN-AND-INK DRAWING
Trestle, broad axe, stone hammer, plane
▼

248a   c.1495–1500
London, British Museum,
Add. MS 17280, fol.168v
So-called Book of Hours of Philippe le Beau and
John of Castile
ILLUMINATION (Bruges)
Axe, drill, bow saw
'Dresdner Gebetbuchmeister', in Brinkmann, Bodo: *Die
flämische Buchmalerei am Ende des Burgunderreiches.*
Turnhout 1997, p.387, col. pl.55
                                        ▶

249   1405–30
London, British Museum,
Add. MS 18850, fol.15v
Book of Hours of the Duke of Bedford
ILLUMINATION (France)
*Wood chisel, drill, broad axe, hammer, plane, mallet,
ladder, nails, hand saw, saw*

Bi/Nu 145; Tyghem, fig.143; Andrews, pl.XIII; Du
Colombier, p.45, fig.26; Harvey (1975), fig.45; Recht,
p.64; Meiss, Millard: *The De Lévis Hours and the
Bedford Workshop.* New Haven, Conn., 1972 (= *Yale
Lectures on Medieval Illumination*), fig.56
▼

248   15th century
London, British Museum,
Add. MS 15692, fol.29v
Euclid
ILLUMINATION (Italy)
Drawing board, square, compasses
Harvey (1975), fig.32
▶

250   1405–30

London, British Museum,

Add. MS 18850, fol.17v

Book of Hours of the Duke of Bedford

ILLUMINATION (France)

Boss hammer, stone hammer, scaffolding, crane with
windlass, mortar bucket, mortar shovel, hod, pointed stone
hammer, carrying basket, shelter, water tub, square, claw
chisel, serrated stone hammer

Bi/Nu 146; Tyghem, fig.105; Andrews, pl.XII; Aubert, figure on
p.207; Brandt I, p.246, fig.331; Du Colombier, p.45, fig.25;
Minkowski, pl.VIII; Recht, p.65; Coldstream (1991), p.8, fig.6

▶

250a   c.1420

London, British Museum,

Add. MS 18856, fol.14v

Bible stories

ILLUMINATION (England)

Hammer, nail

Schöller, p.93, no.32; Meiss, Millard: *The De Lévis Hours and*
the Bedford Workshop. New Haven, Conn., 1972 (= *Yale*
Lectures on Medieval Illumination), fig.57

▼

251   end 15th century

London, British Museum,

Add. MS 19720, fol.27

Pierre Croissens, *Le livre de Rustican des prouffiz rüraulx*

ILLUMINATION

Trestle, broad axe, scaffolding, trowel, crane with windlass, ladder, level, mortar tub, hod, frame saw, wheelbarrow, water pitcher

Bi/Nu 147; Tyghem, fig.135; Andrews, pl.XI; Harvey (1975), fig.14

▶

252   beginning 14th century

London, British Museum,

Add. MS 27210, fol.3

Golden Haggadah

ILLUMINATION (northern Spain)

Bucket, mortar-mixing pick, rope pulley

▼

253   beginning 14th century

London, British Museum,

Add. MS 27210, fol.11

Golden Haggadah

ILLUMINATION (northern Spain)

Tub, scaffolding, trowel, rope pulley

Gimpel, Jean: *Les bâtisseurs de cathédrales*. Bourges 1976, figure on p.54; Recht, p.76

▶

254   c.1500
London, British Museum,
Add. MS 35313, fol.34
Book of Hours
ILLUMINATION (Flanders, Hortulusmeister and his workshop)
Lump hammer, scaffolding, hammer, cart, crane with windlass and external lewis, measuring staff, hod, chisel, saw
Bi/Nu 148; Andrews, pl.IX; Harvey (1975), fig.22; Winston, Richard & Clara: *Notre-Dame*. Wiesbaden 1979, p.49; Coldstream (1991), p.51, fig.54

256   12th century
London, British Museum,
Add. MS 39943, fol.39
Venerable Bede, *Vita S. Cuthberti*
ILLUMINATION
Brooke, Christopher: *Die große Zeit der Klöster, 1000–1300*. Freiburg, Basle & Vienna 1976, p.63, fig.94
▼

257   12th century
London, British Museum,
Add. MS 39943, fol.41
Venerable Bede, *Vita S. Cuthberti*
ILLUMINATION
Mortar shovel
Brooke, Christopher: *Die große Zeit der Klöster, 1000–1300*. Freiburg, Basle & Vienna 1976, p.63, fig.95
▼

255   c.1450
London, British Museum,
Add. MS 38122, fol.78v
Dutch Bible
ILLUMINATION (northern Netherlands)
Work table, wooden template, mortar shovel, shovel, wheelbarrow
Hollestelle, Johanna: *De Steenbakerij in de Nederlanden tot omstreeks 1560*. Arnhem 1976, fig.1; Salzmann, L.F.: *Building in England down to 1540*. Oxford 1952, pl.12a; Recht, p.31

258   1326–31

London, British Museum,
Add. MS 47682, fol.2
Holkham Bible
ILLUMINATION
Compasses
Block Friedman, John: 'The architect's compass in creation
miniatures of the later middle ages', in *Traditio* 30, 1974,
fig.VII (reversed image); Gimpel, Jean: *Les bâtisseurs des
cathédrales*. Bourges 1976, figure on p.32; Zahlten, Johannes:
*Creatio mundi. Darstellungen der sechs Schöpfungstage und
naturwissenschaftliches Weltbild im Mittelalter*. Stuttgart
1979, fig.290 (= *Stuttgarter Beiträge zur Geschichte und
Politik*, vol.13)

▼

259   1326–31

London, British Museum, Add.
MS 47682, fol.27
Holkham Bible
ILLUMINATION
*Double-sided stone hammer, scaffolding, trowel, mallet,
basket, crane, ladder, plumbline, square*
Harvey, John: *Medieval Craftsmen*. London & Sydney 1975,
fig.19; Schöller, p.93, no.B4
▼

260   1482

London, British Museum,
Bib. Reg. 15 E 11, fol.99
Jean du Ries, *Des Proietez des Choses*
ILLUMINATION (Bruges)
Mallet, spoon-bit, chisel
Bi/Nu 142; Tyghem, fig.70; Andrews, pl.I in the appendix;
Foerster, Rolf Hellmut: *Das Leben in der Gotik*. Munich,
Vienna & Basle 1969, figure on p.30; Fremantle, Anne: *Kaiser,
Ritter und Scholaren*. Hamburg 1973, figure on p.94 (extract)

▼

261   1224–35

London, British Museum,
Burney MS 3-f, fol.5v
Bible of Robertus de Bello
ILLUMINATION (Canterbury)
Stone hammer, ramp, pannier
Rickert, Margaret: *Painting in Britain.
The Middle Ages*. Baltimore 1954,
pl.96; Schöller, p.93, no.35

▶

262   15th century
London, British Museum,
Cotton MS Aug. A V, fol.22
French manuscript
ILLUMINATION
Broad axe, scaffolding, ladder, plumbline, level, hod,
wheelbarrow, pointed stone hammer
Bi/Nu 137; Tyghem, fig.134; Coldstream (1991), p.45,
fig.46
▼

264   15th century
London, British Museum,
Cotton MS Aug. A V, fol.416
French manuscript

ILLUMINATION
Basket, hod, wheelbarrow
Bi/Nu 139; Tyghem, fig.136; Andrews, pl.X
▼

263   15th century
London, British Museum,
Cotton MS Aug. A V, fol.51v
French manuscript
ILLUMINATION
Scaffolding, trowel, crane, hod, wheelbarrow
Bi/Nu 138; Tyghem, fig.133

▶

265   second quarter 11th century
London, British Museum,
Cotton MS Claudius B IV, fol.19
Aelfric, metrical paraphrase of the Pentateuch and
Joshua
ILLUMINATION (St Augustine's Abbey, Canterbury)
*Lump hammer, scaffolding, hammer, ladder, mortar
tub, chisel (possibly a punch)*
Bi/Nu 8; Binding (1972), figure on p.19 (outline); Borst,
Arno: *Der Turmbau zu Babel*, vol.II, part 1. Stuttgart
1958, p.550; Foerster, Rolf Hellmut: *Das Leben in der
Gotik*. Munich, Vienna & Basle 1969, p.351; *Meyers
illustrierte Weltgeschichte*, vol.11. Mannheim 1980,
p.51; Minkowski, pic. 4; Rickert, Margaret: *Painting in
Britain. The Middle Ages*. Baltimore 1954, pl.35
▼

266   first half 11th century
London, British Museum,
Cotton MS Cleopatra C VIII
Mixed volume including MS of *Psychmachia*
PEN-AND-INK DRAWING (Anglo-Saxon, after Anglo-
Saxon forerunners of the 9th and 10th centuries)
Measuring staff
Stettiner, Richard: *Die illustrierten
Prudentiushandschriften*. Berlin 1905, pl.45/46, no.2
Compare no.122
▼

267   third quarter 14th century
London, British Museum,
Cotton Nero D I, fol.23
Life of the Offas
PEN-AND-INK DRAWING
*Stone hammer, basket, crane with windlass, level,
square, compasses*
Bi/Nu 136; Tyghem, fig.57; Andrews, pl.II, fig.1; Aubert,
figure on p.251; Binding (1974), p.9, fig.3 (outline);
Brandt II, p.148, fig.183; Du Colombier, p.99, fig.58;
Harvey, fig.11; Hecht, p.70, fig.69, 3 (level outline);
Recht, p.39; Coldstream (1991), p.12, fig.10
Compare no.168 (precursor)
▼

268 c.1300
London, British Museum,
Egerton MS 1894, fol.5v
English manuscript
ILLUMINATION
Scaffolding, ramp, level, mortar shovel, hod,
stretcher, hawk
Colvin, H.M.: *Building accounts of King Henry III.*
Oxford 1971, pl.1; Harvey (1975), fig.16; Schöller, p.93,
no.36; Coldstream (1991), p.53, fig.58

268a beginning 11th century
London, British Museum,
Harleian MS 603, fol.66v
Harley Psalter
PEN-AND-INK DRAWING (Canterbury)
Summary representation of tools
Basing, Patricia: *Trades and Crafts in*
Medieval Manuscripts. London
1990, p.11, fig.1

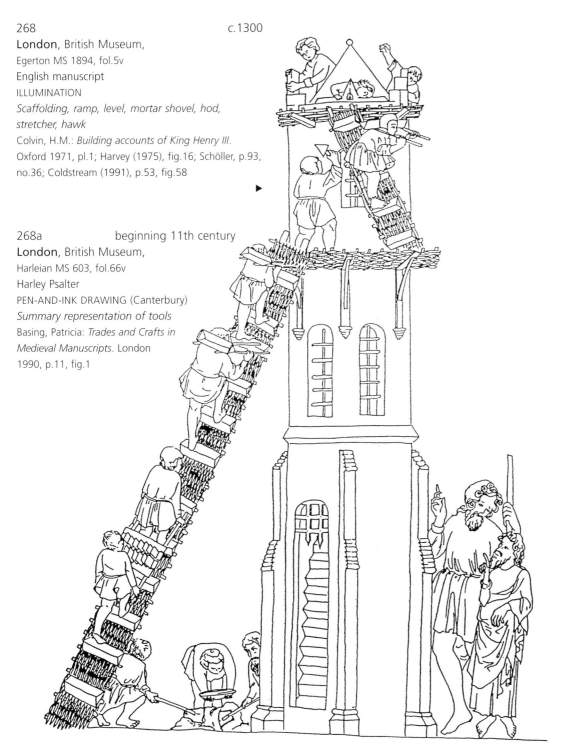

269, 270 ▲ ▲ 1230–40
London, British Museum,
Harleian MS 1526, fols 8v, 14v
Bible moralisée
ILLUMINATION
Pick
Laborde, Tome III, pl. 451, 457
This refers to a three-volume set of the *Bible moralisée*,
of which two examples are known. The older and better
is in the care of Toledo cathedral and the younger is split
between Oxford (Bodley 270b), Paris (Bibliothèque
Nationale, MS lat. 11560) and London (British Museum,
Harleian MS 1526–7). Compare Haussherr, Reiner:
'Templum Salomonis und Ecclesia Christi', in *Zeitschrift*
für Kunstgeschichte 31, 2. Munich & Berlin 1968, p.107

271   1230–40
London, British Museum,
Harleian MS 1527, fol.4v
Bible moralisée
ILLUMINATION
Square, compasses
Laborde, Tome III, pl.475
Compare no.559 and see note to no.269

▼

272   1433
London, British Museum,
Harleian MS 2278, fol.28v
John Lydgate, *Life of St Edmund*
ILLUMINATION (England)
*Stone hammer, scaffolding, trowel,
crane with windlass, mortar tub,
mortar bucket, mortar shovel*
Bi/Nu 144; Tyghem, fig.125; Dammertz,
Victor, *et al.*: *Benedictus. Eine
Kulturgeschichte des Abendlandes.*
Geneva 1980, p.389, fig.358

▶

273   15th century
London, British Museum,
Harleian MS 4431, fol.109
French manuscript
ILLUMINATION
Crane with windlass, serrated stone axe, compasses
Harvey (1975), fig.24
Compare no.463c

▼

273a   c.1410
London, British Museum,
Harleian MS 4431, fol.290
Cité-des-Dames workshop; Christine de Pisan, *La
cité des dames*
ILLUMINATION
Trowel, hod
Schöller, p.94, no.38; Schaefer, Lucie: 'Die Illustrationen
zu den Handschriften der Christine de Pisan', in
Marburger Jahrbuch für Kunstgewerbe 10, 1937,
p.151, fig.39; Meiss (1974), fig.38
Compare nos 118a, 464

▼

273b   c.1410
London, British Museum,
Harleian MS 4431, fol.290
Cité-des-Dames workshop; Christine de Pisan, *La cité des dames*
ILLUMINATION
Crane
Schöller, p.94, no.39; Meiss (1974), fig.42
▼

273c   first half 13th century
London, British Museum,
Harleian Roll Y.6
The Guthlac Roll
ILLUMINATION (Crowland)
Stone hammer, trowel, basket, crane
Schöller, p.94, no.40; Foto Courtauld 9/1 (23); Schöller (1998), fig.4, p.103
▶

274   first quarter 14th century
London, British Museum,
MS Or. 2737, fol.62v
Hebrew manuscript
ILLUMINATION (Spain)
Ladder
Metzger, Thérèse & Mendel: *Jüdisches Leben im Mittelalter nach illuminierten hebräischen Handschriften vom 13.–16. Jahrhundert*. Fribourg & Würzburg 1983, p.164, fig.214
▶

275   c.1350
London, British Museum,
MS Or. 2884, fol.2v
Hebrew manuscript
ILLUMINATION (Spain, Barcelona?)
Axe, hatchet, hammer
Metzger, Thérèse & Mendel: *Jüdisches Leben im Mittelalter nach illuminierten hebräischen Handschriften vom 13.–16. Jahrhundert*. Fribourg & Würzburg 1983, p.158, fig.207
▶

276   1374
London, British Museum,
MS Or. 5024, fol.184v
Hebrew manuscript
ILLUMINATION (Italy)
Plane, bench for plane
Metzger, Thérèse & Mendel: *Jüdisches Leben im Mittelalter nach illuminierten hebräischen Handschriften vom 13.–16. Jahrhundert*. Fribourg & Würzburg 1983, p.175, fig.239
▼

276a   first quarter 14th century
London, British Museum,
Royal MS 2 B VII, fol.65v
Queen Mary's Psalter
ILLUMINATION (England)
Stone hammer, level
Schöller, p.94, no.42; Millar, Eric G.: *La miniature du XIVe et SVe siècles*. Paris & Brussels 1928, pl.30; Recht, p.39

▶

277   c.1340
London, British Museum,
Royal MS 10 E IV, fol.99v
English manuscript
ILLUMINATION
Trestle, two-man saw
Harvey (1975), fig.42

▼

277a   beginning 14th century
London, British Museum,
Royal MS 14 E III, fol.66v
Romance of the Holy Grail
ILLUMINATION
Lump hammer, chisel
Basing, Patricia: *Trades and Crafts in Medieval Manuscripts*. London 1990, p.71, fig.39
Compare no.243a

▼

277b   second quarter 14th century
London, British Museum,
Royal MS 10 E IV, fol.289v
Smithfield Decretales
WASHED PEN-AND-INK DRAWING (England)
Scaffolding, trowel, crane with windlass
Schöller, p.94, no.43; Randall, p.208, no illus.

▼

278   beginning 14th century
London, British Museum,
Royal MS 14 E III, fol.85v
English manuscript
ILLUMINATION (England)
Stone hammer, trowel, centring, ladder
Bi/Nu 140; Tyghem, fig.63; Du Colombier, p.46, fig.27;
Harvey (1975), fig.17; Recht, p.90
▼

280   beginning 15th century
London, British Museum,
Royal MS 15 D III, fol.12
Guyart des Moulins, *Historia Scholastica*
ILLUMINATION (France)
Trestle, broad axe, hammer
Harvey (1975), fig.44; Schöller, p.94, no.44
▼

281   beginning 15th century
London, British Museum,
Royal MS 15 D III, fol.15v
Guyart des Moulins, *Historia Scholastica*
ILLUMINATION (France)
Scaffolding with ramp, trowel, measuring staff, hod,
square, stone hammer
Bi/Nu 141; Tyghem, fig.94; Harvey (1975), fig.23
▼

279   beginning 15th century
London, British Museum,
Royal MS 15 D III, fol.3v
Guyart des Moulins, *Historia Scholastica*
ILLUMINATION (France)
Compasses
Block Friedman, John: 'The architect's compass in
creation miniatures of the later middle ages', in
Traditio 30, 1974, fig.IX; Müller, Christian:
Torheiten des Lebens – Mathias Gerungs
'Melancolia 1558'. Karlsruhe 1983, p.30
(reversed illustration)

282   1482
London, British Museum,
Royal MS 15 E III, fol.102
Bartholomaeus Anglicus, *Des propriétés des choses*
ILLUMINATION (Flanders)
Pointed stone hammer
Harvey (1975), fig.27
▼

283a   beginning 15th century
London, British Museum,
Royal MS 20 Bxx, fol.82
Story of Alexander the Great
ILLUMINATION (France)
◄

*Lump hammer, scaffolding, trowel, ladder, level, hod,
masonry chisel, punch, pointed stone hammer,
square*
Basing, Patricia: *Trades and Crafts in Medieval
Manuscripts*. London 1990, p.68, fig.38

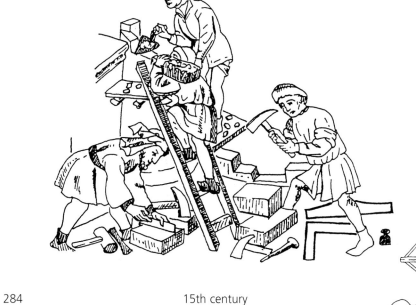

283   1411
London, British Museum,
Royal MS 19 D III, fol.3
Guyart des Moulins, *Historia Scholastica*
ILLUMINATION
(France,
Clairefontaine)
Compasses
Block Friedman, John:
'The architect's
compass in creation
miniatures of the later
middle ages', in
Traditio 30, 1974,
fig.XII
►

284   15th century
London, British Museum,
Royal MS 20 E II, fol.262
Book of hours, Anglo-French Chronique de
France ou de Saint-Denis
ILLUMINATION
*Scaffolding, crane with treadwheel, ladder,
plumbline, pointed stone hammer, square,
compasses, trowel*
Bi/Nu 143; Andrews, pl.VII
►

284a after 1481
London, British Museum,
MS Yates Thompson 33, fol. 74
Normandy Chronicle for Philippe de Crèvecoeur
ILLUMINATION (France)
Trowel, plumbline, mortar tub, mortar-mixing pick, hod
Schöller, p.94, no.45; Pächt, Jenni, Thoss, fig.39; Yates
Thompson, Henry: *Illustrations from 100 Manuscripts in
the Library of Henry Yates Thompson*, vol.6. London,
1916, pl.66

▼

284b second half 14th century
London, British Museum,
MS Yates Thompson 76, 79 A, fol.1
Bible historiale du Duc de Berry
ILLUMINATION
Trowel, hod, pointed stone hammer
Yates Thompson, Henry: *Illustrations from 100
Manuscripts in the Library of Henry Yates Thompson*,
vol.5. London, 1915, pl.4

▶

284c first quarter 15th century
London, Society of Antiquaries
PANEL PAINTING
Trowel, mortar tub, stone hammer
Davenport, Millia, *The Book of Costume*. New York
1976, vol.1, p.353, fig.924

284d 14th century
Lucca, San Martino Cathedral
MS 1, fol.112v
Gradual
ILLUMINATION
*Hammer, trowel, basket, mortar-mixing pick, mortar
shovel, hod, stone hammer*
Baracchini, Clara, & Caleca, Antonio: *Il Duomo di
Lucca*. Lucca 1973, pp.168–9, fig.786

▶

285 1488
Lübeck, Steffen Arndes, printer
Jacobus de Voragine, *Life of the Saints*, fol.162v
WOODCUT
Schramm 11, no.76
Re-use of the printing block for no.397

286 1492
Lübeck, Steffen Arndes, printer
Jacobus de Voragine, *Life of the Saints*
WOODCUT
Trowel, ladder, hod
Schramm 11, no.825

▼

287   1492
Lübeck, Steffen Arndes, printer
Jacobus de Voragine, *Life of the Saints*
WOODCUT
Ladder, mortar tub, mortar-mixing pick
Schramm 11, no.898
▼

289   1475
Lübeck, Lucas Brandis, printer
Rudimentum novitiorum, fol.3 va
WOODCUT
Crane with external lewis, mortar bucket, mortar-mixing pick, pointed stone hammer
Schramm 10, no.9
▼

290   1475
Lübeck, Lucas Brandis, printer
Rudimentum novitiorum, fol.3 vb
WOODCUT
Crane, mortar-mixing pick, wheelbarrow
Bi/Nu 151; Schramm 10, no.16; Minkowski, pic. 75
▼

288   1494
Lübeck, Steffen Arndes, printer
Low German Bible
WOODCUT
Tub, scaffolding, trowel, mallet, crane with treadwheel, ladder, mortar shovel, hod, chisel
Bi/Nu 150; Schramm 11, nos 958, 1031; Tyghem, fig.168; Klemm, fig.5; Minkowski, pic. 93

▶

291   1475
Lübeck, Lucas Brandis, printer
Rudimentum novitiorum, fol.3 vc
WOODCUT
Mortar shovel, wheelbarrow
Schramm 10, no.37
▼

293   1475
Lübeck, Lucas Brandis, printer
Rudimentum novitiorum, fol.3 ve
WOODCUT
Crane with external lewis, mortar-mixing pick
Schramm 10, no.90
▼

294   c.1475
Lübeck, Lucas Brandis, printer
Spiegel menschlicher Behaltnis
WOODCUT
Scaffolding, trowel, ladder, hod
Bi/Nu 149; Schramm 10, no.414; Minkowski, pic. 76
For a re-use of this block see no.295
▼

292   1475
Lübeck, Lucas Brandis, printer
Rudimentum novitiorum, fol.3 vd
WOODCUT
Hammer, crane
Schramm 10, no.19

▶

295   1478
Lübeck, Lucas Brandis, printer
Nye Eee und Passional
WOODCUT
Bi/Nu 317; Schramm 10, no.214; Minkowski, no.77, no
illus.
Re-use of the printing block in no.294

295a   1496
Lübeck, Sankt-Annen-Museum
Henning van der Weide, *Altar der*
Fronleichnamsbruderschaft
PANEL PAINTING
Scaffolding, crane
Schöller, p.94, no.46 and p.85, fig.46; Marburger
Index, fiche 698/F2

295b   c.1150
Liège, Archives de l'Etat, Liasse 1148-5964
A.E. Liège, exue imp. de Wetzlar
Remaklus-Retabel von Stablo; from later drawing
of 1661
PEN-AND-INK DRAWING
Axe, trestle, tub, broad axe, hammer, crane
Bi/Nu 2; Binding (1972), figure on p.23 (outline);
Binding (*Rhein und Maas*), p.94, fig.11 (outline);
Binding (*Ornamenta ecclesiae*), vol.1, p.184; Tyghem,
fig.13; Klötzsche, Dieter, in *Rhein und Maas. Kunst und
Kultur 800–1400*. Cologne 1972, p.249, fig.G10;
Krempel, Ulla: 'Das Remaclusretabel in Stavelot und
seine künstlerische Nachfolge', in *Münchener Jahrbuch
der bildenden Kunst*, 3rd ed., vol.22, 1971, pp.23–45,
fig.1; Recht, p.335
▼

296   11th/12th century
Lyon, Bibliothèque du Palais des Arts,
MS 22
Prudentius, *Psychomachia*
PEN-AND-INK DRAWING (north-eastern
France, from Carolingian forerunners of
c.800)
Stone hammer, level, chisel
Bi/Nu 9; Hecht, p.254, fig.66
▶

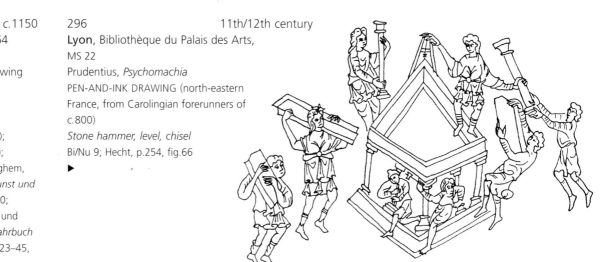

296a   c.1495
Lyon, M. Huss, printer
Prudentius, *Psychomachia*
Werner Rovelinck *père*, Fasciculus temporum
WOODCUT
*Scaffolding, trowel, crane with external lewis,
ladder, hod with brow band, pointed stone hammer*
Vernet, André: *Histoire des bibliothèques
françaises: les bibliothèques médiévales du
VIe siècle à 1530*. n.p., n.d., p.303
▶

296b   1310–20

Lyon, Cathedral

Right-hand wall of the middle doorway on the west façade

ARCHITECTURAL SCULPTURE

Hammer, basket

Schöller, p.94, no.47; *L'index photographique de l'art en France* (ed. Bildarchiv Foto Marburg), Munich 1978–91, fiche 310/G10; Minkowski, Helmut: *Vermutungen über den Turm zu Babel.* Freren 1991, p.149, fig.107

297   c.1180

Maastricht, St Servatius

Capital in the south-west corner of the western aisle   ◄

ARCHITECTURAL SCULPTURE

Mallet, masonry chisel, punch

Bi/Nu 42; Binding (1972), figure on p.56 (outline); Binding (*Rhein und Maas*), p.94, figs 8 & 9 (outlines); Kubach, Hans Erich, & Verbeek, Albert: *Romanische Kirchen an Rhein und Maas.* Neuss 1971, fig.381; Timmers, J.J.M.: *Tijdsbeeld in Steen.* Heerlen 1968, cover picture

297a   c.1480

Macon, Bibliothèque municipale,

MS 1, 5th book, fol.172

St Augustine, *La cité de Dieu*

ILLUMINATION

Schöller, p.94, no.48; Laborde, Alexandre Comte de: *Les manuscrits à peintures de la cité de Dieu de Saint-Augustin.* Paris 1909, vol.3, pl.111

298   1473–80

Macon, Bibliothèque de la Ville,

MS 2, fol.94

St Augustine, *La cité de Dieu*

ILLUMINATION (northern France)

Broad axe, scaffolding, trowel, basket, crane, ladder, plumbline, mortar shovel, hod, pointed stone hammer

Bi/Nu 152; Tyghem, fig.162, Minkowski, pic. 64

                                             ►

298a c.1430
Madrid, Biblioteca Nacional,
MS B. 19 (Vit. 25–7), fol.32
ILLUMINATION (Vienna)
Scaffolding, trowel, crane with lewis, mortar tub,
mortar-mixing pick
Schöller, p.94, no.49; *Wien im Mittelalter*, exhibition
catalogue for Sonderausstellung des Historischen
Museums der Stadt Wien. Vienna 1975, fig.21
▼

299 third quarter 13th century
Madrid, Escorial Biblioteca Real,
MS T I, 1
Las Cantigas de Santa Maria by Alfonso X 'el sabio'
ILLUMINATION (Castile, Toledo (?))
Scaffolding
Meyers illustrierte Weltgeschichte: vol.12, Das späte
Mittelalter. Mannheim 1980, figure on p.55; Llorens,
José Maria, Lovillo, José Guerrero, *et al.: Cantigas de*
Santa Maria de Alfonso X el Sabio. Monumentos
históricos de la Música Española. Madrid 1979
▶

299a end 15th century
Madrid, Escorial,
MS I.J. 3
Spanish Bible
ILLUMINATION
Measuring staff, mortar-mixing pick, sanding board

▶

300 1485–90
Madrid, Museo del Prado Hieronymus Bosch,
'Haycart' triptych
Detail from the right-hand wing
PANEL PAINTING
Broad axe, scaffolding, trowel, crane with windlass,
ladder, mortar tub, hod
Bosman, Anthony: *Hieronymus Bosch*. Deventer 1962,
figure on p.26; Marijnssen, R.-H., *et al.: Hieronymus*
Bosch. Geneva 1972, fig.156; Tolnay, Charles de:
Hieronymus Bosch. Baden-Baden 1965 (German
edition, Eltville 1984), figure on p.130 f.
◀

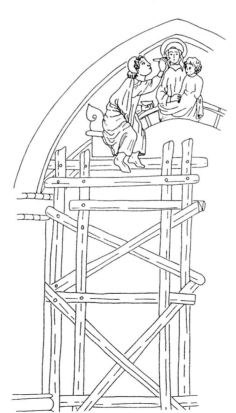

300a   14th century

Milan, Biblioteca Ambrosiana,

cod. F. 119 Sup., fol.60

Martianus Capella, *De nuptis philologiae et mercurii*

ILLUMINATION (Italy)

Square, compasses

Tezmen-Siegel, Jutta: *Die Darstellungen der septem artes liberales in der Bildenden Kunst als Rezeption der Lehrplangeschichte*. Munich 1985 (= tuduv-Studien, Reihe Kunstgeschichte 14), fig.4

▼

301   c.1240–50

Milan, Biblioteca Ambrosiana,

cod. F. 129 Sup

Otto von Freising, *Chronica sive historia de duabus civitatibus*

PEN-AND-INK DRAWING

Pointed stone hammer, square

Bi/Nu 10; Binding (1972), figure on p.61 (outline); Binding (*Ornamenta ecclesiae*), p.172, fig.6; Scheidig, pl.2

Copy of no.210

▼

302   c.1240–50

Milan, Biblioteca Ambrosiana,

cod. F. 129 Sup

Otto von Freising, *Chronica sive historia de duabus civitatibus*

PEN-AND-INK DRAWING

Pointed stone hammer

Gengaro, Maria Luisa, & Guglielmetti, Gemma Villa: *Inventario dei Codici decorati e miniati (sec. VII–XIII) della Biblioteca Ambrosiana*. Florence 1968, pp.100–03, pl.98

Copy of no.209

▼

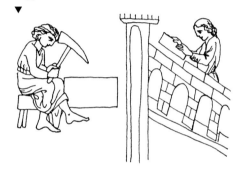

303   1492

Mainz, Peter Schöffer, printer

Botho, *Chronik der Sachsen*, fol.4v

WOODCUT

Crane with external lewis

Bi/Nu 285a; Schramm 14, no.575; Kunze, Horst: *Geschichte der Buchillustration in Deutschland. Das 15. Jahrhundert*. Leipzig 1975, fig.4

The same woodblock was re-used several times in the same work: compare fol. 15v (Schramm 14, no.588), fol. 26v (Schramm 14, no.604), fol. 25r (Schramm 14, no.607)

▶

304   1492

Mainz, Peter Schöffer, printer

Botho, *Chronik der Sachsen*, fol.4v

WOODCUT

Crane with treadwheel

Schramm 14, no.893

▼

305   1492

Mainz, Peter Schöffer, printer

Botho, *Chronik der Sachsen*, fol.4v

WOODCUT

Scaffolding, crane with treadwheel, ladder, mortar tub, mortar-mixing bin, water tub

Schramm 14, no.599

For a reversed derivative see fol. 41 of the same work (Schramm 14, no.632)

▶

306   1492

Mainz, Peter Schöffer, printer

Botho, *Chronik der Sachsen*, fol.4v

WOODCUT

Bucket, scaffolding, ladder, mortar-mixing bin, mortar-mixing pick

Schramm 14, no.895

◀

307   1492

Mainz, Peter Schöffer, printer

Botho, *Chronik der Sachsen*, fol.4v

WOODCUT

Ladder, mortar shovel, hod

Schramm 14, no.896

▼

308   1492

Mainz, Peter Schöffer, printer

Botho, *Chronik der Sachsen*, fol.4v

WOODCUT

Wheelbarrow

Schramm 14, no.901

The same woodblock was re-used several times in the same work: compare Schramm 14, nos 902–04

▼

309   1492

Mainz, Peter Schöffer, printer

Botho, *Chronik der Sachsen*, fol.4v

WOODCUT

Crane with treadwheel and external lewis

Schramm 14, no.905

The same woodblock was re-used several times in the same work: compare Schramm 14, nos 906–08

▶

310   1492

Mainz, Peter Schöffer, printer

Botho, *Chronik der Sachsen*, fol.4v

WOODCUT

Crane with treadwheel

Schramm 14, no.932

◀

311   1492

Mainz, Peter Schöffer, printer

Botho, *Chronik der Sachsen*, fol.4v

WOODCUT

Scaffolding

Schramm 14, no.928

The same woodblock was re-used several times in the same work: compare Schramm 14, no.947

▼

312   c.1353
Malibu, California, J. Paul Getty Museum,
Louis XI 7, fol.56
Hedwig Codex
ILLUMINATION (Silesia, workshop of the court of
Duke Ludwig I of Liegnitz and Brieg)
Scaffolding, trowel, crane with pallet
Van Euw, Anton, & Plotzek, Joachim M.: *Die*
Handschriften der Sammlung Ludwig. Cologne 1985,
vol.4, fig.154; Legner, Anton (ed.): *Die Parler.*
Resultatband zur Ausstellung des Schnütgen-Museums
in der Kunsthalle Köln. Cologne 1980, pl.172 (signature
details incorrect); Recht, p.77
Compare nos 95, 602a
▼

312a   c.1475
Malibu, California, J. Paul Getty Museum,
Louis XIII 5, fol.138
Miroir historial (Vincentius de Beauvais, Speculum
historiale, vol. I)
ILLUMINATION (Gent)
Trowel, pointed stone hammer (?)
Van Euw, Anton, & Plotzek, Joachim M.: *Die*
Handschriften der Sammlung Ludwig. Cologne 1982,
vol.3, pp.243–9 (no illus.)

313   c.1405
Malibu, California, J. Paul Getty Museum,
Louis XV 7, fol.26
Guillaume de Lorris and Jean de Meung, *Le Roman*
de la Rose
ILLUMINATION (Paris)
Scaffolding, trowel, mortar-mixing pick
Van Euw, Anton, & Plotzek, Joachim M.: *Die*
Handschriften der Sammlung Ludwig. Cologne 1985,
vol.4, pp.228–39, fig.154

313a   c.1400
Malibu, California, J. Paul Getty Museum,
83. MP. 146 (Louis XIII 3), fol.1
Histoire ancienne jusqu'à César
ILLUMINATION (Paris)
Compasses
Van Euw, Anton, & Plotzek, Joachim M.: *Die*
Handschriften der Sammlung Ludwig. Cologne 1985,
vol.3, figure on p.235
▼

313b   c.1400

Malibu, California, J. Paul Getty Museum,
83. MP. 146 (Louis XIII 3), fol.8v
Histoire ancienne jusqu'à César
ILLUMINATION (Paris)
Crane with windlass and pallet, mortar-mixing pick,
mortar shovel, hawk
Van Euw, Anton, & Plotzek, Joachim M.: *Die*
Handschriften der Sammlung Ludwig.
Cologne 1985, vol.3,
fig.160; Recht, p.66.
Compare no.351a
▶

313c   c.1475

Malibu, California, J. Paul Getty Museum,
83. MR 178 (Louis XV 8), fol.156v
Quintus Curtius Rufus, *Livre des fais d'Alexandre*
le grant
ILLUMINATION (Bruges)
Crane with windlass, trowel
Van Euw, Anton, & Plotzek, Joachim M.: *Die*
Handschriften der Sammlung Ludwig.
Cologne 1985, vol.4,
fig.183
▶

313d   1400–10

Malibu, California, J. Paul Getty Museum,
MS 33 (88. MP. 70), fol.13
Weltchronik of Rudolf von Ems and Jansen
Enikel
ILLUMINATION (Bavaria)
Scaffolding, trowel, crane with treadwheel
and pallet, mortar tub, mortar-mixing pick
▶

314   beginning 13th century
Manchester, John Rylands Library,
MS fr. 5, fol.13v
French Bible
ILLUMINATION
Trestle, broad axe, hooked dog or staple
Tyghem, fig.25
▼

315   beginning 13th century
Manchester, John Rylands Library,
MS fr. 5, fol.16
French Bible
ILLUMINATION
Hatchet, stone axe, bucket, scaffolding, crane,
ladder, level
Bi/Nu 11; Binding (1972), figure on p.41 (outline);
Binding (*Ornamenta ecclesiae*), p.173, fig.9; Tyghem,
fig.23
▶

315a   1487 (?)
Manchester, John Rylands Library,
MS 39, fol.146a
ILLUMINATION (Flanders)
Crane with treadwheel
James, Montague Rhodes: *A Descriptional Catalogue of*
the Latin Manuscripts in the John Rylands Library at
Manchester. London 1921, vol.II, pl.92
▼

315b   1487 (?)
Manchester, John Rylands Library,
MS 39, fol.150a
ILLUMINATION (Flanders)
Broad axe, scaffolding, hammer, crane with
treadwheel, ladder, mortar-mixing pick, hod
James, Montague Rhodes: *A Descriptional Catalogue of*
the Latin Manuscripts in the John Rylands Library at
Manchester. London 1921, vol.II, pl.93
▶

315c   c.1430
Manchester, John Rylands Library,
MS 82, fol.246v
ILLUMINATION (Paris)
Trowel, mallet, hod, chisel, hawk, cart, compasses
James, Montague Rhodes: *A Descriptional Catalogue of*
the Latin Manuscripts in the John Rylands Library at
Manchester. London 1921, vol.II, pl.173
▼

316   1450

Maulbronn, monastery

Founders' panel in the form of a winged altar in the seminarists' refectory

PANEL PAINTING (Upper Rhine)

Broad axe, crane with treadwheel and external lewis, mortar tub, mortar-mixing bin, mortar-mixing pick, square, stone hammer

Bi/Nu 153; Tyghem, fig.137; Dörrenberg, Irmgard: *Das Zisterzienserkloster Maulbronn.* Würzburg 1938, p.137, fig.130; Schneider, Ambrosius, Wienand, Adam, Bickel, Wolfgang *et al.: Die Cistercienser. Geschichte–Geist–Kunst.* Cologne 1974, figure on p.63

▶

317   after 1424

Maulbronn, monastery church

Console, south aisle of the nave

ARCHITECTURAL SCULPTURE

Hammer

Bi/Nu 244; Gerstenberg, figure on p.35; Dörrenberg, Irmgard: *Das Zisterzienserkloster Maulbronn.* Würzburg 1938, p.128, fig.120 li

▼

318   c.1445
Middleburg, Rijksarchief
Dutch Bible (lost during Second World War)
ILLUMINATION
Stone hammer, scaffolding, trowel, ladder, mortar
tub, mortar-mixing pick, mortar shovel, hod
Bi/Nu 154; Tyghem, fig.116

▼

319   1452–79
Modena, Biblioteca Estense,
MS V.G. 11, vol.I, fol.9
Bibbia di Borso d'Este
ILLUMINATION
Scaffolding, ramp, mortar tub, mortar-mixing pick,
mortar shovel, hod
Tyghem, fig.159

◄

319a   mid-15th century
Modena, Biblioteca Estense,
MS it. 1015, fol.173v
Livy
ILLUMINATION (Flanders)
Bucket, trowel, ladder, mortar shovel, shoulder pole
Limentani Virdis, Caterina: *Codici miniati fiamminghi e*
olandesi nelle Biblioteche dell'Italia nord-orientale.
n.p.1981, fig.28

320   13th century
Modena, Archivio Capitolare, MS O II 11
Relatio Translationis Corporis S. Geminiani
ILLUMINATION
Hod, shovel, shoulder basket, hammer
Tyghem, fig.37

▼

321   c.1120–40

Modena, Cathedral of S. Geminiano, Porta dei Principi, south aisle of nave, archivault
ARCHITECTURAL SCULPTURE
Mallet, three-legged stool, chisel
Leonardi, Cesare, & Armandi, Marina: *Il Duomo di Modena. Atlante fotografico*. Modena 1985, figure on p.348 f.

▶

322   1180–90

Monreale, Cathedral of Santa Maria
Western transept, north side of Capital 20
ARCHITECTURAL SCULPTURE (stone relief)
Broad axe
Binding (1972), figure on p.34; Brandt I, p.244, fig.237; Du Colombier, p.120, pl.5; Minkowski, fig.5; Parrot, A.: *Ziggurats et tour de Babel*. Paris 1949, p.170; Salvini, Roberto: *Il Chiostro di Monreale*. Part of a catalogue, Palermo 1962

▼

323   c.1174–94

Monreale, Cathedral of Santa Maria
Southern wall of the central nave
MOSAIC
Broad axe, two frame saws, roofing axe (?)
Tyghem, fig.16; Brandt I, fig.323; Du Colombier, p.56, fig.32; Demus, Otto: *The Mosaics of Norman Sicily*. London 1949, fig.99b; Kitzinger, Ernst: *The Mosaics of Monreale*. Palermo 1960, figs 24, 25, pl.22

▶

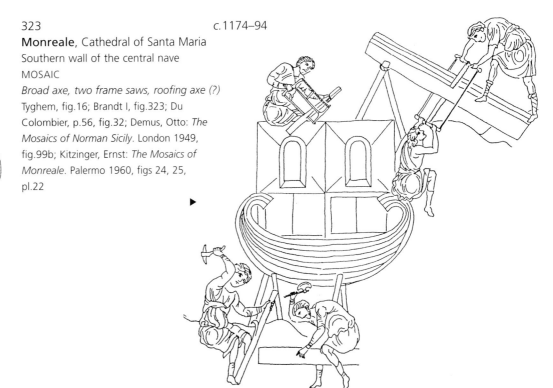

324   c.1185

Monreale, Cathedral of Santa Maria
Southern wall of the central nave, 3rd panel
MOSAIC
Broad axe, scaffolding, trowel, ladder, mortar-mixing pick, hod, pointed stone hammer
Binding (1972), figure on p.29; Tyghem, fig.15; Brandt I, fig.325; Du Colombier, fig.33; Demus, Otto: *The Mosaics of Norman Sicily*. London 1949, fig.102; Kitzinger, Ernst: *The Mosaics of Monreale*. Palermo 1960, figs 29; Minkowski, fig.2b

▶

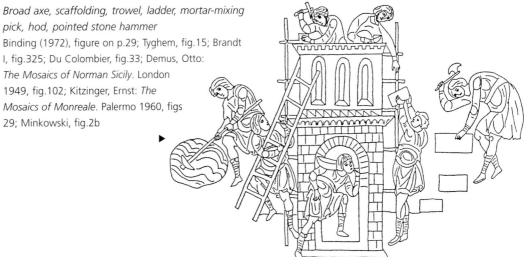

325 1022–3
Monte Cassino, Biblioteca Monte Cassino,
cod. 132, fol.364
Hrabanus Maurus, *De origine rerum*
PEN-AND-INK DRAWING (southern Italy)
Hand saw
Meyers illustrierte Weltgeschichte. Mannheim, Vienna &
Zürich 1980, vol.11, figure on p.11; Saxl, F.: 'Illustrated
Medieval Encyclopedias', in *Lectures*. London 1957, II,
pl.158a

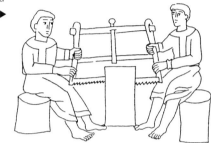

326 1022–3
Monte Cassino, Biblioteca Monte Cassino,
cod. 132, fol.418
Hrabanus Maurus, *De origine rerum*
PEN-AND-INK DRAWING (southern Italy)
Hand saw
Tyghem, p.8, fig.7; Binding (1972), p.70; Du Colombier,
fig.2; Amelli, A.M.: *Miniature sacre e profane dell'anno
1023 illustranti l'enciclopedia medioevale Rabano
Mauro*. Monte Cassino 1896, book 17, pl.119;
Feldhaus, F.M.: *Die Säge. Ein Rückblick auf vier
Jahrtausende*. Berlin & Remscheid 1921, p.22;
Ragghianti, Carlo Ludovico: *L'Arte bizantina e romanica*.
Rome 1968 (= *L'Arte in Italia* 2), fig.266, pl.310

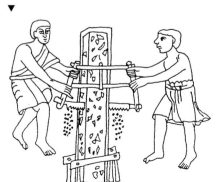

327 1022–3
Monte Cassino, Biblioteca Monte Cassino,
cod. 132, fol.418
Hrabanus Maurus, *De origine rerum*
PEN-AND-INK DRAWING (southern Italy)
Scaffolding, trowel, ladder, hod
Binding (1972), figure on p.18 (outline); Tyghem, fig.6;
Du Colombier, p.117, pl.1; Dammertz, Victor, *et al.*:
*Benedictus. Eine kleine Kulturgeschichte des
Abendlandes*. Geneva 1980, p.338, fig.357

328 after 1181–c.1197
Mozac (Puy-de-Dôme), Church of Saint-Pierre
Reliquary of St. Calminius
ENAMEL
Trowel, ramp, mortar-mixing bin, pannier
Bi/Nu 18; Du Colombier, p.33, fig.21; Gauthier,
Marie-Madeleine: *Emaux du moyen âge
occidental*. Fribourg 1972, cat. no.57,
pp.333–5 (with literary refs, no illus.); Rupin,
Ernest: *L'oeuvre de Limoges*. Paris 1890, p.102,
fig.168

329 after 1181–c.1197
Mozac (Puy-de-Dôme), Church of Saint-Pierre
Reliquary of St. Calminius
ENAMEL
Trowel, hod
François-Souchal, Geneviève: 'Les émaux de Grandmont
au XIIe siècle', in *Bulletin monumental* 131, 1963,
p.311, fig.25; Gauthier, Marie-Madeleine: *Emaux du
moyen âge occidental*. Fribourg 1972, cat. no.57,
pp.333–5 (with literary refs, no illus.); Rupin, Ernest:
L'oeuvre de Limoges. Paris 1890, p.104, fig.170

330   after 1181–c.1197
Mozac (Puy-de-Dôme), Church of Saint-Pierre
Reliquary of St. Calminius
ENAMEL
Hammer, trowel, mortar bucket
Gauthier, Marie-Madeleine: *Emaux du moyen âge
occidental*. Fribourg 1972, cat. no.57, pp.333–5 (with
literary refs, no illus.); Rupin, Ernest: *L'oeuvre de
Limoges*. Paris 1890, p.103, fig.169

▶

331   c.1340
Mulhouse (Alsace), Church of Saint-Etienne
Choir window
STAINED GLASS
Hammer, ladder, mortar-mixing pick, hod
Bi/Nu 155; Aubert, p.185; Minkowski, pic. 39

▼

332   end 15th century
Munich, Bayerische Staatsbibliothek,
Cod. gall. 8, fol.4
Christine de Pisan, *La cité des dames*
ILLUMINATION (France)
Trowel, hod, rope pulley, pick
Bi/Nu 172; Tyghem, fig.175 (with wrong source
information); Brandt II, p.45, fig.42; Schöller, p.95,
no.91

▼

332a   15th century
Munich, Bayerische Staatsbibliothek,
Cod. gall. 8, fol.44v
Christine de Pisan, *La cité des dames*
ILLUMINATION (France)
Trowel, crane
Schöller, p.95, no.52; Schaefer, Lucie: 'Die Illustrationen
zu den Handschriften der Christine de Pisan', in
Marburger Jahrbuch für Kunstgewerbe 10, 1937,
p.185, fig.121

332b   15th century
Munich, Bayerische Staatsbibliothek,
Cod. gall. 8, fol.90v
Christine de Pisan, *La cité des dames*
ILLUMINATION (France)
Crane
Schöller, p.95, no.53; Schaefer, Lucie: 'Die Illustrationen
zu den Handschriften der Christine de Pisan', in
Marburger Jahrbuch für Kunstgewerbe 10, 1937,
p.185, fig.123

331a   15th century
Munich, Bayerische Staatsbibliothek,
Cod. gall. 4, fol.2v
Les grandes chroniques de France
ILLUMINATION (France)
Trowel, mortar-mixing pick (?), hod
Schöller, p.94, no.50; Marburger Index, fiche 2356/C5

333   1458

Munich, Bayerische Staatsbibliothek,
Cod. gall. 6, fol.14
*Jehan Boccace, Des cas des nobles hommes et
femmes* illustrated by Jean Fouquet
ILLUMINATION
*Bucket, basket, crane with treadwheel and pallet,
measuring staff, pointed stone hammer*
Bi/Nu 158; Minkowski, pic. 60; Perels, Klaus Günther:
Jean Fouquet. London, Paris & New York 1940, p.129,
fig.107
▼

334   end 14th century

Munich, Bayerische Staatsbibliothek,
Cod. germ. 4, fol.25
Christ-Herre-Chronik
ILLUMINATION (southern Germany)
*Hammer, mallet, crane with pallet, mortar tub,
mortar-mixing pick, one-legged stool, chisel, pointed
stone hammer, compasses*
Bi/Nu 156; Brandt I, p.248, fig.335; Jacobi, fig.14;
Minkowski, pic. 31; Schultz I, p.58, fig.82 (detail of
stonemason)
Compare no.335
▶

333a   1303–08

Munich, Bayerische Staatsbibliothek,
Cod. gall. 16, fol.24v
Psalter of Queen Isabella of England
ILLUMINATION (England)
*Tub with shoulder pole, stone hammer, trowel, level,
wheelbarrow, shoulder basket*
Schöller, p.95, no.54; Randall, p.67, no illus.
▶

335   c.1370

Munich, Bayerische Staatsbibliothek,

Cod. germ. 5, fol.29

Mixed manuscript (*Christ-Herre-Chronik*, Rudolf von Ems,

Jansen Enikel)

ILLUMINATION (southern Germany)

Masons' lodge, trowel, crane with lewis, mortar tub, mortar-
mixing pick, one-legged stool, pointed stone hammer, square

Bi/Nu 157; Tyghem, fig.72; Brandt I, p.248, fig.334; Jacobi, fig.12;

Minkowski, pic. 24; Philippi, pl.54; Schultz I, p.57, fig.81 (outline);

Recht, p.336; Coldstream 1991, p.59, fig.59

Compare nos 241, 334, 490

336   beginning 14th century

Munich, Bayerische Staatsbibliothek,

Cod. germ. 11, fol.15

Jansen Enikel, *Weltchronik*

ILLUMINATION (Bavaria, southern Germany)

Masons' lodge, tub, hammer, trowel, crane with pallet,
plumbline, measuring staff, pointed stone hammer, square

Bi/Nu 159; Jacobi, fig.11; Minkowski, pic. 9

◀

336a   1457

Munich, Bayerische Staatsbibliothek,

Cod. germ. 206, fol.28v

Hieronymus Müller, Old Testament, psalter and Life of Mary

ILLUMINATION (Augsburg)

Scaffolding, crane with lewis, mortar tub

Schöller, p.95, no.55; Marburger Index, fiche 2365/G6

337   first half 15th century
Munich, Bayerische Staatsbibliothek,
Cod. germ. 250, fol.19
Jansen Enikel, *Weltchronik*
ILLUMINATION (Bavaria, Austria)
Scaffolding, trowel, mortar tub, mortar shovel, rope pulley
Bi/Nu 161; Tyghem, fig.104; Minkowski, pic. 34
▶

337a   end 15th century
Munich, Bayerische Staatsbibliothek,
Cod. germ. 436, fol.9
Thomas Lirer, *Schwäbische Chronik*
COLOURED PEN-AND-INK DRAWING
Scaffolding, crane with lewis, ladder, pointed stone hammer
Schöller, p.95, no.57; Marburger Index, fiche 2366/E14
Compare no.571

338   15th century
Munich, Bayerische Staatsbibliothek,
Cod. germ. 862
Flemish manuscript
ILLUMINATION
Scaffolding, ladder
Bi/Nu 162; background details from Tyghem, fig.141
Compare no.349a
▼

339   1439
Munich, Bayerische Staatsbibliothek,
Cod. germ. 1102, fol.16v
Dutch Bible
ILLUMINATION
Bucket, scaffolding, trowel, crane, ladder, mortar-mixing pick, hod, stand for hod
Bi/Nu 163; Tyghem, fig.114; Minkowski, pic. 69
◀

339a   end 13th century
Munich, Bayerische Staatsbibliothek,
Cod. germ. 8345, fol.11
Weltchronik of Rudolf von Ems
ILLUMINATION (Lake Constance area)
Crane, hod, four-legged stool, pointed stone hammer
Schöller, p.95, no.58; Recht, p.93; Stange, Alfred: 'Studien
zur oberrheinischen Malerei um 1300', *Münchener
Jahrbuch der bildenden Kunst* NF 9, 1932, p.21, fig.4
▶

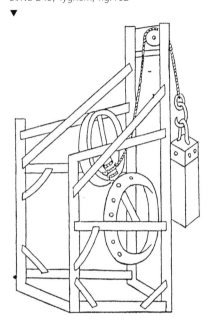

340   mid-14th century
Munich, Bayerische Staatsbibliothek,
Cod. lat. 146
Speculum humanae salvationis
PEN-AND-INK DRAWING (southern Germany)

Scaffolding, trowel, mortar bucket
Bi/Nu 160; Minkowski, pic. 21; *Speculum Humanae
Salvationis. Kritische Ausgabe. Übersetzung von Jean
Mulot 1448. Die Quellen des Speculum une seine
Bedeutung in der Ikonographie besonders in der
elsässischen Kunstwissenschaft des 14. Jahrhunderts.*
Leipzig 1907, vol.II, pl.67
◀

341   c.1430
Munich, Bayerische Staatsbibliothek,
Cod. lat. 197, fol.8v
Unknown author of the *Hussite Wars*
PEN-AND-INK DRAWING
Pile-driving machine
Bi/Nu 245; Tyghem, fig.102
▼

340a   mid-14th century
Munich, Bayerische Staatsbibliothek,
Cod. lat. 146, fol.35
Speculum humanae salvationis
PEN-AND-INK DRAWING (southern Germany)
Trowel
*Speculum Humanae Salvationis. Kritische Ausgabe.
Übersetzung von Jean Mulot 1448. Die Quellen des
Speculum une seine Bedeutung in der Ikonographie
besonders in der elsässischen Kunstwissenschaft des 14.
Jahrhunderts.* Leipzig 1907, vol.II, pl.64
Compare nos 2, 193a   ▶

342   c.1430

Munich, Bayerische Staatsbibliothek,
Cod. lat. 197, fol.8v
Unknown author of the *Hussite Wars*
PEN-AND-INK DRAWING
Crane with windlass and mortar tub
Bi/Nu 246; Tyghem, fig.103; Neher, F.L.: *Alles hing
einmal am Haken*. Simbach am Inn 1961 (= Heraklith-
Rundschau 31), figs 56 & 57 right (derivative drawings)
▼

344   c.1430

Munich, Bayerische Staatsbibliothek,
Cod. lat. 197
Unknown author of the *Hussite Wars*
PEN-AND-INK DRAWING
Demolition crane
Bi/Nu 247; Neher, F.L.: *Alles hing einmal am Haken*.
Simbach am Inn 1961 (= Heraklith-Rundschau 31), fig.59
▼

344b   beginning 11th century

Munich, Bayerische Staatsbibliothek,
Cod. lat. 4454, fol.8v
Gospels
ILLUMINATION (Reichenau)
Broad axe, mallet, chisel
Schöller, p.95, no.60; Leidinger, Georg: *Miniaturen aus
Handschriften der bayerischen Staatsbibliothek zu
München*, vol.6: *Evangeliarium aus dem Domschatz zu
Bamberg (Cod. lat. 4454)*. Munich n.d., pl.1
Compare nos 172, 344a
▼

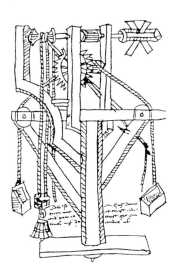

343   c.1430

Munich, Bayerische Staatsbibliothek,
Cod. lat. 197
Unknown author of the *Hussite Wars*
PEN-AND-INK DRAWING
Crane with windlass and hook
Bi/Nu 248; Tyghem, fig.103;
Neher, F.L.: *Alles hing einmal
am Haken*. Simbach am Inn
1961 (= Heraklith-Rundschau
31), figs 56 & 57 right
(derivative drawings)
▶

344a   c.1000

Munich, Bayerische Staatsbibliothek,
Cod. lat. 4453 (Cim 58), fol.18
So-called Gospels of Emperor Otto III
ILLUMINATION (Reichenau)
Broad axe, mallet, chisel
Schöller, p.95, no.59; Leidinger, Georg: *Miniaturen aus
Handschriften der königlichen Hof- und
Staatsbibliothek zu München*, vol.1: *Das sogenannte
Evangeliarium Kaiser Ottos III*. Munich n.d., pl.8
Compare nos 172, 344b
▼

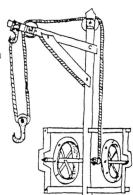

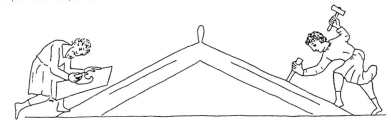

345   1414

Munich, Bayerische Staatsbibliothek,
Cod. lat. 8101d, fol.18
Vita illustrata Sancti Benedicti from Metten
ILLUMINATION (lower Bavaria, with Bohemian
influence)
*Crane with treadwheel and external lewis, measuring
staff, pointed stone hammer*
Bleibrunner, Hans: *Niederbayern. Kulturgeschichte des
bayerischen Unterlandes in zwei Bänden.* Landshüt
1979, vol.I, figure on p.404; Schneider, Ambrosius, &
Wienand, Adam: *Und sie folgten der Regel St
Benedikts.* Cologne 1981, p.68, figure on p.73;
Schöller, p.95, no.61

▼

347   c.1175

Munich, Bayerische Staatsbibliothek,
Cod. lat. 13074, fol.90v
Vitae et passiones apostolorum et sanctorum
PEN-AND-INK DRAWING (Regensburg, Prüfening)
Stone axe, mallet, chisel
Bi/Nu 13; Binding (1972), figure on p.52 (outline);
Binding (*Rhein und Maas*), p.94, fig.10 (outline);
Boeckler, Albert: *Die Regensburg-Prüfeninger
Buchmalerei des 12. und 13. Jahrhunderts.* Munich
1924, pl.55, fig.61; Legner, Anton (ed.): *Ornamenta
ecclesiae.* Exhibition catalogue, Cologne 1985, vol.1,
p.184 f., with illus.; Strobel, Richard: *Romanische
Architektur in Regensburg.* Nuremberg 1965, fig.I

▶

347a   1481

Munich, Bayerische Staatsbibliothek,
Cod. lat. 15711, fol.118v
Berthold Furtmayr von Regensburg, missal
*Lump hammer, level, hod, pointed stone hammer,
treadwheel, internal lewis, compasses*
Schöller, p.95, fig.80, & p.80, fig.2; Leidinger, Georg:
Meisterwerke der Buchmalerei. Munich 1920, pl.41

▶

346   before 1222

Munich, Bayerische Staatsbibliothek,
Cod. lat. 835, fol.10
English psalter (Gloucester?)
ILLUMINATION
*Scaffolding, trowel, basket, mortar-mixing pick,
pannier*
Bi/Nu 12; Binding (1972), figure on p.39 (outline);
Binding (*Ornamenta ecclesiae*), p.173, fig.8; Tyghem,
fig.24; Minkowski, pl.4; Brandt I, p.245, pl.II; Recht,
p.66

▶

348   end 14th century
Munich, Bayerische Staatsbibliothek,
Cod. lat. 23433, fol.36v
Speculum humanae salvationis
PEN-AND-INK DRAWING (southern Germany)
*Ladder, measuring staff, mortar-mixing pick, hod,
pointed stone hammer*
Bi/Nu 164; Minkowski, pic. 32
▼

349   first half 16th century
Munich, Bayerische Staatsbibliothek,
Cod. lat. 23638, fol.5
Simon Benning, Flemish calendar
ILLUMINATION
Axe, two-handed saw
Tyghem, fig.207; Leidinger, Georg (ed.):
*Miniaturen aus Handschriften der
königlichen Hof- und Staatsbibliothek in
München*, vol.2. Munich 1912–38, pl.II, 7
▼

349a   end 15th century
Munich, Bayerische Staatsbibliothek,
Cod. lat. 228346, fol.225v
Prayer book with calendar
ILLUMINATION
Scaffolding, ladder
Marburger Index, fiche 2414/G9
Compare no.338

350   c.1436
Munich, Bayerisches Nationalmuseum,
no. 2505
Weltchronik, attributed to Rudolf von Ems
ILLUMINATION
*Tub, crane with external lewis, mortar-mixing bin,
mortar-mixing pick, pointed stone hammer, compasses*
Bi/Nu 165; Minkowski, pic. 35
▼

351   14th century
Munich, Jacques Rosenthal Collection
Livre d'Orose
ILLUMINATION (France)
Compasses
Zahlten, Johannes: *Creatio mundi. Darstellungen der
sechs Schöpfungstage und naturwissenschaftliches
Weltbild im Mittelalter.* Stuttgart 1979 (= *Stuttgarter
Beiträge zur Geschichte und Politik*, vol.13), fig.288 ▶

351a   c.1390
formerly **Munich**, Jacques Rosenthal Collection
(R 82–3), fol.7
Orosius, *Historiae*
ILLUMINATION
*Stone hammer, crane with
pallet, ramp, hawk, brick kiln*
Schöller (1987), p.96, no.63, &
p.84, fig.5; Marburger Index, fiche
2532/F7
Compare no.313b ▶

351b beginning 14th century
Nancy, Bibliothèque municipale,
MS 249, fol.27
Psalter
ILLUMINATION (France, Flanders)
Mallet, chisel
Randall, fig.C, p.484

351c c.1478
Nantes, Bibliothèque municipale,
MS fr. 8, fol.110
Augustine, *La cité de Dieu*
ILLUMINATION
Schöller, p.96, no.64; Laborde, Alexandre Comte de:
Les manuscrits à peintures de la Cité de Saint-Augustin.
Paris 1909, vol.3, pl.94

352 first half 15th century
Neumarkt (Oberpfalz), Catholic parish church
of St John the Baptist
Console of wall-columns in the choir
ARCHITECTURAL SCULPTURE
Hammer, mallet, one-legged stool
Bi/Nu 250; Gerstenberg, figure on p.167; Brandt II,
p.149, fig.189; Otte, Heinrich: *Handbuch der kirchlichen
Kunst – Archäologie des deutschen Mittelalters.* Leipzig
1884, 2 vols, p.482, fig.437 (outline)
▼

353
New York, Guennol Collection
Catherine of Cleves' Book of Hours, fol. 64
ILLUMINATION (Utrecht)
Hatchet, hammer, long-handled drill
Plummer, John: *Die Miniaturen aus dem Stundenbuch
der Katharina von Kleve.* Berlin 1966, fig.25
▼

354 c.1200
New York, Pierpont Morgan Library,
MS 43, fol.10v
Huntingfield Psalter
ILLUMINATION (England)
*Stone hammer, scaffolding, trowel, basket,
ladder, mortar tub, mortar shovel, mortar
spade, hod*
Bi/Nu 14; Tyghem, fig.12; Binding (1972),
figure on p.37 (outline); Binding (1985),
p.173, fig.7 (outline); Brandt I, p.244,
fig.326; Minkowski, p.17, fig.10 ▶

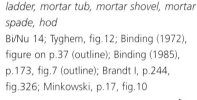

354a 1417
New York, Pierpont Morgan Library,
MS 232, fol.11
Petrus Crescentius, *Le livre de Profits champêtres et
ruraux*
ILLUMINATION (Bruges)
Carpenter's chisel, roofing axe, mallet
▼

354b   c.1200

New York, Pierpont Morgan Library,

MS 338, fol.168v

Latin psalter (Morgan Psalter)

ILLUMINATION (Tournai)

Stone hammer, trowel, ramp, plumbline, pannier,
hawk, compasses

Schöller, p.96, no.65; Deuchler, Florens: *Der*
Ingeborgpsalter. Berlin 1967, pl.xlvi, fig.137

▼

355   mid-13th century

New York, Pierpont Morgan Library,

MS fr. 638, fol.3

Marcierjowsky, Old Testament

ILLUMINATION

Hammer, trowel, mallet, crane with treadwheel,
ladder, measuring staff, hod, chisel, square

Bi/Nu 166; Tyghem, fig.65; Du Colombier, frontispiece
(outline); de Smidt, p.47, fig.20; Schöller (1998), p.112,
fig.8   ▶

355a   mid-13th century

New York, Pierpont Morgan Library,

MS fr. 638, fol.7

ILLUMINATION (Paris)

Lump hammer, scaffolding, trowel, ladder, hod,
chisel, shoulder basket, square

Schöller, p.96, no.66; Cockerell, Sydney C.: *Old*
Testament Miniatures. A Medieval Picture Book with
283 Paintings from the Creation to the Story of David.
London 1969, p.51

     ▶

355b   14th century

New York, Pierpont Morgan Library,

MS fr. 638, fol.2v

Marcierjowsky, Old Testament

ILLUMINATION

Broad axe, long-handled drill

Cockerell, Sydney C.: *Old Testament Miniatures. A*
Medieval Picture Book with 283 Paintings from the
Creation to the Story of David. London 1969

▼

356   c.1125–50

New York, Pierpont Morgan Library,
MS 736
Miracula S. Edmundis regis et martyris
ILLUMINATION (Bury St Edmunds)
Pickaxe, hammer, ladder, shovel
Pächt, Otto, Dodwell, C.R., & Wormald,
Francis: *The St Albans Psalter*. London
1960, pl.159a

▶

357   1200–30

New York, Pierpont Morgan Library,
MS 739, fol.10
Cursus Sanctae Mariae
ILLUMINATION (presumably from the Louka
monastery, Moravia)
Trestle, broad axe
Bi/Nu 43; Husa, Václav: *Homo faber. Der Mensch und
seine Arbeit*. Wiesbaden 1971, fig.85

▶

357a   c.1375–80

New York, Pierpont Morgan Library,
MS 769, fol.28v
Weltchronik of Rudolf von Ems
ILLUMINATION (south-eastern Bavaria)
*Trowel, crane with external lewis, ramp, mortar tub,
mortar-mixing pick, one-legged stool, pointed stone
hammer*
*Mediaeval and Renaissance Manuscripts. Major
Acquisitions of the Pierpont Morgan Library 1924–74.*
New York 1974, no.31

▼

358   c.1440
New York, Pierpont Morgan Library,
MS 917, fol.105
Catherine of Cleves' Book of Hours
ILLUMINATION (Utrecht)
Broad axe, guide line
Plummer, John: *Die Miniaturen aus dem Stundenbuch
der Katharina von Kleve*. Berlin 1966, fig.64
▼

358a   c.1460
Norwich, Cathedral
Keystone
ARCHITECTURAL SCULPTURE
Stone hammer, various chisels, square
Svanberg, Jan: *Master Masons*, Sweden 1983, p.80,
no.38
▼

359   c.1465
Nuremberg, Germanisches Nationalmuseum (on
loan from St Sebaldus' church)
EMBROIDERY (Franken)
Trestle, broad axe
▼

360   end 15th century
Nuremberg, Germanisches Nationalmuseum,
Kapsel 1532, sheet 196 (16th-cent. copy)
History of Schönau monastery
PEN-AND-INK DRAWING
*Crowbar, scaffolding, crane with lewis, ramp, mortar-
mixing bin, mortar-mixing pick, template, shovel,
four-legged stool, square*
Tyghem, fig.204; Du Colombier, fig.28, 1; Derwein,
Herbert: *Das Zisterzienserkloster Schönau mit den
Zeichnungen des 16 Jahrhunderts aus dem Germanischen
Nationalmuseum in Nürnberg*. Frankfurt am Main 1931,
fig.2; Elm, Kaspar: *Die Zisterzienser. Ordensleben zischen
Ideal und Wirklichkeit*. Exhibition catalogue, Aachen &
Bonn 1980, cat. no.B3d (= *Schriften des Rheinischen
Museumsamtes* no.10); von Essenwein, August: 'Bauleute
und Bauführungen im Mittelalter', *Anzeiger für Kunde
der deutschen Vorzeit* 29, 1882, 193/4, fig.3
▼

361   end 15th century
Nuremberg, Germanisches Nationalmuseum,
Kapsel 1532, sheet 201 (16th-cent. copy)
History of Schönau monastery
PEN-AND-INK DRAWING
*Hod, trowel, crane with treadwheel and external
lewis, ramp, pointed stone hammer, pannier*
Derwein, Herbert: *Das Zisterzienserkloster Schönau mit
den Zeichnungen des 16. Jahrhunderts aus denm
Germanischen Nationalmuseum in Nürnberg.* Frankfurt
am Main 1931, fig.7; Elm, Kaspar: *Die Zisterzienser.
Ordensleben zischen Ideal und Wirklichkeit.* Exhibition
catalogue, Aachen & Bonn 1980, cat. no.B3d (=
Schriften des Rheinischen Museumsamtes no.10)

▶

362   1468
Nuremberg, Germanisches Nationalmuseum,
MS 4028, fol.19
Melusine
ILLUMINATION (south-western Germany)
*Broad axe, scaffolding, trowel, crane, mortar tub,
mortar shovel*
Keller, Béatrice: *Der Erker. Studie zum mittelalterlichen
Begriff nach literarischen, bildlichen und
architektonischen Quellen.* Berne & Frankfurt am Main
1981, figure on p.133

▼

363   second half 14th century
Nuremberg, Germanisches Nationalmuseum,
MS 5970   ▶
Speculum humanae salvationis
PEN-AND-INK DRAWING (mid-Rhine area)
*Scaffolding, crane with treadwheel, mortar tub,
mortar-mixing pick, pointed stone hammer*
Bi/Nu 167; Tyghem, fig.69; Minkowski, pic. 30 (outline);
von Essenwein, August: 'Bauleute und Bauführungen
im Mittelalter', *Anzeiger für Kunde der deutschen
Vorzeit* 29/8, 1882, Sp, 189–90, fig.1

364   c.1500
Nuremberg, Germanisches Nationalmuseum,
MS 7121
Haggadah
PEN-AND-INK DRAWING
Basket, ladder
von Essenwein, August: 'Bauleute und Bauführungen
im Mittelalter', *Anzeiger für Kunde der deutschen
Vorzeit* 29/8, 1882, Sp, 189–90, fig.1

▶

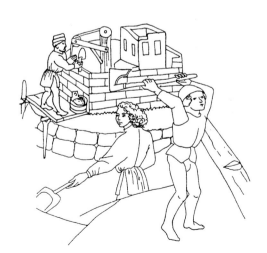

365   c.1030–40
Nuremberg, Germanisches Nationalmuseum,
MS 156142, fol.13
Codex aureus Epternacensis
ILLUMINATION
Broad axe
Bi/Nu 45; Binding (1972), figure on p.65 (outline);
Binding (*Rhein und Maas*), p.95, fig.15 (outline);
Goldschmidt, Adolf: *Die deutsche Buchmalerei 2.*
Munich 1928, p.49,
fig.47; Metz, Peter:
Das goldene
Evangelienbuch von Echternach
im Germanischen
Nationalmuseum zu Nürnberg.
Munich 1956, fig.20
▶

366   c.1030–40
Nuremberg, Germanisches Nationalmuseum,
MS 156142, fol.12v
Codex aureus Epternacensis
ILLUMINATION
Broad axe
Bi/Nu 44; Binding (1972), figure on p.66 (outline);
Binding (*Rhein und Maas*), p.95, fig.15 (outline); Metz,
Peter: *Das goldene Evangelienbuch*
von Echternach im
Germanischen Nationalmuseum
zu Nürnberg. Munich 1956,
fig.19f; Verheyen, Egon: *Das*
goldene Evangelienbuch von
Echternach. Munich
1963, p.58f   ▶

366a   c.1410–15
Nuremberg, Germanisches Nationalmuseum,
Germany, Hebrew text
Marburger Index, fiche 8007/F5

367   1425–36
Nuremberg, Stadtbibliothek
Hausbuch der Mendelschen Zwölfbrüderstiftung,
fol.4
PEN-AND-INK DRAWING
Level, template, one-legged stool, pointed stone
hammer, square
Bi/Nu 251; Tyghem, fig.86; Treue, pl.11
For copies see nos 368, 369, 370
▼

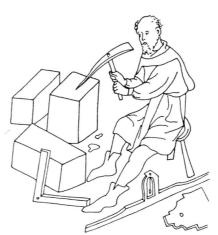

368   1425–36
Nuremberg, Stadtbibliothek
Hausbuch der Mendelschen Zwölfbrüderstiftung,
fol.36v
PEN-AND-INK DRAWING
Level, three-legged stool, pointed stone hammer,
square
Bi/Nu 252; Tyghem, fig.92; Friederich, fig.112; Treue,
pl.264
Reversed free copy of no.367
▶

369   c.1448
Nuremberg, Stadtbibliothek
Hausbuch der Mendelschen Zwölfbrüderstiftung,
fol.70v
PEN-AND-INK DRAWING
Level, one-legged stool, pointed stone hammer
Treue, pls 264 & 121
Reversed free copy of no.367
▼

369a   1456
Nuremberg, Stadtbibliothek
Hausbuch der Mendelschen Zwölfbrüderstiftung,
fol.77
PEN-AND-INK DRAWING
Hammer, trowel, stool
Treue, pl.116
Compare no.107
▼

370   1457
Nuremberg, Stadtbibliothek
Hausbuch der Mendelschen Zwölfbrüderstiftung,
fol.79
PEN-AND-INK DRAWING
*Level, one-legged stool, pointed
stone hammer, square*
Treue, pl.121
Reversed free copy of no.367
▼

371   1425–36
Nuremberg, Stadtbibliothek
Hausbuch der Mendelschen Zwölfbrüderstiftung,
fol.2v
PEN-AND-INK DRAWING
Tub, mortar-mixing bin, mortar-mixing pick
Treue, pl.10
See nos 372, 373
▼

372   1425–36
Nuremberg, Stadtbibliothek
Hausbuch der Mendelschen Zwölfbrüderstiftung,
fol.36
PEN-AND-INK DRAWING
Treue, pl.264
Reversed free copy of no.371
▼

373   c.1450
Nuremberg, Stadtbibliothek
Hausbuch der Mendelschen Zwölfbrüderstiftung,
fol.72
PEN-AND-INK DRAWING
Treue, pl.109
Copy of no.372

374   1425–36
Nuremberg, Stadtbibliothek
Hausbuch der Mendelschen Zwölfbrüderstiftung,
fol.31v
PEN-AND-INK DRAWING
Crane with external lewis
Bi/Nu 252a; Treue, pl.59
See no.375
▶

375   1428
Nuremberg, Stadtbibliothek
Hausbuch der Mendelschen Zwölfbrüderstiftung,
fol.49v
PEN-AND-INK DRAWING
Treue, plate on p.85; Ganßauge, Gottfried: 'Hebeklaue
und Wolf', in *Deutsche Kunst- und Denkmalpflege*
1937, pp.199–205, fig.201
Copy of no.374

376   c.1425
Nuremberg, Stadtbibliothek
Hausbuch der Mendelschen Zwölfbrüderstiftung,
fol.24v
PEN-AND-INK DRAWING
Trowel, ladder, mortar bucket
Tyghem, fig.178; Treue, plate on p.46
▼

377   1425–36
Nuremberg, Stadtbibliothek   ▶
Hausbuch der Mendelschen Zwölfbrüderstiftung,
fol.30v
PEN-AND-INK DRAWING
Trowel, mortarboard, mortar-mixing bin, mortar-
mixing pick
Treue, plate on p.57; RDK VII, Sp.275, fig.1

378   1425–36
Nuremberg, Stadtbibliothek
Hausbuch der Mendelschen Zwölfbrüderstiftung,
fol.37
PEN-AND-INK DRAWING
Trestle, broad axe, hooked dog or staple
Treue, plate on p.67
See nos 379, 380

379   1434–36
Nuremberg, Stadtbibliothek
Hausbuch der Mendelschen Zwölfbrüderstiftung,
fol.56v
PEN-AND-INK DRAWING
Treue, plate on p.263, 3
Copy of no.378

▶

380   1437
Nuremberg, Stadtbibliothek
Hausbuch der Mendelschen Zwölfbrüderstiftung,
fol.61
PEN-AND-INK DRAWING
Treue, plate on p.263, 4
Copy of no.378

381   1446
Nuremberg, Stadtbibliothek
Hausbuch der Mendelschen Zwölfbrüderstiftung,
fol.67
PEN-AND-INK DRAWING
Broad axe, long-handled drill, crowbar
Treue, plate on p.105
▼

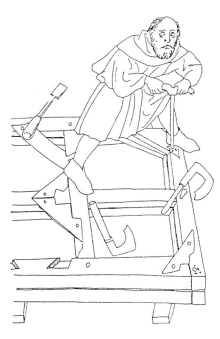

382   1454

Nuremberg, Stadtbibliothek

Hausbuch der Mendelschen Zwölfbrüderstiftung,
fol.76

PEN-AND-INK DRAWING

Broad axe, long-handled drill

Treue, plate on p.114

▼

383   1425–36

Nuremberg, Stadtbibliothek   ▶

Hausbuch der Mendelschen Zwölfbrüderstiftung,
fol.1

PEN-AND-INK DRAWING

Trestle, frame saw

Treue, pl.263

See nos 384, 385

384   1425–36

Nuremberg, Stadtbibliothek

Hausbuch der Mendelschen Zwölfbrüderstiftung,
fol.39

PEN-AND-INK DRAWING

Treue, plate on p.70

Copy of no.383

▶

385   1443

Nuremberg, Stadtbibliothek

Hausbuch der Mendelschen Zwölfbrüderstiftung,
fol.65v

PEN-AND-INK DRAWING

Bi/Nu 252a; Treue, pl.263

Copy of no.383

386   1483

Nuremberg, Anton Koberger, printer

German Bible, fol. IXb

WOODCUT

Bi/Nu 319; Minkowski, no.82 (no illus.)

Re-use of the woodblock for no.225

387   1488

Nuremberg, Anton Koberger, printer

Jacobus de Voragine, Life of the Saints

WOODCUT

Bucket, scaffolding, trowel, ladder, mortar tub,
mortar-mixing pick

Schramm 17, no.109

▼

388   1488

Nuremberg, Anton Koberger, printer

Jacobus de Voragine, Life of the Saints

WOODCUT

Trowel, crane with treadwheel and external lewis,
ladder, mortar tub

Schramm 17, no.146

▼

389   1488

Nuremberg, Anton Koberger, printer
Jacobus de Voragine, Life of the Saints
WOODCUT
Scaffolding, trowel, ramp, mortar tub, mortar-mixing
bin, mortar-mixing pick
Schramm 17, no.198
▼

391   ▲   1488

Nuremberg, Anton Koberger, printer
Jacobus de Voragine, Life of the Saints
WOODCUT
Stone hammer, scaffolding, trowel, ladder, mortar
tub, mortar-mixing pick, stool
Schramm 17, no.220

393   1488

Nuremberg, Anton Koberger, printer
Jacobus de Voragine, Life of the Saints
WOODCUT
Trowel, crane with lewis, ladder, mortar tub, mortar-
mixing bin, mortar-mixing pick, one-legged stool,
pointed stone hammer
Schramm 17, no.272
▼

390   1488

Nuremberg, Anton Koberger, printer
Jacobus de Voragine, Life of the Saints
WOODCUT
Scaffolding, mallet, crane with treadwheel and lewis,
ladder, mortar tub, one-legged stool, chisel
Schramm 17, no.209
▼

392   1488

Nuremberg, Anton Koberger, printer
Jacobus de Voragine, Life of the Saints
WOODCUT
Crane with lewis
Schramm 17, no.233
▼

394   1491

Nuremberg, Anton Koberger, printer

Schatzbehälter, fig. 69

WOODCUT

Trowel, mortar tub, mortar-mixing bin, mortar-mixing pick,
hod, one-legged stool

Schramm 17, no.385

395   1493
Nuremberg, Anton Koberger, printer
Hartmann Schedel, *Liber chronicarum*
WOODCUT
Hatchet, trestle, drill, broad axe, lump hammer,
hammer, ladder
Schramm 17, no.417
▼

396   1493
Nuremberg, Anton Koberger, printer
Hartmann Schedel, *Liber chronicarum*, fol.17v
WOODCUT
Crane with lewis
Bi/Nu 168; Schramm 17, no.424; Minkowski, pic. 92
▶

397   1475
Nuremberg, Johann Sensenschmidt, printer
Jacobus de Voragine, Life of the Saints
WOODCUT
Schramm 18, no.88
Free derivative of no.24
▶

398   1476–8
Nuremberg, Johann Sensenschmidt, printer
Bible
WOODCUT
Schramm 18, no.254
Derivative of no.25
▼

399   1494
Nuremberg, Peter Wagner, printer
Sebastian Brant, *Das Narrenschiff*
WOODCUT
Schramm 18, no.430
Free derivative of no.37
▼

400   1494
Nuremberg, Peter Wagner, printer
Sebastian Brant, *Das Narrenschiff*
WOODCUT
Schramm 18, no.481
Reversed free derivative of no.38
▼

401   1493
Nuremberg, Peter Wagner, printer
Allegorical representation of Geometry as master
mason
WOODCUT (fragment of a large-format single-sheet
printing block)
Crane with lewis, pointed stone hammer, square,
compasses
Omm, Peter: *Meßkunst ordnet die Welt*, 1958; Reicke,
Emil: *Der Gelehrte in der deutschen Vergangenheit*.
Cologne 1924 (reprint), fig.28
▶

401a   1470–1500
Nuremberg, Peter Wagner, printer
Allegorical representations
SINGLE-SHEET WOODCUT
Trestle, broad axe
Wirth, Karl-August: 'Neue Schriften zur deutschen
Kunst des 15. Jahrhunderts. Einträge in einer
Sammelhandschrift des Sigismund Gossembrot', in
Städel Jahrbuch, NF 6 (1977), p.336, figs 5–7
▼

402 1163–66

Otranto, Cathedral of Santa Maria Annunziata
Floor in central nave
MOSAIC
Hatchet, frame saw
Willemsen, Carl Arnold: *Apulien.* Cologne 1958,
fig.229f; Haug, Walter: *Das Mosaik von Otranto.*
Darstellung, Deutung und Bilddokumentation.
Wiesbaden 1977, fig.5
▼

403 1163–66

Otranto, Cathedral of Santa Maria Annunziata
Floor in central nave
MOSAIC ▶
Trowel, ladder, hammer
Kier, Hiltrud: *Der mittelalterliche Schmuckfußboden.*
Düsseldorf 1970, fig.408 (= *Die Kunstdenkmäler des*
Rheinlandes, suppt 14); Willemsen, Carl Arnold:
Apulien. Leipzig 1944, p.61, fig.275; Willemsen, Carl
Arnold: *Apulien.* Cologne 1958, figs 229–30;
Willemsen, Carl Arnold: *Apulien. Kathedralen und*
Kastelle. Cologne 1971, pp.197f, fig.110; Haug,
Walter: *Das Mosaik von Otranto. Darstellung, Deutung*
und Bilddokumentation. Wiesbaden 1977, fig.3

404 1487–92

Ottawa, National Gallery of Canada
Piero di Lorenzo, a.k.a. Piero di Cosimo, *Vulcano ed*
Eolo
PANEL PAINTING
Hammer, hand saw
Bacci, Mina: *L'opera completa di Piero di Cosimo.* Milan
1976, pl.xvii, xix (= *Classici dell'Arte* 88)
▶

404a c.1370

Oxford, Bodleian Library,
MS Auct. D 4.4
Latin psalter
ILLUMINATION (England)
Ladder, hod, pointed stone hammer
Schöller, p.96, no.67; Montague Rhodes, James: *The*
Bohun Manuscripts. A group of five manuscripts
executed in England about 1370 for the members of the
Bohun family. Oxford 1936, pl.25/b; Harrison, Fr: *English*
Illumination of the 13th and 14th Centuries, pl.18–19

404b end 13th century

Oxford, Bodleian Library,
MS Auct. D 5.17, fol.197v
Latin Bible
ILLUMINATION (Paris)
Trowel, ramp, hawk, serrated stone
hammer
Schöller, p.96, no.68; Pächt, Otto,
Alexander, H., & Graham, Jonathan
James: *Illuminated Manuscripts in the*
Bodleian Library, Oxford. vol.1: *German,*
Dutch, Flemish, French and Spanish
Schools. Oxford 1966, pl.41, fig.544
▶

404c   1420–30

Oxford, Bodleian Library,
MS Barlow 53 (R)
Compendium historiae in genealogia Christi
ILLUMINATION (England)
Carpenter's chisel, drill, broad axe, saw,
square, compasses
Pächt, Otto, Alexander, H., & Graham,
Jonathan James: *Illuminated Manuscripts in*
the Bodleian Library, Oxford. vol.3: British,
Irish and Icelandic Schools. Oxford 1973,
pl.lxxxiv, fig.883

▶

405   1230-40

Oxford, Bodleian Library,
MS Bodley 270b, fol.1
Bible moralisée
ILLUMINATION
Compasses
Friedman, John Block: 'The architect's compass in
creation miniatures of the later middle ages', in *Traditio*
30, 1974, fig.V
Compare no.555
This refers to a three-volume set of the *Bible moralisée*,
of which two examples are known. The older and better
is in the care of Toledo cathedral and the younger is split
between Oxford (Bodley 270b), Paris (Bibliothèque
Nationale, MS lat. 11560) and London (British Museum,
Harleian MS 1526–7). Compare Haussherr, Reiner:
'Templum Salomonis und Ecclesia Christi', in *Zeitschrift*
für Kunstgeschichte 31, 2. Munich & Berlin 1968, p. 107

▶

406   1230–40

Oxford, Bodleian Library,
MS Bodley 270b, fol.9v
Bible moralisée
ILLUMINATION
Drill, broad axe
Laborde, vol.I, pl.9

▶

407   1230–40

Oxford, Bodleian Library,
MS Bodley 270b, fol.11v
Bible moralisée
ILLUMINATION
Stone hammer, ladder, mortar-mixing pick, pannier,
hawk
Bi/Nu 282; Tyghem, fig.88; Brandt I, p.247, fig.332;
Laborde, vol.I, pl.11; Schöller, p.96, no.69

▼

408   1230–40

Oxford, Bodleian Library,
MS Bodley 270b, fol.36
Bible moralisée
ILLUMINATION
Double-headed serrated stone hammer, hammer,
trowel, level, pannier
Bi/Nu 283; Tyghem, fig.89; Brandt I, p.258, fig.350;
Laborde, vol.I, pl.36
▼

409   1230–40

Oxford, Bodleian Library,
MS Bodley 270b, fol.163v
Bible moralisée
ILLUMINATION
Hammer, mallet, chisel, square
Laborde, vol.I, pl.163
Compare no.556
▼

410   1230–40

Oxford, Bodleian Library,
MS Bodley 270b, fols 180, 181v
Bible moralisée
ILLUMINATION
Axe, trestle, broad axe, square
Laborde, vol.I, pls 180, 181
▼

411   1230–40

Oxford, Bodleian Library,
MS Bodley 270b, fol.184, 185
Bible moralisée
ILLUMINATION
Double-headed serrated stone hammer, trowel,
mallet, ramp, chisel, pannier, square
Laborde, vol.I, pls 184, 185
▼

412   1230–40

Oxford, Bodleian Library,
MS Bodley 270b, fol.197v
Bible moralisée
ILLUMINATION
Broad axe
Laborde, vol.I, pl.197
▶

412a   first quarter 14th century
Oxford, Bodleian Library,
MS Douce 6, fol.95
Psalter
ILLUMINATION (Flanders)
Mallet, chisel
Schöller, p.96, no.70; Randall, fig.430

412b   first quarter 14th century
Oxford, Bodleian Library,
MS Douce 6, fol.129
Latin Psalter
ILLUMINATION (Flanders)
Trowel, hod
Schöller, p.96, no.71; Randall, p.162 (no illus.)

▼

412c   1485–90
first quarter 14th century
Oxford, Bodleian Library,
MS Douce 219 (SC 21793), fol.41
ILLUMINATION (Flanders)
Scaffolding
Schöller, p.96, no.72; Pächt, Otto: *The Master of Mary
of Burgundy*. London 1947, pl.21b

413   end 15th century
first quarter 14th century
Oxford, Bodleian Library,
MS Douce 353, fol.43v
French manuscript
ILLUMINATION
*Scaffolding, trowel, crane with windlass, ladder,
mortar tub, mortar-mixing pick, hod, pointed stone
hammer*
Bi/Nu 89; Harvey, John: *Medieval Craftsmen*. London
1975, fig.20 (detail); Platt, Colin: *The English Medieval
Town*. London 1976, fig.18, p.41

▼

413a   c.1000
Oxford, Bodleian Library,
MS Junius 11 (SC 5123), fol.82
Genesis (Caedmon Genesis), Exodus etc.
ILLUMINATION (Canterbury)
Summary representation of tools
Schöller, p.96, no.73; Henderson, G.: 'Late antique
influences in some illustrations of Genesis', in *Journal of
the Wartburg and Courtauld Institutes* 25, 1962, pl.34c

413b   mid-15th century
Oxford, Bodleian Library,
MS Lyell 75, fol.4v
ILLUMINATION (Siena?)
*Stone hammer, scaffolding, trowel, basket, ladder,
plumbline, mortar tub, mortar-mixing pick, mortar
shovel, hod, four-legged stool, chisel*
Pächt, Otto, Alexander, H., & Graham, Jonathan James:
Illuminated Manuscripts in the Bodleian Library, Oxford.
vol.2: *Italian School*. Oxford 1970, pl.xxiii, fig.255

▼

414 1166–80

Palermo, Palazzo dei Normanni (Reale)
South wall of the central nave, Capella Palatina
MOSAIC
Drill, hammer, crowbar
Demus, Otto: *The Mosaics of Norman Sicily*. London
1949, fig.30b; Kitzinger, Ernst: *The Mosaics of
Monreale*. Palermo 1960, fig.23

415 1135–40

Palermo, Palazzo dei Normanni (Reale)
South wall of the central nave, Capella Palatina
MOSAIC
*Broad axe, stone axe, trowel, mortar tub, mortar-
mixing bin, mortar-mixing pick, mortar shovel*
Binding (1972), figure on p.27; Tyghem, fig.17;
Minkowski, fig.2a; Demus, Otto: *The Mosaics of
Norman Sicily*. London 1949, fig.32b

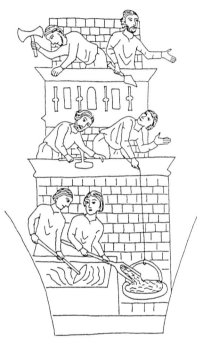

415a 1276

Paris, Archives nationales,
pièce S1626, fol.20
Census of the abbey of Ste-Geneviève, Paris
ILLUMINATION
Trowel, ramp, pannier
Schöller, p.96, fig.74; Folda, Jaroslaw: *Crusader
Manuscript Illumination at St Jean d'Acre 1275–1291*.
Princeton 1976, fig.35; Gimpel (1980), figure on p.35

416 after 1485

Paris, Sainte-Chapelle
Detail from the western rose window
STAINED GLASS
Measuring staff
Propyläen Kunstgeschichte, vol.VII. Bialostocki, Jan:
Spätmittelalter und beginnende Neuzeit. Berlin 1984,
fig.153

416a 1248

Paris, Sainte-Chapelle
STAINED GLASS
Trowel, hawk
Binding, Günther: *Hochgotik*. Cologne 1999, p.130

417   c.1460
Paris, Musée des Arts décoratifs
EMBROIDERY (Tournai, workshop of Pasquier
Grenier)
Axe, hand saw
Brandt II, p.32, fig.21; *Lexikon der Kunst.* Leipzig 1976,
vol.2, p.320; Warburg, A.: 'Arbeitende Bauern auf
burgundischen Teppichen', in *Zeitschrift für bildende
Kunst* 1907, p.41, fig.1

▶

418   13th century
Paris, Musée de Cluny
Gravestone of master mason Guérin and his wife
(from the parish church of Saint-Marcel in Saint-Denis)
ENGRAVING
Stone hammer, trowel, plumbline, measuring staff
Bi/Nu 234; Du Colombier, p. 102, fig. 61; Kimpel,
Dieter, & Suckale, Robert: *Die gotische Architektur in
Frankreich 1130–1270.* Munich 1985, p. 229, fig. 229
(Drawings after Guilhermy, François de: *Inscriptions de
la France du Ve au XVIIIe siècle.* 5 vols, Paris 1873–83,
vol.II, pp.199f)

▼

419   c.1220–30
Paris, Musée de Cluny, inv. 2826
Reliquary of St Fausta of Kyzikos
ENAMEL
Basket, ladder, plumbline
François-Souchal, Geneviève: 'Les émaux de Grandmont
au XIIe siècle (suite)', in *Bulletin monumental*, vol.cxxi.
4, Paris 1963, p.313, fig.26; Gauthier, Marie-
Madeleine: *Emaux du moyen âge occidental.* Fribourg
1972, cat. no.132, figure on p.189

▼

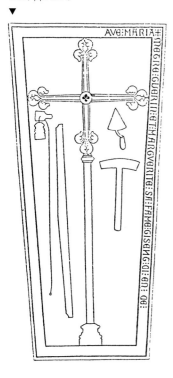

420   c.1360
Paris, Bibliothèque de l'Arsenal,
MS 667, fol.10
Histoire romaine (so-called
Romuléon of Bologna)
ILLUMINATION
*Scaffolding, trowel, mallet, crane,
ladder, measuring staff, mortar-
mixing pick, hod, chisel, square,
compasses*
Brandt II, p.51, fig.47

▶

421 15th century
Paris, Bibliothèque de l'Arsenal,
MS fr. 5064
Pierre de Crescens, *Livre des profits champêtres*
ILLUMINATION
*Trestle, broad axe, scaffolding, hammer, trowel,
ladder, mortar shovel, hod, pointed stone hammer*
Bi.Nu 184; Evans, fig.59

▶

422 1409–11
Paris, Bibliothèque de l'Arsenal,
MS fr. 5193, fol.11v
Boccaccio, *Des cas des nobles hommes et femmes*
by Jean Sans Peur
ILLUMINATION (France)
Crane with treadwheel and pallet, mortar-mixing pick
Bi/Nu 185; Minkowski, pic. 59; Martin, Henry: *Le
Boccace de Jean Sans Peur. Des cas des nobles hommes
et femmes.* Brussels & Paris 1911, pl.1, fig.2

▼

422a 1409–19
Paris, Bibliothèque de l'Arsenal,
MS 5193, fol.16v
Boccaccio, *Des cas des nobles hommes et femmes*
by Jean Sans Peur
ILLUMINATION (France)
Scaffolding, chisel
Schöller, p.96f., no.75; Martin, Henry: *Le Boccace de
Jean Sans Peur. Des cas des nobles hommes et femmes.*
Brussels & Paris 1911, pl.1, fig.4

423 second half 14th century
Paris, Bibliothèque de l'Arsenal,
MS 5212, fol.294v
Guyart des Moulins, *Bible historiale*
ILLUMINATION (Maître aux Bouqueteaux)
Trowel, pointed stone hammer, square
Du Colombier, fig.10; Martin, Henry: *La miniature
française du XIIIe au XVe siècle.* Brussels & Paris 1923,
pl.50, fig.lxx; Schöller, p.97, no.76

▶

424 second half 14th century
Paris, Bibliothèque de l'Arsenal,
MS 5212, fol.91v
Guyart des Moulins, *Bible historiale*
ILLUMINATION (Maître aux Bouqueteaux)
Trowel, hod, pointed stone hammer, square
Bi/Nu 186; Tyghem, fig.74; Martin, Henry: *La miniature
française du XIIIe au XVe siècle.* Brussels & Paris 1923,
pl.49, fig.lxvii

▼

425   end 14th century

Paris, Bibliothèque de l'Arsenal,

MS 5223, fol.2

Chronique des royes de France

ILLUMINATION

Stone hammer, trowel, ladder, plumbline, hod

Bi/Nu 187; Tyghem, fig.87; Martin, Henry: *La miniature française du XIIIe au XVe siècle.* Brussels & Paris 1923, pl.76, fig.4

▼

426   15th century

Paris, Bibliothèque de la Chambre des députés,

MS 1265, fol.72

Livy, *Histoire Romaine*

ILLUMINATION

Trowel, crane, plumbline, level, mortar tub, precision hammer

Bi/Nu 190; Tyghem, fig.130; Recht, p.68

▶

427   c.1475

Paris, Bibliothèque Sainte-Geneviève,

MS fr. 246, fol.284v

French Augustine manuscript

ILLUMINATION

Bi/Nu 327; Minkowski, no.65 (no illus.)

427a   14th century

Paris, Bibliothèque Sainte-Geneviève,

MS 777, fol.7

Livy, *Histoire Romaine*

ILLUMINATION (Paris)

Trowel, hod, serrated stone hammer

Schöller, p.98, no.94; Martin, Henry: *La miniature française du XIIIe au XVe siècle.* Brussels & Paris 1923, pl.52, fig.lxxiii; Avril, François: *Buchmalerei am Hofe Frankreichs 1310–1380* (= *Die großen Handschriften der Welt* 8). Munich 1978, pl.38

▶

428   14th century

Paris, Bibliothèque Sainte-Geneviève,
MS 777, fol.100
Workshop of the Maître aux Bouqueteaux, Livy of
Charles V
ILLUMINATION
Trowel, hod, pointed stone hammer, square
Bi.Nu 188; Tyghem, fig.73; Gimpel, Jean: *Les bâtisseurs
de cathédrales.* Bourges 1976, figure on p.77;
Martin, Henry: *La miniature française du XIIIe au
XVe siècle.* Brussels & Paris 1923, pl.52, fig.lxxv
▶

429   1430–40

Paris, Bibliothèque Sainte-Geneviève,
MS 1015, fol.1
Livre du Gouvernement des Rois et des Princes
ILLUMINATION
*Trowel, mallet, crane, ramp, level, measuring staff,
hod, chisel, pointed stone hammer, compasses*
Bi/Nu 189; Foerster, Rolf Hellmut: *Das Leben in der
Gotik.* Munich, Vienna & Basle 1969, p.179; *Meyers
illustrierte Weltgeschichte.* Mannheim, Vienna & Zürich
1980, vol.12, figure on p.58f.
▼

429a   1378

Paris, Bibliothèque Historique de la Ville de Paris
ILLUMINATION
Crane with pallet
Stejskal, Karl: *Karl IV und die Kulture und Kunst seiner
Zeit.* Hanau 1978, fig.77; Schöller (1998), fig.1
▼

430   end 12th century

Paris, Bibliothèque de l'Ecole des Beaux-Arts,
donation J. Masson
Homélies de Saint-Basile from the abbey of Lambert
de Liessies
PEN-AND-INK DRAWING
*Axe, carpenter's chisel, trestle, drill, broad axe,
mallet, mortar-mixing pick*
Bi/Nu 17; Binding (1972), figure on p.61 (outline);
Tyghem, fig.22
▼

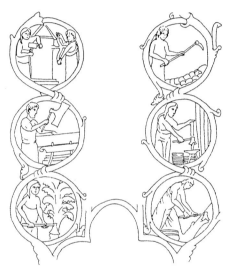

431 first half 11th century
Paris, Bibliothèque Nationale,
MS lat. 6 III, fol.89v
Bible from Noailles
PEN-AND-INK DRAWING
Stone hammer, four-wheeled cart, trowel, plumbline
Bi/Nu 15; Binding (1972), figure on p.17 (outline);
Tyghem, fig.5; Le Goff, fig.99; Lacroix, Paul: *Les arts au moyen âge et à l'époque de la renaissance*. Paris 1977, p.429, fig.308; Recht, p.333
▶

433 1469–89
Paris, Bibliothèque Nationale,
MS lat. 920, fol.198
Book of Hours of Louis de Laval
ILLUMINATION
Lump hammer, scaffolding
Bi/Nu 325
▼

432 1469–89
Paris, Bibliothèque Nationale,
MS lat. 920, fol.38v
Book of Hours of Louis de Laval
ILLUMINATION
Scaffolding, mallet, crane, chisel, pointed stone hammer
Bi/Nu 324; Leroquais I, p.21 (no illus.)
▶

433a   end 15th century
Paris, Bibliothèque Nationale,
MS lat. 4266, fols 44v, 45
Carolus da Gouda, *Figurale cognationum*
opusculum
ILLUMINATION
Crane with treadwheel
Schad, Hermann: *Die Darstellungen der Arbores*
Consanguinitatis un der Arbores Affinitatis. Tübingen
1982, fig.159
▼

435   end 15th century
Paris, Bibliothèque Nationale,
MS lat. 6067
Guillaume Caoursin, *De casu regis Zizimi*
ILLUMINATION
Carpenter's chisel, broad axe, scaffolding, trowel,
mallet, ladder, hod, pointed stone hammer, square,
compasses
Bi/Nu 177; Tyghem, fig.177; Du Colombier, p.53,
fig.30; Delort, Robert: *Life in the Middle Ages*. Oxford
1974, p.299; Recht, p.345
▶

434   1448–9
Paris, Bibliothèque Nationale,
MS lat. 4915, fol.46v
Livre des Rois, Mers des Histoires
ILLUMINATION
Axe, square, claw chisel
Bi/Nu 176l Du Colombier, p.111, fig.74; Coldstream
(1991), p.23, fig.17
▶

435a end 15th century
Paris, Bibliothèque Nationale,
MS lat. 6067 (–68)
Guillaume Caoursin, *De casu regis Zizimi* or *De bello Rhodio*
ILLUMINATION
Trowel
Recht, p.343, fig.A9; Comte Riant: 'Inventaire sommaire des manuscrits relatifs à l'histoire et à la géographie de l'Orient latin', in *Archives de l'Orient latin* II, 1884

436 c.1450
Paris, Bibliothèque Nationale,
MS lat. 7239, fol.21
Tractatus Pauli Sanctini
PEN-AND-INK DRAWING
Crane with windlass
Bi/Nu 254; Tyghem, fig.119
▼

437 end 10th century
Paris, Bibliothèque Nationale,
MS lat. 8085
Prudentius, *Psychomachia*
PEN-AND-INK DRAWING
Stettiner, Richard: *Die illustrierten Prudentiushandschriften*. Berlin 1905, pl.79
For a copy from Leiden, compare no.237

438 beginning 13th century
Paris, Bibliothèque Nationale,
MS lat. 8846, fol.1
Illuminated psalter (copy of the Utrecht Psalter)
ILLUMINATION (Canterbury)
Compasses
Steinen, Wolfram von den: *Homo caelestis*. Berne & Munich 1965, vol.II, fig.238; Zahlten, Johannes: *Creatio mundi. Darstellungen der sechs Schöpfungstage und naturwissenschaftliches Weltbild im Mittelalter.* Stuttgart 1979, fig.283 (= *Stuttgarter Beiträge zur Geschichte und Politik*, vol.13)
▼

439 14th century
Paris, Bibliothèque Nationale,
MS lat. 8846, fol.94
Illuminated psalter
ILLUMINATION (England, produced by Catalan artists)
Mortar tub, mortar-mixing pick, pulley, stone hammer
Bi/Nu 179; Gimpel (1980), p.45; Tyghem, fig.42
▼

440   14th century
Paris, Bibliothèque Nationale,
MS lat. 8846, fol.170v
Illuminated psalter
ILLUMINATION (England, produced by Catalan artists)
Basket, ladder, mortar tub, mortar-mixing pick,
pulley, pointed stone hammer
Bi/Nu 180; Tyghem, fig.41; Brandt I, p.266, fig.366;
Gimpel (1980), p.44

441   first half 15th century
Paris, Bibliothèque Nationale,
MS lat. 9471, fol.23v
Grandes Heures de Rohan
ILLUMINATION
Ladder, pointed stone hammer, square, serrated
stone hammer
Bi/Nu 326

440a   beginning 11th century
Paris, Bibliothèque Nationale,
MS lat. 8851, fol.12
Sainte-Chapelle Gospels
ILLUMINATION (Trier)
Schöller, p.98, no.92; *L'index photographique de l'art*
en France, fiche 554/D9

442   1230–40
Paris, Bibliothèque Nationale,
MS lat. 11560, fol.35v
Bible moralisée
ILLUMINATION
Double-headed serrated stone hammer, mallet, chisel
Coldstream (1991), p.13, fig.12; Laborde, vol.II, pl.259
This refers to a three-volume set of the *Bible*
moralisée, of which two examples are known. The
older and better is in the care of Toledo cathedral
and the younger is split between Oxford (Bodley
270b), Paris (Bibliothèque Nationale, MS lat. 11560)
and London (British Museum, Harleian MS 1526–7).
Compare Haussherr, Reiner: 'Templum Salomonis
und Ecclesia Christi', in Zeitschrift für
Kunstgeschichte 31, 2. Munich & Berlin 1968, p. 107

443   1230–40
Paris, Bibliothèque Nationale,
MS lat. 11560, fol.46
Bible moralisée
ILLUMINATION
Mallet, chisel
Laborde, vol.II, pl.270
Compare no.557
▼

443a   1327
Paris, Bibliothèque Nationale,
MS lat. 11935, fol.5
Jean Pucelle, Bible of Robert de Billying
ILLUMINATION
Compasses
Martin, Henry: *La miniature française du XIIIe au XVe
siècle.* Brussels & Paris 1923, pl.34, fig.xliii

444   1230–40
Paris, Bibliothèque Nationale,
MS lat. 11560, fol.63v
Bible moralisée
ILLUMINATION
Trowel, square
Laborde, vol.II, pl.287
                           ▶

445   1230–40
Paris, Bibliothèque Nationale,
MS lat. 11560, fol.108
Bible moralisée
ILLUMINATION
Trestle, broad axe, hand saw
Laborde, vol.II, pl.332
▼

446   1230–40
Paris, Bibliothèque Nationale,
MS lat. 11560, fol.114
Bible moralisée
ILLUMINATION
*Double-headed serrated
stone hammer*
Laborde, vol.II, pl.338
                    ▶

447   1230–40
Paris, Bibliothèque Nationale,
MS lat. 11560, fol.122
Bible moralisée
ILLUMINATION
Hammer, ladder, pannier
Laborde, vol.II, pl.346
▼

448   1230–40
Paris, Bibliothèque Nationale,
MS lat. 11560, fol.147v
Bible moralisée
ILLUMINATION
Mallet, ramp, pannier
Laborde, vol.II, pl.371
▶

449   1230–40
Paris, Bibliothèque Nationale,
MS lat. 11560, fol.233v
Bible moralisée
ILLUMINATION
Ladder, pannier
Laborde, vol.II, pl.233

▲

450   1289
Paris, Bibliothèque Nationale,
MS lat. 15158
Prudentius, *Psychomachia*
PEN-AND-INK DRAWING (Abbey of St Victor, Paris)
Measuring staff, template, square, compasses
Bi/Nu 181; Hecht, p.234, fig.56; Stettiner, Richard: *Die
illustrierten Prudentiushandschriften*. Berlin
1905, pl.199f, no.14

▲

451   after 1189
Paris, Bibliothèque Nationale,
MS lat. 17716, fol.43
Miscellanea secundum usum ordinis Cluniacensis
ILLUMINATION (Cluny, St Peter)
Rope
Bi/Nu 16; Binding (*Ornamenta ecclesiae*), vol.I, p.185;
Du Colombier, p.86, fig.53; Gimpel, Jean: *Les bâtisseurs
de cathédrales*. Auvergne 1976, figure on p.144; Hecht,
p.213, fig.45; L'Huillier, A.: *Viede Saint Hugues, abbé
de Cluny 1024–1109*. Paris 1888, p.360 (col. illus.)

▼

452   1040–50
Paris, Bibliothèque Nationale,
nouv. acq. lat. 2196, fol.6v
Fragment of Gospels from Luxeuil
ILLUMINATION (Echternach)
Axe, ladder, shovel
Grodecki, Louis, et al.: *Die Zeit der Ottonen und Salier*.
Munich 1973, p.176, fig.167

▼

452a   7th century
Paris, Bibliothèque Nationale,
nouv. acq. lat. 2334, fol.58
Ashburnham Pentateuch (Spain?)
ILLUMINATION
Summary representation of tools
Schöller, p.98, no.93; *Der Stuttgarter Bilderpsalter. Bibl.
Fol. 23. Württembergische Landesbibliothek Stuttgart.
Untersuchungen*. Stuttgart 1968, vol.2, fig.38

452b   c.1412

Paris, Bibliothèque Nationale,

MS fr. 9, fol.13

Guiart des Moulins, *Bible historiale*

ILLUMINATION (France)

Trestle, hammer, ladder, measuring staff, hand saw

Schöller, p.97, no.77; Meiss, Millard, *The De Lévis-*
Hours and the Bedford Workshop (= *Yale Lectures on*
Medieval Illumination). New Haven 1972, fig.55

▶

453   1473

Paris, Bibliothèque Nationale,

MS fr. 19, fol.81v

Augustine manuscript

ILLUMINATION (France, Tours school)

Bucket, scaffolding, trowel, basket, crane, ladder,
hod, shoulder pole, pointed stone hammer, square

Bi/Nu 168a; Minkowski, pic. 63

▼

454   c.1400

Paris, Bibliothèque Nationale,

MS fr. 21, fol.87

French Augustine manuscript   ▶

ILLUMINATION

Scaffolding, trowel, ramp, measuring staff, hod

Bi/Nu 320

455   c.1390

Paris, Bibliothèque Nationale,

MS fr. 23, fol, 119v

Augustine manuscript

ILLUMINATION (Flanders or northern France)

Bucket, mallet, crane, pointed stone hammer

Bi/Nu 169; Minkowski, pic. 53

◀

456   c.1460
Paris, Bibliothèque Nationale,
MS fr. 27, fol 112
French Augustine manuscript
ILLUMINATION
Scaffolding, trowel, crane with treadwheel, mortar
shovel, hod
Bi/Nu 321
Compare 145a
▼

457   14th century
Paris, Bibliothèque Nationale,
MS fr. 167, fol.18
Bible moralisée
ILLUMINATION
Trowel, ladder, plumbline, serrated stone hammer
Bi/Nu 170; Minkowski, pic. 50
▼

457a   1402
Paris, Bibliothèque Nationale,
MS fr. 166, fol.5v
Limburg Brothers, *Bible moralisée*
ILLUMINATION
Trowel, ramp, plumbline, hod
Schöller, p.97, no.79; Meiss, 1974, vol.3, fig.289

▶

457b   1403–04
Paris, Bibliothèque Nationale,
MS fr 166, fol.18
Limburg Brothers, Exodus I
ILLUMINATION
Mallet, basket, crane, square, chisel, table
Meiss (1974), fig.314

458   c.1380
Paris, Bibliothèque Nationale,
MS fr. 171, fol.135v
French Augustine manuscript
ILLUMINATION
Ladder, plumbline, hod, serrated stone hammer
▼

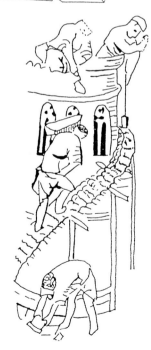

459   c.1392
Paris, Bibliothèque Nationale,
MS fr. 172, fol.117v
French Augustine manuscript
ILLUMINATION
Crane with lewis, pointed stone hammer
Bi/Nu 323
▼

460   mid-14th century
Paris, Bibliothèque Nationale,
MS fr. 185, fol.205v
Collected volume, fols 202–09v: *Vie de Saint-Denis*
ILLUMINATION
Trowel, ladder, hod, serrated stone hammer
Bähr, Ingeborg: *St Denis und seine Vita im Spiegel der Bildüberlieferung der französischen Kunst des Mittelalters*. Worms 1984, p.102f., fig.64
▼

461   c.1470
Paris, Bibliothèque Nationale,
MS fr. 247, fol.3
Jean Fouquet, *Antiquités Judaïques*
ILLUMINATION
Drill, mallet, level, square, compasses
Bi/Nu 253; Binding (1974), pl.14
▼

462   end 15th century
Paris, Bibliothèque Nationale,
MS fr. 247, fol.163
Jean Fouquet, *Antiquités Judaïques*
ILLUMINATION
Bucket, lump hammer, crane with treadwheel and pallet, mortar-mixing pick, pointed stone hammer, chisel (possibly a punch)
Bi/Nu 171; Tyghem, fig.173; Aubert, figure on p.189; Brandt I, p.265, fig.365; Coldstream (1991), p.4, fig.1; Du Colombier, p.23, fig.7; Delort, Robert: *Life in the Middle Ages*. London 1974, figure on p.267; Harvey (1975), figs 15, 21; Recht, p.69; Schib, Karl: *Das Mittelalter*. Erlenbach & Zürich 1956 (*Weltgeschichte* vol.2), fig.29; Winston, Richard & Clara: *Notre-Dame*. Wiesbaden 1976, figure on p.62
[OVERLEAF]

462a   1412–13
Paris, Bibliothèque Nationale,
MS fr. 259, fol.150v
Boucicaut workshop, Livy's *Histoire Romaine*
ILLUMINATION
Trestle, broad axe, square, stone hammer
Schöller, p.97, no.81; Meiss, Millard: *French Painting in the time of Jean de Berry. The Boucicaut Master*, plate volume. London & New York 1968, fig.435; Schöller (1998), fig.2, p.100
▼

462b   c.1475
Paris, Bibliothèque Nationale,
MS fr. 273, fol.7
Jean Fouquet, Livy's *Histoire Romaine*
ILLUMINATION
Mallet, chisel, pointed stone hammer
Schöller, p.97, no.82; Perels, Klaus Günther: *Jean Fouquet*. London, Paris & New York 1940, p.227, fig.251

462

463   1396
Paris, Bibliothèque Nationale,
MS fr. 312, fol.102
Vincent de Beauvais, *Miroir historial*
ILLUMINATION (Raoulet d'Orléans, active at the court
of Charles V)
Trowel, plumbline
Bi/Nu 171a; Warnke, Martin: *Bau und Überbau.*
Soziologie der mittelalerlichen Architektur nach den
Schriftquellen. Frankfurt am Main 1976, p.213, fig.10
▼

463a   1396
Paris, Bibliothèque Nationale,
MS fr. 312, fol.130
Vincent de Beauvais, *Miroir historial*
ILLUMINATION
Schöller, p.97, no.83; *L'index photographique de l'art*
en France (ed. Bildarchive Foto Marburg). Munich
1978–81, fiche 527/C14

463b   shortly after 1410
Paris, Bibliothèque Nationale,
MS fr. 603, fol.207
Cité des Dames Workshop: Christine de Pisan, *La*
mutacion de fortune
ILLUMINATION
Bucket, crane, hawk
Schöller, p.97, no.84; Schaefer, Lucie: 'Die Illustrationen
zu den Handschriften der Christine de Pisan', in
Marburger Jahrbuch für Kunstwissenschaft 10, 1987,
p.191, fig.156

463c   c.1402
Paris, Bibliothèque Nationale,
MS fr. 606, fol.19
ILLUMINATION (Christine de Pisan artist)
Crane with windlass, compasses
Schöller, p.97, no.85; *Europäische Kunst um 1400.*
Exhibition catalogue of Kunsthistorisches Museum,
Vienna, 1962, no.115, pl.138
Compare no.273
▼

464   c.1407
Paris, Bibliothèque Nationale,
MS fr. 607, fol.2
Christine de Pisan, *La cité des dames*
ILLUMINATION
Trowel, hod
Schöller, p.97, no.86; Swaan, Wim: *Kunst und Kultur*
der Spätgotik. Freiburg, Basle & Wien 1978, fig.137;
Meiss (1974), vol.3, fig.36
Compare nos 118a, 273a, 464c   ▶

464a   c.1405
Paris, Bibliothèque Nationale,
MS fr. 607, fol.31v
Christine de Pisan, *La cité des dames*
ILLUMINATION
Crane with windlass
Schöller, p.97, no.87; Meiss (1974), vol.3, fig.39
Compare nos 118b, 464b
▼

464b   c.1406
Paris, Bibliothèque Nationale,
MS fr. 1178, fol.64v
Christine de Pisan, *La cité des dames*
ILLUMINATION
Crane
Schöller, p.98, no.88; Meiss (1974), fig.41
Compare nos 464a, 118b

464c   c.1406
Paris, Bibliothèque Nationale,
MS fr. 1178, fol.3
Christine de Pisan, *La cité des dames*
ILLUMINATION
Trowel, hod
Schöller, p.98, no.89; Meiss (1974), fig.35
Compare nos 118a, 273a, 464

▼

465   14th century
Paris, Bibliothèque Nationale,
MS fr. 2092, fol.75v
La Légende de Saint-Denis
ILLUMINATION
Trestle, broad axe
Bi/Nu 173; Tyghem, fig.62; Brandt I, p.287, fig.402; Du
Colombier, p.32, fig.19; Recht, p.72

466   15th century
Paris, Bibliothèque Nationale,
MS fr. 2685, fol.159
Jean de Courcy, *La Bouquechardière*
ILLUMINATION
*Trowel, mallet, ladder, measuring staff, hod, chisel,
pointed stone hammer*
Bi/Nu 174; Du Colombier, p.108, fig.71; Recht, p.339

466a   c.1413
Paris, Bibliothèque Nationale,
MS fr. 2810, fol.7
Boucicaut Workshop, *Livre des merveilles du monde*
ILLUMINATION
Schöller, p.98, no.90; Omont, H.: *Livre des merveilles.*
Paris n.d., vol.1, fig.10

467   before 1379
Paris, Bibliothèque Nationale,
MS fr. 2813, fol.4
Grandes Chroniques de France
ILLUMINATION
Stone hammer, trowel, ladder, plumbline, hod
Bi/Nu 175; Tyghem, fig.75; Martin, Henry: *La miniature
française du XIIIe au XVe siècle.* Paris & Brussels
1923,pl.55, fig.lxxx   ◄

▶

468   *c.1485*

Paris, Bibliothèque Nationale,
MS fr. 6465, fol.96
Jean Fouquet, *Les Grandes Chroniques de France*
ILLUMINATION
Scaffolding, ramp, precision hammer
Bi/Nu 178; Tyghem, fig.165; Perels, Klaus Günther: *Jean Fouquet*. London, Paris & New York 1940, p.93, fig.62
▼

468a   1409/10–14

Paris, Bibliothèque Nationale,
MS fr. 9141, fol.9
ILLUMINATION (Boucicaut workshop)
Compasses
Meiss, Millard: *French Painting in the time of Jean de Berry. The Boucicaut Master*, plate vol.London & New York 1968, fig.447

468b   mid-15th century

Paris, Bibliothèque Nationale,
MS fr. 9343, fol.249v
PEN-AND-INK DRAWING
Hatchet, trowel, ladder, mortar shovel, hod
Small, Graeme: 'Les origines de la ville de Tournai dans les chroniques légendaires du bas moyen âge', in Dumoulin, Chanoine Jean, & Pycke, Jacques (eds): *Les grands siècles de Tournai (12e–15e siècles)*. Tournai 1993, p.88, fig.31
▼

469

Paris, Bibliothèque Nationale,
MS fr. 19093
Sample book of Villard de Honnecourt
PEN-AND-INK DRAWING
*Fol. 20: Measuring staff, template, cord, square,
compasses*
*Fol. 20v: Triangulation board and hanging staff for
measuring height; square*
Fol. 21: Measuring staff, template, cord
*Fol. 22v: Crane with windlass, mechanical water-
powered saw*

c.1225–35

fol.23: Level, stabilising structure, underwater saw
fol.32: Cord
Bi/Nu 182; Bechmann, Roland: *Villard de Honnecourt.
La pensée téchnique au XIIIe siècle et sa
communication.* Paris 1991; Hahnloser, Hans R.: *Villard
de Honnecourt. Kritische Gesamtausgabe des
Bauhüttenbuches MS fr. 19093 der Pariser
Nationalbibliothek.* Graz 1972, pls 39–41, 44f., 63
▼

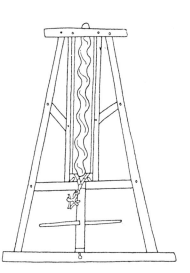

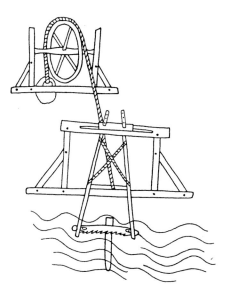

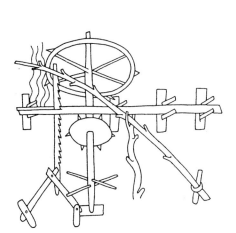

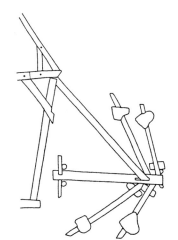

470   15th century

Paris, Bibliothèque Nationale,

MS fr. 20065, fol.26v

Bible of Raoul de Presles

ILLUMINATION

Trestle, drill, bucket, trowel, mallet, crane with lewis, ramp, measuring staff, mortar-mixing bin, hod, chisel, pointed stone hammer, crowbar, square, claw chisel, compasses; in the marginal scenes: broad axe, plane, saw

Bi/Nu 183; Tyghem, fig.127; Du Colombier, p.107, fig.70

▼ ▼ ▶

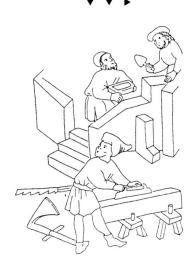

470a   c.1480

Paris, Bibliothèque Nationale,

MS fr. 20071, fol.1

Jean Fouquet workshop, Livy's *Histoire Romaine*

ILLUMINATION (Tours)

Mallet, crane with treadwheel, chisel, pointed stone hammer

Schöller, p.98, no.91; König, Eberhard: *Französische Buchmalerei um 1450*. Berlin 1982, pl.81, fig.167

471   1376

Paris, Bibliothèque Nationale,

MS fr. 22913, fol.2v

Augustine, *La cité de Dieu*

ILLUMINATION (France)

Compasses

Zahlten, Johannes: *Creatio mundi. Darstellungen der sechs Schöpfungstage und naturwissenschaftliches Weltbild im Mittelalter.* Stuttgart 1979, fig.180 (= *Stuttgarter Beiträge zur Geschichte und Politik*, vol.13)

▶

472   15th century

Paris, Bibliothèque Nationale
Manuscript
ILLUMINATION
Pointed stone hammer, square
Comte, Suzanne: *Everyday Life in the Middle
Ages*. Geneva 1978, figure on p.18

▶

473   15th century

Paris, Bibliothèque Nationale
French manuscript (extract)
Construction of the church of Saint-Denis
ILLUMINATION (France)
*Mallet, crane with treadwheel, ladder,
chisel, pointed stone hammer, hawk, cart,
square*
Winston, Richard & Clara: *Notre-Dame*.
Wiesbaden 1976, figure on p.35

◀

474   end 15th century

Parma, Biblioteca Palatina,
MS Parm. 3143 – De Rossi 958, fol.4v
(extract)
Hebrew manuscript
ILLUMINATION (northern Italy)
*Scaffolding, trowel, ladder, mortar-
mixing pick, hod*
Metzger, Thérèse & Mendel: *Jüdisches
Leben im Mittelalter nach illuminierten
hebräischen Handschriften vom13.–16.
Jahrhundert*. Fribourg & Würzburg 1983,
p.172, fig.232

▶

475   c.1220–5

Peterborough, Cathedral
Ceiling of central nave
CEILING PAINTING
Square, compasses
Clapham, Alfred: *English Romanesque
Architecture*. Oxford 1934, vol.II, pl.46;
Morriss, Richard: *Cathedrals and Abbeys of
England and Wales*. London, Toronto &
Melbourne 1979, pp.67, 110, fig.46

▶

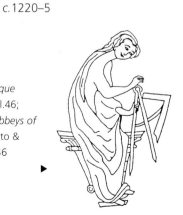

475a   c.1410
Philadelphia, Museum of Art,
MS 45-65-1, fol.66v
Orosius master, Augustine's *Cité de Dieu*
ILLUMINATION
*Trowel, ladder, mortarboard, hod, pointed stone
hammer, hawk*
Schöller, p.98, no.96; Meiss (1974), fig.277

476   c.1470
Pforzheim, Schloß- und Stiftskirche St Michael
Eastern keystone in the choir; master mason Hans
Sprysz von Zaberfeld
ARCHITECTURAL SCULPTURE
Pointed stone hammer, compasses, stone hammer
Gerstenberg, p.182; Hecht, p.232, fig.55.2 (outline);
Lacroix, Emil, *et al.*: *Die Kunstdenkmäler der Stadt
Pforzheim* (= *Die Kunstdenkmäler Badens* 9,6).
n.p.1939, p.130, fig.163

▼

476a   c.1440
Philadelphia, Free Library, Widener MS 1
Jacques Bruyant, *Le castel de labour*
ILLUMINATION (northern France)
*Level, frame saw, summary representation of
carpenter's tools*
Schöller, p.98, no.95; *Illuminated Books of the Middle
Ages and Renaissance*. Exhibition catalogue, Baltimore
Museum of Art 1949. Baltimore 1949, pl.41, no.103

477   1389–91
Pisa, Camposanto, extension to the north wing
Piero di Puccio, 'Building Noah's Ark'
MURAL
*Hatchet, trestle, hammer, plane, frame saw, guide
line*
Tyghem, fig.82; Ramalli, Giuseppe, *et al.*: *Camposanto
Monumentale di Pisa*. Pisa 1960, pp.18ff., figs 108ff.

▼

477a 1468–85
Pisa, Camposanto
Mural by Benozzo Gozzoli
Tub, bucket, trowel, crane with windlass, ladder, plumbline, scaffolding, square, pointed stone hammer, measuring staff (?)
Davenport, Millia: *The Book of Costume*. New York 1976, vol.1, p.279, fig.757f.; Ehrenstein, Theodor: *Das Alte Testament im Bilde*. Vienna 1923, p.128, fig.11; Papini, Roberto: *Pisa* (= *Catalogo delle cose d'arte di antichità d'Italia*). Rome 1912, 1, vol.2,2, pls xxxii, xxxiii, cat. 470

▶

478 1361-64
Pistoia, Cathedral of SS Zeno and Jacopo, chapel of S. Jacopo
Giovanni & Francesco di Niccolò: Silver altar to S. Jacopo
SILVERWORK
Hammer
Lessing, Ernst: *Die Arche Noah in Bildern*. n.p., n.d., figures on pp.18f., 110
▼

479 end 12th century
Plieningen, Protestant parish church
Frieze beneath the eaves ledge
Pointed stone hammer
Bi/Nu 50; Binding (1972), figure on p.54 (outline); Binding (1985), p.180, fig.20 (outline), Bock, Emil: *Romanische Baukunst und Plastik in Württemberg*. Stuttgart 1958, p.157, fig.81

▶

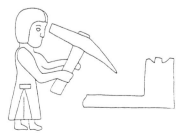

480 c.1300
Poitiers, Cathedral of Notre-Dame-la-Grande
Choirstalls
WOOD RELIEF
Level, drawing board, square, compasses
Bi/Nu 255; Du Colombier, p.91, fig.56; Hecht, p.256, fig.69, 2 (drawing of level); Aubert, figure on p.31; Mussat, André: 'Les cathédrales dans leurs cités', in *Revue de l'art* 55, 1982, pp.9–22, fig.I, p.9

▶

481 10th century (?)
Poitiers, Musée de Poitiers
Stone relief from Saint-Hilaire
ARCHITECTURAL SCULPTURE
Stone hammer
Oursel, Raymond: *Haut-Poitou Romain*. Paris 1975 (= *La nuit des temps* 42), fig.48

▶

481a first half 14th century
Pommersfelden, Schloßbibliothek,
cod. 215, fol.161
Alanus ab Insulis, *Anticlaudianus*
ILLUMINATION
Hatchet, broad axe
Mütherisch, Florentine: 'Ein Illustrationszyklus zum
Anticlaudianus des Alanus ab Insulis', in *Münchener
Jahrbuch der bildenden Kunst*. Munich 1951, 3rd ed.,
vol.2, pp.73–88

482 14th century
Prague, Archiv Pražkého hradu,
cod. A 10, fol.166v
Manuscript
ILLUMINATION
Hammer, crane with treadwheel, mortar tub
Neuwirth, Josef: *Geschichte der bildenden Kunst in
Böhmen*. Prague 1893, vol.I, pl.III
▼

483 c.1400
Prague, Národní Knihovna, University Library
division, Sign. VII C 8, fol.168b
Peter de Crescentiis, *Rurarium comodorum libri decem*
ILLUMINATION
Trestle, broad axe, ladder
Bi/Nu 192; Husa, Václav: *Homo faber. Der Mensch und
seine Arbeit. Die Arbeitswelt in der bildenden Kunst des
11.–17. Jahrhunderts*. Wiesbaden 1971, figure on p.11;
Neuwirth, Josef: *Geschichte der bildenden Kunst in
Böhmen*. Prague 1893, vol.I, fol. 176, p.408

484 c.1400
Prague, Národní Knihovna, University Library
division, Sign. VII C 8, fol.176
Peter de Crescentiis, *Rurarium comodorum libri decem*
ILLUMINATION
Ladder
Bi/Nu 193; Husa, Václav: *Homo faber. Der Mensch und
seine Arbeit. Die Arbeitswelt in der bildenden Kunst des
11.–17. Jahrhunderts*. Wiesbaden 1971, figure on p.11;
Neuwirth, Josef: *Geschichte der bildenden Kunst in
Böhmen*. Prague 1893, vol.I, fol. 168, p.408

485 c.1432
Prague, Národní Knihovna, University Library
division, Sign. XVII A 34, fol.180b
Bible
PEN-AND-INK DRAWING
Broad axe, ladder
Bi/Nu 194; Husa, Václav: *Homo faber. Der Mensch und
seine Arbeit. Die Arbeitswelt in der bildenden Kunst des
11.–17. Jahrhunderts*. Wiesbaden 1971, figure on p.11
▼

486 c.1500
Prague, Národní Knihovna, University Library
division, Sign. XXIII A 1, fol.199b
Lobkowitz songbook
ILLUMINATION
*Crane with lewis, mortar-mixing bin, mortar-mixing
pick, wheelbarrow*
Bi/Nu 194; Husa, Václav: *Homo faber. Der Mensch und
seine Arbeit. Die Arbeitswelt in der bildenden Kunst des
11.–17. Jahrhunderts*. Wiesbaden 1971, fig.94
▼

487   c.1340

Prague, Národní Knihovna, University
Library division,
Sign. Lob. 412, fol.11b
Welislaw Bible
PEN-AND-INK DRAWING
Scaffolding, hammer, trowel, crane with
treadwheel and pallet, ramp, mortar
tub, hod, pannier
Bi/Nu 195; Tyghem, fig.61; Minkowski, pl.V; Brandt
I, p.245, fig.330; Du Colombier, p.28, fig.13;
Menclová, Debroslava: *České hrady*, Prague
1972, figure on p.116

488   first quarter 15th century

Prague, Knihovna Národního Muzea,
Sign. III B 10, p. 76
Collection of religious tracts from Krumlov
(southern Bohemia)
ILLUMINATION
Scaffolding, trowel, mortar-mixing pick
Bi/Nu 191; Husa, fig.96 & title page

▼

489   1246–54

Regensburg, Dominikanerkirche
'Brother Diemar' console figure in northern choir
chapel
ARCHITECTURAL SCULPTURE
Compasses
Bi/Nu 258; Gerstenberg, fig.34; Du Colombier, p.100,
fig.59; Grote, pl.1; Kletzl, Otto: 'Ein Werkriss des
Frauenhauses in Straßburg', in *Marburger Jahrbuch für*
Kunstwissenschaft 11, 1938, p.141, fig.24; Kobler,
Friedrich: 'Stadtkirchen der frühen
Gotik', in *Wittelsbach und Bayern.*
Exhibition catalogue, Munich
1980, vol.I, 1, p.428; RDK II,
under 'Baumeisterbildnis', fig.1

▶

490   c.1380

Regensburg, Fürstliche Thurn- und Taxissche
Hofbibliothek
Enikel, *Weltchronik*, fol.21
ILLUMINATION
Trowel, crane with lewis, mortar tub, mortar shovel,
one-legged stool, pointed stone hammer, square
Bi/Nu 328; Jacobi, Franz: *Studien zur Geschichte der*
bayerischen Miniatur (= *Studien zur deutschen*
Kunstgeschichte 102). Strasbourg 1908, fig.13;
Minkowski, no.25 (no illus.)
Compare nos 241, 335 ▶▼

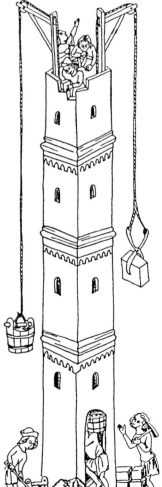

491   end 13th century
Reims, Notre-Dame Cathedral (formerly in Saint-Nicaise)
Gravestone of master mason Hugues Libergier (d.1263)
STONE CARVING
Measuring rod, square, compasses
Bi/Nu 260; Tyghem, fig.50; Du Colombier, p.91, fig.55; Hecht, p.224, fig.50; Andrews, figure on p.24; Aubert, figure on p.32; Binding (1974), pl.16a; Binding (1975), p.182, fig.32; Recht, p.210
▼ ▼

492   1494
Reutlingen, Michael Greyff, printer
Sebastian Brant, *Das Narrenschiff*
WOODCUT
Schramm 9, no.502
Derivative of no.37

493   1494
Reutlingen, Michael Greyff, printer
Sebastian Brant, *Das Narrenschiff*
WOODCUT
Schramm 9, no.553
Derivative of no.38

494   1482
Reutlingen, Johannes Otmar, printer
Conrad Schlafer, Saints' legends
Trowel, mortar-mixing bin, mortar-mixing pick
Schramm 9, no.739

495   15th century
Rome, Pinacoteca Vaticana, no. 288
Scuola Fiorentina, *Storie della Vita di S. Barbara*
(no illus.)

496   15th century
Rome, Pinacoteca Vaticana, no. 308
Guidoccio Cozzarelli (1450–1516), *Vita di S. Barbara*
PANEL PAINTING
(no illus.)

496a   15th century
Rome, Biblioteca Angelica,
MS 1146
ILLUMINATION
Hammer, trowel, mortar-mixing pick, mortar shovel, hod, pointed stone hammer
Conrad, Dietrich: *Kirchenbau im Mittelalter. Bauplannung und Bauausführung.* Leipzig 1990, fig.16
▼

497   10th century
Rome, Biblioteca Vaticana,
cod. reg. lat. 596
Roman fragment (2 sheets, fols 26 & 27, of a mixed volume in Paris, Bibliothèque Nationale, MS lat. 8318)
PEN-AND-INK DRAWING (France; after late Classical antecedents)
Measuring staff
Stettiner, Richard: *Die illustrierten Prudentiushandschriften.* Berlin 1905, pl.14
Compare no.238
▼

159

498   c.1120

Rome, Biblioteca Vaticana,
Vat. lat. 4939, fol.28
History of Santa Sophia in Benevento
ILLUSTRATION
Ladder, trowel
Binding (1972), figure on p.46; Boeckler, Albert:
Abendlandische Miniaturen der romanischen Zeit. Berlin
& Leipzig, 1930, fig.106

▼

498a   1282–3

Rome, Biblioteca Vaticana,
Vat. lat. 5895, fol.14v
Histoire ancienne jusqu'à César
ILLUMINATION
Hammer, crane, mortar-mixing pick, hod
Perricioli Saggense, Alessandra: *I romanzi cavallereschi
minati a Napoli.* Naples 1979, p.87f., pl.V

499   c.1340–50

Rottweil, Kapellenkirche
West doorway, tympanum
ARCHITECTURAL SCULPTURE
Pointed stone hammer
Bi/Nu 261; Gerstenberg, figures on
pp.36–7; Du Colombier, p.134

▶

500   first half 14th century

Rouen, Abbey church of Saint-Ouen
Sainte-Cécile chapel, gravestone of a master mason
ENGRAVING
Drawing board, compasses
Bi/Nu 262; Du Colombier, p.103,
fig.62 (outline); Binding (1974),
p.108, fig.11 (outline)

▶

501   after 1441

Rouen, Abbey church of Saint-Ouen
Sainte-Cécile chapel, gravestone of foremen
Alexandre and Colin de Berneval
ENGRAVING
Drawing board (depicting rose window), compasses
Bi/Nu 263; Binding (1974), p.50, fig.4; Du Colombier,
p.64, fig.35 (outline); Masson, André: *L'Eglise Abbatiale
Saint-Ouen de Rouen.* Paris 1927, figure on p.69; RDK
8, Sp.106 (detail)

▶

501a   fourth quarter 14th century

Rouen, Bibliothèque municipale,
MS Y26, fol.101 R°
ILLUMINATION
Stone hammer

502   1210–20

Rouen, Notre-Dame Cathedral
Window in north aisle of the nave, Chapelle Saint-
Jean-dans-la-Nef dite des 'Belles-Verrières'
STAINED GLASS
Hammer, measuring rod, template
Bi/Nu 197; Du Colombier (1953), p.85, fig.18; Grodecki,
Louis: 'Les vitraux', in *La cathédrale de Rouen. Les
monuments historiques de la France.* Paris 1956,
pp.101–10; Grodecki, Louis, & Brisac, Catherine: *Le vitrail
gothique au XIIIe siècle.*
Fribourg 1984, p.48;
Ritter, Georg: *Les
vitraux de la
Cathédrale de
Rouen.* Cognac
1926, pl.3

▶

503   1210–20
Rouen, Notre-Dame Cathedral
Window in north aisle of the nave, Chapelle Saint-Jean-dans-la-Nef dite des 'Belles-Verrières'
STAINED GLASS
Trestle, broad axe
Binding (1985) (*Ornamenta ecclesiae*), p.181, fig.23; Grodecki, Louis: 'Les vitraux', in *La cathédrale de Rouen. Les monuments historiques de la France*. Paris 1956, pp.101–10; Grodecki, Louis, & Brisac, Catherine: *Le vitrail gothique au XIIIe siècle*. Fribourg 1984, p.48; Ritter, Georg: *Les vitraux de la Cathédrale de Rouen*. Cognac 1926, pl.1

504   1210–20
Rouen, Notre-Dame Cathedral
Window in north aisle of the nave, Chapelle Saint-Jean-dans-la-Nef dite des 'Belles-Verrières'
STAINED GLASS
Trowel, mallet, hod, engraving chisel, pointed stone hammer
Bi/Nu 198; Tyghem, fig.44; Du Colombier (1953), p.85, fig.19; Grodecki, Louis: 'Les vitraux', in *La cathédrale de Rouen. Les monuments historiques de la France*. Paris 1956, pp.101–10; Grodecki, Louis, & Brisac, Catherine: *Le vitrail gothique au XIIIe siècle*. Fribourg 1984, p.48; Ritter, Georg: *Les vitraux de la Cathédrale de Rouen*. Cognac 1926, pl.3

504a   c.1250
Rouen, Saint-Julien-du-Sault church
Left-hand window, south-eastern ambulatory chapel, chancel
Theophilus legend
STAINED GLASS
Hammer, ramp, hod, stone axe
Schöller, p.98, no.97; Cothren, Michael W.: 'The iconography of Theophilus windows in the first half of the thirteenth century', in *Speculum* 59, 1984, p.314, fig.3a

504b   end 13th century
Saint-Omer, Bibliothèque municipale,
MS 5, vol.2, fol.140
Bible
ILLUMINATION (France or Flanders)
Schöller, p.98, no.98; Randall, p.162 (no illus.)

505   second half 11th century
Salerno, Cathedral of S. Matteo
Cathedral Museum, antependium
IVORY CARVING
Mortar-mixing pick, hod
Binding (1972), figure on p.20; Borst, Arno: *Der Turmbau zu Babel*. Stuttgart 1958, vol.II, part 1, p.588; Brandt I, p.243, fig.324; Minkowski, p.13; Parrot, André: *Ziggurats et tour de Babel*. Paris 1949, p.169, fig.109

506   second half 11th century
Salerno, Cathedral of S. Matteo
Cathedral Museum, antependium
IVORY CARVING
*Trestle, broad axe, roofing axe, drill, hammer, frame
saw*
Lessing, Erich: *Die Arche Noah in Bildern.* n.p., n.d.,
figures on pp.16, 106
▼

507   1456
Salzburg, Franziskanerkirche
South-eastern round pillar in front of the high altar
*Bildnisse der Meister Hans Stethaimer und Stefan
Krumenauer,* by painter from the circle of master
Pfenning
MURAL
Mallet, chisel (possibly a punch), stone hammer
Bi/Nu 264, Gerstenberg, figure on p.216; Liedke,
Volker: *Die Baumeister- und Bildhauerfamilie Rottaler
(1480–1533).* Munich 1976, figs. 145f.; Liedke, Volker:
'Hans Purghauser, genannt Meister
Hanns vom Burghausen', in *Ars
Bavarica 35/36,*
1984, p.19,
fig.16

507a   1430–40
Salzburg, Universitätsbibliothek,
MS lat. et germ. M III 36, fol.239v
COLOUR-WASHED PEN-AND-INK DRAWING
Axe
Tezmen-Siegel, Jutta: *Die Darstellungen der septem
artes liberales in der Bildenden Kunst als Rezeption der
Lehrplangeschichte.* Munich 1985, fig.49
▶

507b   1430–40
Salzburg, Universitätsbibliothek,
MS lat. et germ. M III 36, fol.240
COLOUR-WASHED PEN-AND-INK DRAWING
Broad axe, trestle
Tezmen-Siegel, Jutta: *Die Darstellungen der septem
artes liberales in der Bildenden Kunst als
Rezeption der Lehrplangeschichte.*
Munich 1985, fig.50
▶

507c   third quarter 14th century
St Petersburg, Imperial Public Library,
vol.1, fol.207
ILLUMINATION (France)
Crane with windlass, ladder, mortar-mixing bin

507d   third quarter 14th century
St Petersburg, Imperial Public Library,
vol.1, fol.12v
ILLUMINATION (France)
Ladder, mortar-mixing bin, pointed stone hammer
▼

507e   third quarter 14th century
St Petersburg, Imperial Public Library, vol.1,
fol.138
ILLUMINATION (France)
Trowel, mallet, ladder, mortar hod, level, chisel,
pointed stone hammer, square
Compare no.466
▼ ▼ ▼ ▶

507f   beginning 15th century
St Petersburg, Imperial Public Library,
vol.1, fol.4v
ILLUMINATION (France)
Broad axe, trowel, mallet, ladder, mortar basket,
mortar-mixing bin, chisel
▼

507g   beginning 14th century
St Petersburg, Imperial Public Library,
vol.1, fol.12v
ILLUMINATION (France)
Basket, ladder, rod

▶

508, 509   shortly after 1350
Sarajevo, Zemaljski Muzej Bosne i Hercegovine
Haggadah
ILLUMINATION (northern Spain, Barcelona?)
Ladder, light pulley, frame saw, pointed stone
hammer
Roth, Cecil (ed.): *Die Haggadah von Sarajevo*. Belgrade
1963
▼ ▼

510   1168–80
Schulpforte bei Naumburg, Bibliothek der
Landesschule Pforte,
MS lat. A. 10, fol.3
Augustine, *De civitate Dei*
ILLUMINATION (Upper Saxony)
Stone axe, scaffolding
Bi/Nu 20; Binding (1972), figure on p.33 (outline); de
Laborde, Alexandre: *Les manuscrits à peinture de la Cité
de Dieu de Saint-Augustin*. Paris 1909, pls 2, 3;
Minkowski, pic. 9

▼

511   1456 (renovated 1586)
Schwäbisch Hall, Protestant town parish church
of St Michael
Vaulting at the western end of the south aisle
CEILING PAINTING (Master Heinrich der Barlierer)
*Measuring staff, square (the
compasses and template listed
by E. Gradmann do not
belong to the original
version – see Gerstenberg,
pp. 216f.)*
Bi/Nu 265; Gerstenberg, figure on
p.217; Hecht, p.230, fig.54, 1
(drawing of compasses)

▶

512   beginning 15th century
Schwäbisch Gmünd, Catholic church
Illustrated Bible (High Germany)
ILLUMINATION
*Scaffolding, trowel, crane, mortar tub, wheelbarrow,
pointed stone hammer*
Friederich, Karl: *Die Steinbearbeitung in ihrer
Entwicklung vom 11. bis zum 18. Jahrhundert.*
Augsburg 1932, fig.111; Lacroix, Emil: 'Die
mittelalterlichen Baugerüste', in *Deutsche Kunst und
Denkmalpflege* 1934, p.220, fig.217

▶

513   1151–56
Schwarzrheindorf, former town chapel of
St Klemens
South-western cross vault of the crypt
CEILING PAINTING
Measuring rod, rope
Bi/Nu 48; Binding (1972), figure on p.14 (outline);
Binding (*Rhein und Maas*), p.93, fig.3 (outline);
Verbeek, Albert: *Schwarzrheindorf*. Düsseldorf 1953,
p.43, fig.30

▶

514   1151–56
Schwarzrheindorf, former town chapel of
St Klemens
South-western cross vault of the crypt
CEILING PAINTING
Measuring rod, rope
Bi/Nu 47; Binding (1972), figure on p.13 (outline);
Binding (1985), p.182, fig.27 (outline); Verbeek, Albert:
Schwarzrheindorf. Düsseldorf 1953, p.43, fig.28

▶

515

Schwarzrheindorf, former town chapel of
St Klemens
Eastern cap of the western vault in the crypt
CEILING PAINTING
Pointed stone hammer
Bi/Nu 49; Binding (1972), figure on p.53 (outline);
Binding (1985), p.180, fig.19 (outline); Verbeek, Albert:
Schwarzrheindorf. Düsseldorf 1953, figs 18, 20, 21a

▼

516 second quarter 13th century

Schweinfurt, Protestant parish church of
St Johannes
Vault console, south-western corner of the crossing
ARCHITECTURAL SCULPTURE
Hammer, one-legged stool
Bi/Nu 266; Gerstenberg, figure on p.19

▼

517 c.1235

Sémur-en-Auxois (Côte d'Or), Collegiate
church of Notre-Dame
Keystone, south aisle
ARCHITECTURAL SCULPTURE
Square, compasses
Bi/Nu 267; Brandt II, p.148, fig.184; Binding (1985),
p.182, fig.29

 ▶

518 1440–4

Siena, Santa Maria della Scala, hospital
Domenico di Bartolo, 'The Bishop's Visit'
MURAL
Tyghem, fig.115; Richter, Luise M.: *Siena*. Leipzig &
Berlin 1901, p.112, fig.78

 ▶

519 after 1407

Siena, Palazzo Pubblico, Sala di Balia
Spinello Aretino & Parri Spinello, 'Storie dal ciclo del
Papa Alessandro III'
MURAL
*Bucket, lump hammer, scaffolding, hammer, trowel,
crane with rope winch, hod*
Cairola, Aldo, & Carli, Enzo: *Il Palazzo Pubblico di Siena*.
Rome 1963, fig.105; Decker, Heinrich: *Gotik in Italien*.
Vienna 1964, figure at pl.63

▼

520 1337–40

Siena, Palazzo Pubblico, Sala della Pace
Ambrogio Lorenzetti, 'La vita cittadina del buon
governo'
MURAL (part)
*Scaffolding, trowel, basket, mortar tub, pointed
stone hammer (?)*
Tyghem, fig.58; Brandt II, p.72

▼

521   1477
Speyer, Peter Drach, printer
Werner Rovelinck,
Fasciculus temporum, fol.4v
WOODCUT
Crane with lewis
Bi/Nu 199; Schramm 16,
no.3; Minkowski, pic. 80;
Recht, p. 78
For the first edition of the
Fasciculus temporum see
no.223; for a re-use of the
blocks, see no.227

522   1478
Speyer, Peter Drach, printer
Spiegel menschlicher Behaltnis, fol.137
WOODCUT
*Builder's hut, scaffolding, trowel, mallet, crane with
lewis, mortar tub, hod, chisel, stone hammer*
Bi/Nu 201; Schramm 16, no.464; Tyghem, fig.158;
Brandt I, p.249, fig.337; Lacroix, Emil: 'Die
mittelalterlichen Baugerüste', in *Deutsche Kunst- und
Denkmalpflege* 1934, p.220, fig.218

523   1478
Speyer, Peter Drach, printer
Spiegel menschlicher Behaltnis,
fol.113v
WOODCUT
Bi/Nu 200; Schramm 16, no.450; Brandt I, p.276,
fig.387; Recht, p.72
Reversed derivative of no.45

524   c.1493
Speyer, Peter Drach, printer
Petrus de Crescentiis, *Commodorum ruralium libri*,
fol.8
WOODCUT
*Trestle, tub, broad axe,
mortar-mixing pick*
Schramm 16, no.27

525   c.1493
Speyer, Peter Drach,
printer
Petrus de Crescentiis,
*Commodorum ruralium
libri*, fol.148
WOODCUT
*Mortar shovel, pointed
stone hammer*
Schramm 16, no.240

525a   15th century
Stockholm, Kungliske Bibliothek,
Vu 74 a
Weltchronik of Rudolf von Ems
WASHED PEN-AND-INK DRAWING
*Trowel, crane with lewis, mortar tub, mortar-mixing
pick, level, four-legged stool, pointed stone hammer*
Svanberg, Jan: *Master Masons*. Sweden 1983, p.60,
no.23

525b   1489
Stockholm, St Nikolai
Bernt Notke, 'George group' of St Nikolai church
WOOD CARVING
Plumbline
Braunsfeld-Esche, Sigrid: *Sankt Georg.*
Legende, Verehrung, Symbol. Munich
1976, p.24, fig.14; Paatz, Walter:
Bernt Notke und sein Kreis. Berlin
1939, vol.2, fig.94

526   1175–91
Strasbourg
Herrad von Landsberg, *Hortus Deliciarum*, fol.27
ILLUMINATION
Mallet, plumbline, mortar-mixing bin, mortar-mixing
pick, hod, chisel, square, stone hammer
Bi/Nu 63; Binding (1972), figure on p.35 (outline);
Binding (*Rhein und Maas*), p.94, fig.6 (outline); Du
Colombier, p.31, fig.18; Philippi, pl.17; Gillen, Otto:
Herrad von Landsberg, Hortus Deliciarum. Neustadt an
der Weinstraße 1979, p.43; Green, Rosalie, *et al.*:
Herrad of Hohenbourg, Hortus Deliciarum. London &
Leiden 1979, fig.26; Heinsius, Maria: *Der*
Paradiesgarten der Herrad von Landsberg. Colmar, Paris
& Freiburg 1968, fig.7; Neher, F.L.: 'Alles hing einmal
am Haken', in *Heraklith-Rundschau* 31, 1961, fig.48;
Recht, p.73

527   1175–91
Strasbourg
Herrad von Landsberg, *Hortus Deliciarum*, fol.32
ILLUMINATION
Measuring staff, compasses
Bi/Nu 62; Binding (1972), figure on p.14 (outline);
Binding (1985), p.182, fig.28 (outline); Du Colombier,
p.118, fig.4; Gillen, Otto: *Herrad von Landsberg, Hortus*
Deliciarum. Neustadt an der Weinstraße 1979, p.43;
Green, Rosalie, *et al.*: *Herrad of Hohenbourg, Hortus*
Deliciarum. London & Leiden 1979, fig.34; Heinsius,
Maria: *Der Paradiesgarten der Herrad von Landsberg.*
Colmar, Paris & Freiburg 1968, fig.8

528   1485
Strasbourg, Johann Grüninger, printer
German Bible
WOODCUT
Lump hammer, trowel, crane with treadwheel and
external lewis, ramp, chisel, hawk
Bi/Nu 202; Schramm 20, no.9; Tyghem, fig.106;
Minkowski, pic. 88
Reversed, free derivative of nos 225, 386

▼

529   1494
Strasbourg, Johann Grüninger, printer
Das neue Narrenschiff
WOODCUT
Schramm 20, no.184.
Reversed, free derivative of no.37

530 1477–85
Strasbourg, Heinrich Knoblochtzer, printer
Johannes Hildeshemensis, *Life of the Three Holy Kings*
WOODCUT
Trestle, broad axe
Schramm 19, no.170
▼

531 1477–85
Strasbourg, Heinrich Knoblochtzer, printer
Duke Ernst von Bayern
WOODCUT
Schramm 19, no.228
Derivative of no.18

532 c.1478
Strasbourg, Heinrich Knoblochtzer, printer
Melusine
WOODCUT
Schramm 19, no.358
Free derivative of no.44

533 c.1484
Strasbourg, Johann Prüss, printer
Melusine
WOODCUT
Schramm 20, no.1665
Reversed derivative of no.44

534 c.1482
Strasbourg, 'Antichrist' printer at Johann Prüss's works
Antichrist
WOODCUT
Crane with treadwheel and external lewis, mortar-mixing pick, one-legged stool, pointed stone hammer
Wallrath, Rolf: *Das schöne gedruckte Buch*. Cologne 1968, fig.on p.41
▼

534a mid-15th century
Strasbourg, Bibliothèque Nationale et Universitaire,
MS 523, fol.3
St Augustine, *Cité de Dieu*
ILLUMINATION (Netherlands)
Scaffolding, trowel, mallet, mortar tub, mortar shovel, mortar pounder, hod, chisel, water jug
Recht, p.344, fig.A8; Laborde, Alexandre Comte de: *Les manuscrits à peintures de la Cité de Dieu de saint Augustin*. Paris 1909, fig.42; Winckler, Friedrich: *Die flämische Buchmalerei des XV. und XVI. Jahrhunderts*. Leipzig 1925; 'Le siècle de la miniature flamande – Le mécénat de Philippe le Bon'. Exhibition catalogue, Brussels & Amsterdam 1959, fig.223
▶

535 end 15th century
Stuttgart, Protestant parish church of the Holy Cross
Console on inner east wall
ARCHITECTURAL SCULPTURE
Stone hammer (?)
Bi/Nu 268; Gerstenberg, fig.on p.173; Sorg, Theo: *Die Stiftskirche in Stuttgart*. Königstein n.d., fig.on p.35
▼

536   1479
Stuttgart, Protestant hospital church
Console figures in the Counts' Gallery
ARCHITECTURAL SCULPTURE
Axe, scaffolding, hammer, level, chisel, hand saw,
compasses, stone hammer
Bi/Nu 269; Gerstenberg, figs on p.70 ff.
▼

536a   14th century
Stuttgart, Württembergische Landesbibliothek,
cod. bibl. 2° 3a, fol.271v
Latin Bible
ILLUMINATION (Paris)
Ladder, hod, pointed stone hammer
Schöller, p.98, no.99; Marburger Index, fiche 2965/F9

537   1383
Stuttgart, Württembergische Landesbibliothek,
cod. bibl. 2° 5, fol.9v
Rudolf von Ems, *Weltchronik*
ILLUMINATION (French influence)
Scaffolding, trowel, crane with treadwheel, mortar
tub, mortar-mixing pick, hod, pointed stone hammer,
serrated stone hammer
Bi/Nu 203; Tyghem, fig.79 (outline); Coldstream (1991),
p.55, fig.60; Minkowski, pic. 27; Schultz I, p.55,
fig.79;Lacroix, Emil: 'Die mittelalterlichen Baugerüste',
in *Deutsche Kunst und Denkmalpflege* 1934, p.220,
fig.216
▼

538   c.1380
Stuttgart, Württembergische Landesbibliothek,
cod. bibl. 2° 6, fol.5v
Bible stories
ILLUMINATION (France)
Compasses
Zahlten, Johannes: *Creatio mundi. Darstellungen der*
sechs Schöpfungstage und naturwissenschaftliches
Weltbild im Mittelalter. Stuttgart 1979, fig.287
(= Stuttgarter Beiträge zur Geschichte und Politik,
vol.13)
◄

538a c.1380–90
Stuttgart, Württembergische Landesbibliothek,
cod. bibl. 2° 6, fol.233
Bible stories
ILLUMINATION (France)
Trowel, plumbline, pointed stone hammer
Schöller, p.98, no.100; Marburger Index, fiche
2970/C10

▲

538b 13th century
Stuttgart, Württembergische Landesbibliothek,
cod. bibl. 2° 8, fol.167v
Bible
ILLUMINATION (France)
Trowel, ramp, hawk
Schöller, p.99, no.101; Marburger Index, fiche
2971/A13

538c 820–30
Stuttgart, Württembergische Landesbibliothek,
cod. bibl. 2° 23, fol.147
'Stuttgart Psalter'
ILLUMINATION (Saint-Germain-des-Prés)
Trowel
Schöller, p.99, no.102; *Der Stuttgarter Bilderpsalter.*
Bibl. Fol. 23. Württembergische Landesbibliothek
Stuttgart facsimile. Stuttgart 1965, vol.1, fol. 147

538d third quarter 13th century
Stuttgart, Württembergische Landesbibliothek,
cod. bibl. 4° 8, fol.163
Latin Bible
ILLUMINATION (France)
Ladder, hod
Schöller, p.99, no.103; Marburger Index, fiche 2987/F8

538e second half 12th century
Stuttgart, Württembergische Landesbibliothek,
cod. poet. et philol. 2° 33, fol.28v
Isidore of Seville, *Etymologiae*
PEN-AND-INK DRAWING (duplicate)
Measuring staff, compasses
Schöller, p.99, no.104, p.79, fig.1; Wirth, Karl-August:
'Eine illustrierte Martianus-Capella-Handschrift aus dem
13. Jahrhundert', in *Städel-Jahrbuch* NF 2, n.p., 1969,
p.63, fig.22

▼

539 end 12th century
San Cugat del Vallés, church at Benedictine
monastery
Sculpture by Arnaldo Catell, on capital at NE corner
of the crossing
ARCHITECTURAL SCULPTURE
Mallet, one-legged stool
Durliat, Marcel, & Dieuzaide, Jean: *Hispania Romanica*.
Vienna 1962, fig.57

▶

540 mid-9th century
St Gallen, Stiftsbibliothek,
cod. sang. 22, fol.64
Psalterium aureum
ILLUMINATION (St Gallen)
Broad axe, chisel
Bi/Nu 21; Binding (1972), fig.on p.45 (outline);
Mehnert, Gottfried: *Ansgar, Apostel des Nordens*. Kiel
1969, fig.26; Recht, p.40

▼

540a second half 15th century
St Gallen, Stiftsbibliothek,
cod. 602, p. 377
ILLUMINATION
Scaffolding, trowel, crane with hook, crane with
windlass, ladder, mortar tub, pointed stone hammer
Gerber, Roland: 'Finanzierung und Bauaufwand der
ersten Oswaldkirche in Zug (1478–1486)', in *Unsere*
Kunstdenkmäler 43, 1992, vol.1, p.60, fig.9

▶

541 c.1000
St Gallen, Stiftsbibliothek,
MS 135, fol.434
Prudentius, *Psychmachia*
ILLUMINATION (southern Germany or Switzerland)
Axe, long saw, measuring staff, pannier
Bi/Nu 1a; Tyghem, fig.2; Binding (1972), fig.on p.16
(outline); Brandt II, figs 72 ff.; Stettiner, Richard: *Die*
illustrierten Prudentiushandschriften. Berlin 1905, plate
vol., pl.191, 17

▼

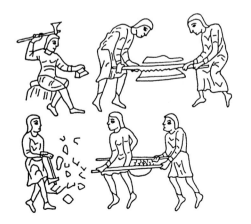

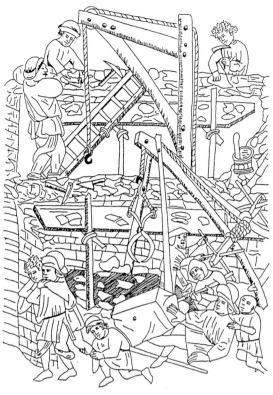

542 c.1260
Saint-Germer-de-Fly (Oise), Benedictine church
Window in Sainte-Chapelle
STAINED GLASS
Mallet, measuring staff, chisel, serrated stone
hammer
Bi/Nu 126; Tyghem, fig.43; Aubert, fig.on p.246;
Binding (1974), p.74, fig.6; Du Colombier, p.37, fig.22;
Grodecki, Louis, & Brisac, Catherine: *Le vitrail gothique*
au XIIIe siècle. Fribourg 1984, p.153; Kimpel, Dieter, &
Suckale, Robert: *Die gotische Architektur in Frankreich*
1130–1270. Munich 1985, p.429, fig.445 (outline by
Emile Boeswillwald)

▶

543 1402
San Gimignano, Pinacoteca Civica
Lorenzo dei Niccolò Gerini, *I miracoli di Santa Fina*
PANEL PAINTING (Florentine school)
Hatchet, scaffolding, hammer, plane, dog or staple
Tyghem, fig.95; Cecchini, Giovanni, & Carli, Enzo: *San*
Gimignano. Milan 1962, pl.73

◀

543a 1367
San Gimignano, Collegiata
MURAL
Hatchet, trestle, roofing axe, scaffolding, hammer,
plane, measuring staff, hand saw, water jug
Meiss, Millard: *The De Levis Hours and the Bedford*
Workshop (= Yale Lectures on Illumination). New
Haven, CT 1972, fig.54
▼

544 c.1100
Saint-Savin-sur-Gartempe (Vienne), abbey
church
Barrel vaulting in middle nave
MURAL
Bucket, crane, square
Bi/Nu 19; Binding (1972), fig.on p.22 (outline); Tyghem,
fig.18; Minkowski, pic. 8
▼

545 14th century
Saint-Thibault (Côte d'Or), church of St Thibault
High altar screen
WOOD CARVING (relief)
Pannier
Bi/Nu 204; Aubert, fig.on p.311; Bußmann, Klaus:
Burgundische Kunst, Geschichte, Landschaft. Cologne
1981, pp.223–5, fig.146; Oursel, Charles: *L'Art de*
Bourgogne. Paris & Grenoble 1953, figs 135–6
▶

546 1471–81
St Wolfgang, parish church of St Wolfgang
High altar, right-hand lower outside panel
Michael Pacher, St Wolfgang healing a possessed
woman
PANEL PAINTING
Scaffolding, mortar-mixing bin, trowel
Bi/Nu 225a; Kühnel, Harry (ed.): *Alltag im Spätmittelalter.*
Graz, Vienna & Cologne 1984, fig.16; Rasmo, Niccolò:
Michael Pacher. Munich 1969, figs 104ff.
▼

547 1471–81
St Wolfgang, parish church of St Wolfgang
High altar, left-hand lower outside panel
Michael Pacher, St Wolfgang building the church
PANEL PAINTING
Hammer, trowel, mortar-mixing pick, mortar shovel,
mortar-mixing bin, hod
Bi/Nu 225; Tyghem, fig.163; Brandt I, p.288, fig.404;
Kühnel, Harry (ed.): *Alltag im Spätmittelalter.* Graz,
Vienna & Cologne 1984, fig.25
▼

548 1452–61
Tamsweg bei Salzburg, pilgrimage church of
St Leonhard
St Leonhard master, Foundation of a monastery
PANEL PAINTING
Trowel, mortar tub, mortar shovel, one-legged stool,
pointed stone hammer
Kühnel, Harry (ed.): *Alltag im Spätmittelalter.* Graz,
Vienna & Cologne 1984, fig.241

549 1433
Tamsweg bei Salzburg, pilgrimage church of
St Leonhard
Representation of master Peter Harperger, northern
choir wall
Square
Bi/Nu 270; Gerstenberg, fig.on p.214

549a 1458
Tegernsee, circular wooden medallion, formerly
the 'keystone' in the vault of Tegernsee
monastery
RELIEF
Broad axe, hand saw
Buchenieder, Fritz: *Gefaßte Bildwerke. Arbeitsheft 40.*
Bayerischer Landesamt für Denkmalpflege, Munich
1990

550 1423
Thann (Alsace), Saint-Thiébaut
Upper panel strip, north choir window
STAINED GLASS
Inventaire général des monuments et des richesses
artistiques de la France. Haut-Rhin, Canton Thann. Paris
1980, p.330, fig.374

551 1423
Thann (Alsace), Saint-Thiébaut
Genesis, north choir window
STAINED GLASS
Compasses
Bi/Nu 330; *Inventaire général des monuments et des*
richesses artistiques de la France. Haut-Rhin, Canton
Thann. Paris 1980, p.338, fig.392, p.330, fig.374

552 1423
Thann (Alsace), Saint-Thiébaut
Genesis, building the Ark, north choir window
STAINED GLASS
Broad axe, trestle, long saw, long-handled drill
Inventaire général des monuments et des richesses
artistiques de la France. Haut-Rhin, Canton Thann. Paris
1980, p.330, fig.374, p.338, fig.393

553 1423

Thann (Alsace), Saint-Thiébaut

Genesis, Cain builds the town of Henoch, north
choir window

STAINED GLASS

Trowel, hod

*Inventaire général des monuments et des richesses
artistiques de la France. Haut-Rhin, Canton Thann.* Paris
1980, p.330, fig.374, p.338, fig.392

▼

554 end 15th century

Thorn, Bezirksmuseum

Altar to St Barbara from the Marienkirche in
Gdańsk

PANEL PAINTING

*Scaffolding, trowel, crane with pallet, level, hod,
pointed stone hammer*

Drost, Willi: *Danziger Malerei.* Leipzig 1938, pl.32; *ibid.*:
Die Marienkirche in Danzig und ihre Kunstschätze.
Stuttgart 1963, pls 126–9; Kussin, Werner:
'Spätgotische Tafelmalerei in Danzig', in *Danziger
Dissertationen.* Erlangen 1937, pp.61–7 (no illus.)

▶

555 c.1230

Toledo, Cathedral, church treasures

Bible moralisée, vol.1, fol.1v

ILLUMINATION

Compasses

Bi/Nu 51; Binding (*Ornamenta ecclesiae*), p.182, fig.30;
Haussherr, Reiner: 'Sensus litteralis und sensus spiritualis
in der Bible moralisée', in *Frühmittelalterliche Studien* 6,
1972, fig.63; Laborde, Alexandre Comte de: *La Bible
moralisée conservée à Oxford, Paris et Londres.* vol.IV,
Paris 1921, pl.625; Swaan, Wim: *Die großen
Kathedralen.* Cologne 1969, p.265, fig.313

A more recent copy of this Bible moralisée has survived
in three separate volumes: Oxford, Bodleian Library, MS
Bodley 270b (cf. nos 405–12); Paris, Bibliothèque
Nationale, MS lat. 11560 (cf. nos 444–9); London,
British Museum, Harleian MS 1526–7 (cf. nos 269–71)

▶

556 c.1230

Toledo, Cathedral, church treasures

Bible moralisée, vol.1, fol.131v

ILLUMINATION

Hammer, mallet, chisel, square

Bi/Nu 22; Haussherr, Reiner: 'Templum Salomonis und
Ecclesia Christi', in *Zeitschrift für Kunstgeschichte* 31, 2,
Munich & Berlin 1968, p.107, fig.5

Compare no.409

▶ ▶

557 c.1230

Toledo, Cathedral, church treasures

Bible moralisée, vol.2, fol.46

ILLUMINATION

Mallet, chisel

Bi/Nu 23; Haussherr, Reiner: 'Templum Salomonis und
Ecclesia Christi', in *Zeitschrift für Kunstgeschichte* 31, 2,
Munich & Berlin 1968, p.112, fig.18; *ibid.*: 'Sensus
litteralis und sensus spiritualis in der Bible moralisée', in
Frühmittelalterliche Studien 6, 1972, fig.71

Compare no.443

▶

558   c.1230
Toledo, Cathedral, church treasures
Bible moralisée
ILLUMINATION
Brick-making press
Bi/Nu 284; Brandt I, p.258, fig.349
▼

559   c.1230
Toledo, Cathedral, church treasures
Bible moralisée, vol.3, fol.1v
ILLUMINATION
Square
Laborde, Alexandre Comte de: *La Bible moralisée conservée à Oxford, Paris et Londres*. vol.IV, Paris 1921, pl.638
Compare no.271

560   second quarter 13th century
Toulouse, Musée des Augustins inv. no. 493.
Capital of corner column from crossing in church of Notre-Dame de la Daurade
Four-legged stool
Legner, Anton (ed.): *Ornamenta ecclesiae*. Exhibition catalogue, Cologne 1985, vol.I, p.257

561   **1402**

Tournai, Notre-Dame cathedral
Treasure chamber
Pierre Ferré, Scenes from the lives of SS Piatus and
Eleutherius
TAPESTRY (Arras)
Stone hammer, trowel, mortar shovel, hod, pannier
Bi/Nu 123; Tyghem, fig.91; Legner, Anton (ed.): *Die
Parler und der schöne Stil*. Exhibition catalogue,
Cologne 1978, vol.I, pp.106–08; conclusions, 1980,
pl.26

▶

562   **c.1000**

Tournus, Abbey church of St Philibert
Vestibule, vaulting towards central nave,
right-hand impost
ARCHITECTURAL SCULPTURE
Stone hammer
Oursel, Raymond: *Bourgogne romaine*.
Zodiaque 1974, p.79, fig.16

▶

563   **before 1260–70**

Tours, Cathedral of St Gatien
Fourth window on north side of choir, Genesis 4:17
– Cain builds the town of Henoch
STAINED GLASS
Brandt I, p.254, no.illus.

564   **15th century**

Tours, Bibliothèque municipale,
MS 984, fol.1
Jacques Besançon, Livy manuscript
ILLUMINATION
*Trowel, basket, plumbline, mortar tub, mortar shovel,
hod, pointed stone hammer*
Bi/Nu 205; Du Colombier, p.109, fig.72; Schöller, p.99,
no.105

▶

565   **end 14th century**

Trento, Castello di Buonconsiglio
Eagle Tower, calendar picture for
December
FRESCO (Lombardy or Bohemia)
Axe, sledge, four-wheeled cart
Kühnel, Harry (ed.): *Alltag im
Spätmittelalter*. Graz, Vienna & Cologne
1984, fig.238, p.191

▼

566 second quarter 13th century
Troyes, St Peter's Cathedral
Window on south side of choir
STAINED GLASS
Plumbline
Bi/Nu 206; Aubert, p.27; Recht, p.99 ▶

567 1383
Turnisce (Hungary), village church, frescoes
Johannes von Aquila, St Ladislaus legend
MURAL
Ladder, hod
Henszlmann, E.: 'Die vierthürmigen Kirchen in Ungarn',
in *Mitteilungen der kaiserlichen königlichen Central-
Commission zur Erforschung und Erhaltung der
Baudenkmale.* Vienna 1870, XV year, p.9, fig.9 ▼

568 after 1463
Ulm, Minster church of Our Lady, south wall
Memorial tablet to Matthäus Ensinger (d. 1463)
RELIEF
Compasses
Gerstenberg, p.179; Hecht, p.230, fig.53.7 (outline of
compasses) ▶

569 c.1390
Ulm, Minster church of Our Lady, northern choir
chapel, ground floor (Neithardkapelle)
Gravestone with the Parler master's sign
RELIEF
Pointed stone hammer
Gerstenberg, p.178; ibid.: *Das Ulmer Münster.* Burg bei
Magdeburg, fig.on p.64; Wortmann, Reinhard: *Das
Ulmer Münster.* Stuttgart 1972, fig.on p.80 ▼

570 1483
Ulm, Conrad Dinckmut, printer
Seelenwurzgarten (probably by Johann von
Arnsheim)
WOODCUT
Crane with lewis
Schramm 6, no.100; Weil, Ernst: *Der Ulmer Holzschnitt
im 15. Jahrhundert.* Berlin 1923, pp.58ff., no illus.
▼

571 1486
Ulm, Conrad Dinckmut, printer
Thomas Lirar, *Schwäbische Chronik*
WOODCUT
Scaffolding, crane with lewis, ladder
Schramm 6, no.133; Weil, Ernst: *Der Ulmer Holzschnitt
im 15. Jahrhundert.* Berlin 1923, pp.74ff., fig.52
▼

572   1483
Ulm, Lienhart Holle, printer
Book of Wisdom, fol. 19v
Broad axe
Schramm 7, no.49
▼

573   1487
Ulm, Johannes Reger, printer
Wallfahrt Mariae, fol.17v
WOODCUT
Trestle, guide line
Schramm 7, no.171; Weil, Ernst: *Der Ulmer Holzschnitt im 15. Jahrhundert*. Berlin 1923, pp.74ff., no illus.
▼

574   1496
Ulm, Johannes Reger, printer
Guillaume Caoursin, *Stabilimenta Rhodiorum militum*, fol.15v
WOODCUT
Builders' hut, stone hammer, scaffolding, trowel, mallet, crane with lewis, ladder, mortar tub, pick
Bi/Nu 285; Schramm 7, no.261; Kunze, Horst: *Geschichte der Buchillustration in Deutschland. Das 15. Jahrhundert*. Leipzig 1975, fig.164
▼

575   1498
Ulm, Johann Schäffler, printer
Calendar
WOODCUT
Broad axe, mallet
Schramm 7, no.358
▶

576   1473
Ulm, Johann Zainer, printer
Boccaccio, *De mulieribus claris*, fol.42v
WOODCUT
Trowel, crane with lewis, mortar tub, mortar bucket, mortar-mixing pick
Schramm 5, no.53; Weil, Ernst: *Der Ulmer Holzschnitt im 15. Jahrhundert*. Berlin 1923, pp.24ff., no illus.
▼

577   c.1500
Urach, lower level of market fountain
Peter von Koblenz, likeness of a master mason
ARCHITECTURAL SCULPTURE
Mallet, chisel
Bi/Nu 272; Gerstenberg, fig.on p.175
▶

578   1481
Urach, Konrad Fyner, printer
Jacobus de Voragine, Lives of the Saints, fol. 138v
WOODCUT
Mallet, crane with lewis, one-legged stool, chisel
Schramm 9,no.215
For a derivative see no.23
▼

579   1481
Urach, Konrad Fyner, printer   ▶
Jacobus de Voragine, Lives of the Saints, fol. 180v
WOODCUT
Scaffolding, trowel, mortar bucket, stool,
treadwheel, stone hammer
Schramm 9, no.136
For a derivative see no.21, and compare no.22

580   not dated, c.1481–2
Urach, Konrad Fyner, printer
Book of Wisdom of the Elders, fol. 14
WOODCUT
Broad axe
Schramm 9, no.291
                                                    ▶

581   second half 13th century
USA (formerly in the Bibliothek Fürst Stolberg,
Wernigerode)
Wernigeroder Weltchronik of Rudolf von Ems
ILLUMINATION
Crane, hod, four-legged stool, pointed stone
hammer
Bi/Nu 277; Minkowski, pic. 18
▼

582   c.830
Utrecht, university library,
cod. 32, fol.38
Utrecht Psalter
PEN-AND-INK DRAWING (Reims)
Bi/Nu 25; Binding (1972), fig.on p.16 (outline)
▼

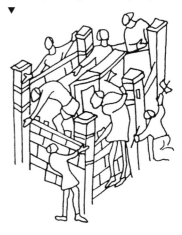

583   c.830
Utrecht, university library,
cod. 32, fol.58
Utrecht Psalter
PEN-AND-INK DRAWING (Reims)
Summary representation of carpenter's tools
Bi/Nu 24; Binding (1972), fig.on p.15 (outline); Brandt I,
p.263, fig.364; Tselos, Dimitri: *The Sources of the*
Utrecht Psalter Miniatures. Minneapolis 1960, fig.166
▼

584   c.830
Utrecht, university library,
cod. 32, fol.62v
Utrecht Psalter
PEN-AND-INK DRAWING (Reims)
Summary representation of carpenter's tools
Engelbrecht, J.H.A.: *Het Utrechts Psalterium, een eeuw*
wetenschapelijkke Bestudering. Utrecht 1965, pl.65, fig.9
▼

585   c.830
Utrecht, university library, cod. 32, fol.62v
Utrecht Psalter
PEN-AND-INK DRAWING (Reims)
Summary representation of carpenter's tools
Engelbrecht, J.H.A.: *Het Utrechts Psalterium, een eeuw*
wetenschapelijkke Bestudering. Utrecht 1965, pl.65,
fig.11
▼

585a   c.1465–74
Utrecht, university library,
MS 42, fol.228
St Augustine, *De civitate Dei*
ILLUMINATION
Crane, wheelbarrow, pointed stone hammer

586   c.1455
Utrecht, university library,
MS 400, fol.63v
Pontificale ecclesiasticum beatae Mariae Trajectensis
ILLUMINATION
Pointed stone hammer
Bi/Nu 208; RDK IV, sp.709, fig.1
▼

586a   c.1417–90
Utrecht, Reichsmuseum Katharinenkonvent, i
nv. no. ABM. b. 471
WOOD CARVING BY ADRIAEN VAN WESEL
Drill, guide line
Adriaen van Weseleen Utrechtse beeldhouwer ut de
late middeleeuwen. Exhibition catalogue, Amsterdam
1980, p.103, cat. 13
▼

587   beginning 11th century
Valenciennes, Bibliothèque publique,
MS 563
Prudentius, *Psychmochia*
PEN-AND-INK DRAWING (Lower Rhine, Saint-Armand
monastery)
Stettiner, Richard: *Die illustrierten*
Prudentiushandschriften. Berlin 1905, pl.81
A copy of a Leiden original; compare no.237

588   11th century
Vendôme, Sainte-Trinité
Console in north transept
Compasses
Bi/Nu 52; Kletzl, Otto: 'Ein Werkriß des Frauenhauses in
Straßburg', in *Marburger Jahrbuch für*
Kunstwissenschaft 11, 1938, p.141, fig.23; von Naredi-
Reiner, Paul: *Architektur und Harmonie*. Cologne 1982,
frontispiece

▶

591   c.1220–1300
Venice, St Mark's
Barrel vaulting in west
vestibule
MOSAIC
Trestle, drill, broad axe, plane,
frame saw
Brandt I, fig.312

▶

589   first quarter 14th century
Venice, Doge's Palace
Capital
ARCHITECTURAL SCULPTURE
Mallet, chisel (possibly a
punch)
Brandt I, fig.446, p.312

▶

592   second quarter 13th century
Venice, St Mark's
West vestibule, between second and third domes
MOSAIC
Bucket, stone hammer, scaffolding, trowel, ramp,
mortar-mixing pick, hod, stand for hod, square
Tyghem, fig.14; Binding (1972), fig.on p.31; Binding
(1985), p.180, fig.18; Brandt I, p.244, fig.329;
Minkowski, p.15, pl.2c

◀

593   third quarter 13th century
Venice, St Mark's
West façade, main doorway
ARCHITECTURAL SCULPTURE
Trowel, ramp, plumbline, hod, pointed stone hammer
Wolters, Wolfgang (ed.): *Die*
Skulpturen von San
Marco in Venedig (=
Deutsches
Studienzentrum in
Venedig. Studien III).
Munich & Berlin 1979,
pp.47–9, fig.152

▶

590   first quarter 14th century
Venice, Doge's Palace
Capital
ARCHITECTURAL SCULPTURE
Broad axe
Brandt I, fig.447, p.313

▶

594   third quarter 13th century
Venice, St Mark's
West façade, main doorway
ARCHITECTURAL SCULPTURE
Broad axe, roofing axe
Brandt I, p.316, fig.454; Wolters, Wolfgang (ed.): *Die Skulpturen von San Marco in Venedig* (= Deutsches Studienzentrum in Venedig. Studien III). Munich & Berlin 1979, pp.47–9, fig.157
▼

595   third quarter 13th century
Venice, St Mark's
West façade, main doorway
ARCHITECTURAL SCULPTURE
Trestle, broad axe, frame saw
Brandt I, p.316, fig.454;
Wolters, Wolfgang (ed.):
Die Skulpturen von San Marco in Venedig
(= Deutsches Studienzentrum in Venedig. Studien III).
Munich & Berlin 1979, pp.47–9, fig.158
►

596   1490
Venice
J. Filippo Forsti di Bergamo, *Supplementum chronicarum*
WOODCUT
Trestle, scaffolding, plane, trowel, mallet, ladder, mortar shovel, hod, chisel
Tyghem, fig.126
▼

597   1489
Venice, Biblioteca Nazionale Marciana, cod. Marc. lat. VIII, 2, fol.5
Averulinus Codex from the Biblioteca Corvina
ILLUMINATION (Ofen)
Scaffolding, hammer, crane with pallet, plumbline, measuring staff, mortar-mixing bin, mortar shovel
Matthias Corvinus und die Renaissance in Ungarn 1458–1541. Catalogue of the Niederösterreichisches Landesmuseum, Vienna 1982, cat. no.172c, fig.on p.281

598   c.1138
Verona, San Zeno
Right-hand wing of the bronze door at the west end
Lump hammer, chisel
Brandt II, p.146, fig.179; Legner, Anton (ed.): *Ornamenta Ecclesiae.* Exhibition catalogue, Cologne 1985, vol.I, p.226; Mende, Ursula: *Die Bronzetüren des Mittelalters.* Munich 1983, pp.57–73, fig.95
◄

599   c.1138
Verona, San Zeno
Right-hand wing of the bronze door at the west
end: lowest row, middle
Trestle, broad axe
Boeckler, Albert: *Die Bronzetür von San Zeno*.n.p.1931,
fig.III; Gazzola, Piero, & Drayer, Walter: *San
Zeno*.Lausanne 1956, fig.84; Leisinger, Hermann:
Romanesque Bronzes. London 1956, fig.66; Mende,
Ursula: *Die Bronzetüren des Mittelalters*. Munich 1983,
pp.57–73, fig.97; Winzinger, Franz, & Drayer, Walter:
Das Tor von San Zeno in Verona. Munich 1958, fig.5
▼

600   1300–25
Vitoria (Basque province of Alava), Catedral
Vieja Santa Maria
Tympanum, left-hand side door of the vestibule
RELIEF
Minkowski, pic. 67

601   c.1300
Volkmarsen, Catholic parish church of St Mary
Buttress on south side
STONE CARVING
*Crane with treadwheel and
external lewis*
Bi/Nu 272a; Ganssauge, Gottfried:
'Hebeklaue und Wolf', in
*Deutsche Kunst und
Denkmalpflege*, n.p.1937,
pp.199–205, fig.202
▶

601a   c.1465
Waddesdon Manor, Rothschild Collection,
MS 11, fol.9
Jean de Courcy, *La Bouquechardière*
ILLUMINATION (Rouen)
*Trowel, mallet, measuring staff, hod, chisel, pointed
stone hammer, square*
Schöller, p.99, no.106; Delaissé, J.M.L., Marrow, James,
& de Wit, John: *The James A. de Rothschild Collection
at Waddesdon Manor. Illuminated Manuscripts*.
Fribourg 1977, p.235, fig.11
Compare no.619a
▼

601b   c.1465

Waddesdon Manor, Rothschild Collection,
MS 11, fol.153
Jean de Courcy, *La Bouquechardière*
ILLUMINATION (Rouen)
Stone hammer, trowel, mallet, measuring staff, hod,
chisel, pointed stone hammer
Schöller, p.99, no.107; Delaissé, J.M.L., Marrow, James,
& de Wit, John: *The James A. de Rothschild Collection*
at Waddesdon Manor. Illuminated Manuscripts.
Fribourg 1977, p.239, fig.13; *Gatherings in Honor of*
Dorothy E. Miner. Baltimore 1974, p.222, fig.15
Compare nos 466, 619b

▼

601c   c.1465

Waddesdon Manor, Rothschild Collection,
MS 11, fol.201
Jean de Courcy, *La Bouquechardière*
ILLUMINATION (Rouen)
Scaffolding, trowel, ladder, measuring staff, mortar
shovel, hod
Schöller, p.99, fig.108; Delaissé, J.M.L., Marrow, James,
& de Wit, John: *The James A. de Rothschild Collection*
at Waddesdon Manor. Illuminated Manuscripts.
Fribourg 1977, p.241, fig.14
Compare no.619c

▶

602   end 14th century
Warsaw, library,
MS Q. v. XIV, fol.37
G. de Lorris, J. de Meung, *Roman de la Rose*
ILLUMINATION
Scaffolding, trowel, pointed stone hammer, square
Bi/Nu 209; Tyghem, fig.84

►

602a   1430–40
Warsaw, National Museum
Altar piece
PANEL PAINTING
Scaffolding, trowel, crane with treadwheel and external lewis
Swiechowskiego, Zygmunta: *Wrocław. Jego Dzieje i Kultura.* Warsaw 1978, p.180, fig.265
Compare nos 95, 312

▼

603   1295–1305
Weißenburg (Alsace), former Benedictine abbey and church of SS Peter and Paul
Chancel window
STAINED GLASS
Mallet, crane with lewis, chisel
Bi/Nu 210; Minkowski, pic. 37

▼

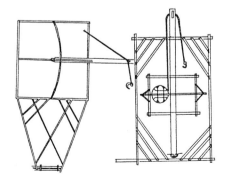

604   first half 12th century
Wettringen, SS Nicholas and Katherine
East side of tower
ARCHITECTURAL SCULPTURE
Mallet, ruler
Bi/Nu 53; Gerstenberg, fig.on p.168

►

605   before 1258
Vienna, Stephansdom, Riesentor
ARCHITECTURAL SCULTPURE
Hatchet
Bi/Nu 54; Gerstenberg, p.12, fig.a; Feuchtmüller, Rupert: *Der Wiener Stephansdom*. Vienna 1978, fig.on p.62

►

606   end 15th century (?)
Vienna, Akademie der bildenden Künste,
inv. no. 16853
PEN-AND-INK DRAWING
Construction machinery
Koepf, Hans: *Die gotischen Planrisse der Wiener Sammlungen*. Vienna, Cologne & Graz 1969, fig.218, cat. no.38

◄

607 c.1490–1500

Vienna, Museum mittelalterlicher österreichischer Kunst

Heiligenmartyrien master, Building of Klosterneuburg monastery

PANEL PAINTING

Crane with lewis, mortar tub, pointed stone hammer, square

Dworschak, Fritz, & Kühnel, Harry: *Die Gotik in Niederösterreich*. Vienna 1963, pl.29; Schmidt, Leopold, & Kühnel, Harry: *Alltag und Fest im Mittelalter*. Exhibition catalogue, Vienna 1970,no.49, figs 24ff. and cover picture; Schöller, p.99, no.109; Toussaint, Fritz: *Lastenförderung durch fünf Jahrtausende*. Demag AG, Duisburg 1965, fig.on p.27

▼

608 c.1400

Vienna, Kunsthistorisches Museum, inv. no. 239

Heiligenkreuz master, *Verkündigung Mariae*

PANEL PAINTING (Heiligenkreuz monastery, Lower Austria)

Tub, scaffolding, winch

▼

609 end 10th century

Vienna, Österreichische Nationalbibliothek, cod. 177, fol.14

Marcianus Capella, *Satyrae de septem artibus liberalibus*

PEN-AND-INK DRAWING (south-west Germany; uses Reichenau techniques)

Measuring staff

Bi/Nu 55; Hermann, Hermann Julius: *Die frühmittelalterlichen Handschriften des Abendlandes*. Leipzig 1923, p.183, fig.125

▼

610 c.1360

Vienna, Österreichische Nationalbibliothek, cod. 370

Krumau illustrated codex

PEN-AND-INK DRAWING

Broad axe

Schmidt, Gerhard: *Krumauer Bilderkodex*. Facsimile edition, Graz 1965

▼

611 1208–13

Vienna, Österreichische Nationalbibliothek, cod. Vindobonensis 507, fol.1v

Reiner Musterbuch (Rein monastery, Steiermark)

PEN-AND-INK DRAWING

Broad axe, hammer, guide line

Bi/Nu 26 & 278; Brandt II, fig.123; Unterkircher, Franz: *Reiner Musterbuch*. Facsimile edition, Graz 1979

▼

612   1247
Vienna, Österreichische Nationalbibliothek,
cod. 1115, fol.185v
Biblia sacra
ILLUMINATION (northern France)
Trowel, basket
Bi/Nu 331

614   second quarter 13th century
Vienna, Österreichische Nationalbibliothek,
cod. 1179, fol.7v
Bible moralisée
ILLUMINATION (Paris)
Stone axe, ramp with interlaced surface, square
Bi/Nu 211; Minkowski, p.29, pic. 49

616   second quarter 13th century
Vienna, Österreichische Nationalbibliothek,
cod. 1179, fol.190
Bible moralisée
ILLUMINATION (Paris)
Pick
Laborde, Alexandre Comte de: *La Bible moralisée conservée à Oxford, Paris et Londres*. vol.IV, pl.687. Paris 1921

613   second quarter 13th century
Vienna, Österreichische Nationalbibliothek,
cod. 1179, fol.1v
Bible moralisée
ILLUMINATION (Paris)
Compasses
Bi/Nu 273; Binding (1974), pl.13b; Friedman, fig.VI; Hermann 1, pl.X; Thoss, Dagmar: *Französische Gotik und Renaissance in Meisterwerken der Buchmalerei*. Exhibition catalogue, Österreichische Nationalbibliothek, Vienna 1978, pp.66–9; Laborde, Alexandre Comte de: *La Bible moralisée conservée à Oxford, Paris et Londres*. vol.IV, pl.672. Paris 1921

615   second quarter 13th century
Vienna, Österreichische Nationalbibliothek,
cod. 1179, fol.113v
Bible moralisée
ILLUMINATION (Paris)
Trowel, mortar bowl
Bi/Nu 56; Haussherr, Reiner: 'Templum Salomonis und Ecclesia Christi', in *Zeitschrift für Kunstgeschichte* 1968, p.104, fig.3

617   second quarter 13th century
Vienna, Österreichische Nationalbibliothek,
cod. 1179, fol.196
Bible moralisée
ILLUMINATION (Paris)
Trowel, level, mortar bowl, pick
Laborde, vol.IV, pl.692

617a   c.1480
Vienna, Österreichische Nationalbibliothek,
cod. 1819, fol.181
Pontificale Romanum
ILLUMINATION (southern France)
Pächt/Thoss, fig.171

618   1422–5
Vienna, Österreichische Nationalbibliothek,
cod. 1855, fol.94v
Duke of Bedford's master, Book
of Hours
ILLUMINATION
Compasses
Bi/Nu 332

▶

618a   before 1467
Vienna, Österreichische Nationalbibliothek,
cod. 2533, fol.12v
History of Jerusalem
ILLUMINATION (France, for Duke Philip the Good of Burgundy)
Scaffolding, trowel, mallet, crane, ladder, plumbline, level,
mortar tub, mortar-mixing bin, mortar-mixing pick, one-legged
stool, chisel, pointed stone hammer
Schöller (1987), p.99, no.111, & p.82, fig.4; Pächt & Thoss, fig.115;
Schöller (1998), fig.6, p.105
Compare no.619

619   before 1467
Vienna, Österreichische Nationalbibliothek,
cod. 2533, fol.17
History of Jerusalem
ILLUMINATION (France, for Duke Philip the Good of Burgundy)
Bucket, scaffolding, trowel, crane, level, mortar tub, mortar-
mixing bin, mortar-mixing pick, one-legged stool, shoulder pole,
stone hammer
Bi/Nu 212; Tyghem, fig.188; Recht, p.74; Schöller (1998), fig.7, p.105
Partial copy of no.620   ▶

619a   c.1470

Vienna, Österreichische Nationalbibliothek,
cod. 2543, fol.9
Jean de Courcy, *La Bouquechardière*
ILLUMINATION (Normandy)
Trowel, mallet, measuring staff, hod, chisel, pointed
stone hammer
Schöller, p.99, no.112; Pächt & Thoss, fig.100
Compare no.601a

▼

619b   c.1470

Vienna, Österreichische Nationalbibliothek,
cod. 2543, fol.163
Jean de Courcy, *La Bouquechardière*
ILLUMINATION (Normandy)
Trowel, mallet, measuring staff, hod, chisel, pointed
stone hammer
Schöller, p.99, no.113; Pächt & Thoss, fig.102; Duby,
Georges: *Wirklichkeit und höfischer Traum. Zur Kultur*
des Mittelalters. Berlin 1986, p.20
Compare nos 466, 601b

▶

619c   c.1470

Vienna, Österreichische Nationalbibliothek,
cod. 2543, fol.218
Jean de Courcy, *La Bouquechardière*
ILLUMINATION (Normandy)
Scaffolding, trowel, crane, ladder, mortar shovel, hod
Schöller, p.100, no.114; Pächt & Thoss, fig.103
Compare no.601c

▼

619d   1447–50
Vienna, Österreichische Nationalbibliothek,
cod. 2549, fol.18
Girat de Roussillon manuscript
ILLUMINATION
*Trowel, crane, mortar tub, mortar-mixing bin, mortar
shovel*
Thoss, p.72, middle fig.

▶

619e   1447–50
Vienna, Österreichische Nationalbibliothek,
cod. 2549, fol.111
Girat de Roussillon manuscript
ILLUMINATION
Crane, mortar-mixing pick, hod
Thoss, p.134, middle fig.

▼

619f   after 1488
Vienna, Österreichische Nationalbibliothek,
cod. 2549, fol.158
Girat de Roussillon manuscript
ILLUMINATION
Scaffolding (sketch only)
Schöller, p.100, no.115; Pächt & Thoss, fig.94

620   1447–50
Vienna, Österreichische Nationalbibliothek,
cod. 2549, fol.164
Girat de Roussillon manuscript
ILLUMINATION
*Tub, roofing axe, bucket, scaffolding, trowel, basket,
crane, ladder, level, mortar-mixing bin, mortar-mixing
pick, one-legged stool*
Bi/Nu 213; Tyghem, fig.117; Coldstream (1991), p.48,
fig.49; Du Colombier, p.11, fig.4; Förster, p.339; Recht,
p.75; Winston, fig.on p.53

▶

620a   1447–50
Vienna, Österreichische Nationalbibliothek,
cod. 2549, fol.164
Girat de Roussillon manuscript
ILLUMINATION
Hammer, ladder
Thoss, p.175, middle fig., p.176, top and middle figs;
Schöller (1998), p.104, fig.5

◀

620b   1447–50
Vienna, Österreichische Nationalbibliothek,
cod. 2549, fol.167v
Girat de Roussillon manuscript
ILLUMINATION
*Lump hammer, scaffolding, ladder, mortar tub,
mortar-mixing bin, mortar shovel, hod, shoulder
pole, pointed stone hammer, water tub*
Thoss, pl.47, p.177, lower fig.

◀

621   c.1220

Vienna, Österreichische Nationalbibliothek,
cod. 2554, fol.1v, frontispiece
Bible moralisée
ILLUMINATION (Champagne/Reims?)
Compasses
Bi/Nu 274; Binding (1974), pl.13a; Binding (1985),
p.182, fig.31; Tyghem, fig.28; Friedman, fig.VII;
Gerstenberg, fig.on p.33; Hermann 1, pl.XIV, pp.47–57;
Thoss, Dagmar: *Französosche Gotik und Renaissance in
Meisterwerken der Buchmalerei*. Exhibition catalogue,
Österreichische Nationalbibliothek, Vienna 1978,
pp.69–71 (with literature list)

▼

623   c.1220

Vienna, Österreichische Nationalbibliothek,
cod. 2554, fol.50
Bible moralisée
ILLUMINATION (Champagne/Reims?)
Two-headed stone hammer, mallet, chisel, square
Bi/Nu 28; Binding (*Ornamenta ecclesiae*), p.179, fig.17;
Haussherr, Reiner: 'Templum Salomonis und Ecclesia
Christi', in *Zeitschrift für Kunstgeschichte* 1968, p.103,
fig.2; Recht, p.63

624, 625   c.1220

Vienna, Österreichische Nationalbibliothek,
cod. 2554, fol.50
Bible moralisée
ILLUMINATION (Champagne/Reims?)
*Two-headed stone hammer, two-headed serrated
stone hammer, ramp with interlaced surface, level,
shoulder basket, shoulder pannier, pannier*
Bi/Nu 28; Binding (*Ornamenta ecclesiae*), p.179, fig.17;
Haussherr, Reiner: 'Templum Salomonis und Ecclesia
Christi', in *Zeitschrift für Kunstgeschichte* 1968, p.103,
fig.2; Recht, p.63

▼   ▼

622   c.1220

Vienna, Österreichische Nationalbibliothek,
cod. 2554, fol.3v
Bible moralisée
ILLUMINATION (Champagne/Reims?)
*Ramp with interlaced surface, mortar-mixing pick,
shoulder pannier, pannier*
Bi/Nu 27; Tyghem, fig.29; Minkowski, pic. 48

▶

626   end 14th century
Vienna, Österreichische Nationalbibliothek,
cod. 2576, fol.9v
Histoire universelle
ILLUMINATION (Provence)
Scaffolding, trowel, ladder, mortar shovel, hod, stand for hod
Bi/Nu 334; Coldstream (1991), p.62, fig.55; Schöller, p.100, no.117
▼

626b   c.1475
Vienna, Österreichische Nationalbibliothek,
cod. 2577, fol.200
Sébastien Mamerot, *Histoire et faits du neuf Preux et des neuf Preues*
ILLUMINATION
Bucket, scaffolding, mallet, crane, chisel, pointed stone hammer
Schöller, p.100, no.119; Pächt & Thoss, fig.132
▼

626c   c.1475
Vienna, Österreichische Nationalbibliothek,
cod. 2578, fol.26v
Sébastien Mamerot, *Histoire et faits du neuf Preux et des neuf Preues*
ILLUMINATION
Bucket, scaffolding, mallet, crane, chisel, pointed stone hammer
Schöller, p.100, no.120; Pächt & Thoss, fig.133
▼

626a   c.1475
Vienna, Österreichische Nationalbibliothek,
cod. 2577, fol.152
Sébastien Mamerot, *Histoire et faits du neuf Preux et des neuf Preues*
ILLUMINATION
Scaffolding, mallet, chisel
Schöller, p.100, no.118; Pächt & Thoss, fig.130

627   second quarter 14th century
Vienna, Österreichische Nationalbibliothek,
cod. 2590, fol.8
Sydrac, *Livre de la fontaine de toutes sciences*
ILLUMINATION (northern France)
Trowel, ramp, mortar bucket, serrated stone hammer
Bi/Nu 214; Tyghem, fig.56, Hermann 2, pl.XIV, pp.51–3
▶

627a   c.1470
Vienna, Österreichische Nationalbibliothek,
cod. 2605, fol.67
Christine de Pisan, *La cité des dames*
ILLUMINATION
*Scaffolding, mallet, crane, measuring staff,
hod, chisel, compasses*
Pächt & Thossm fig.81; Mazal, O.: *Prinz
Eugens schönste Bücher. Handschriften
aus der Bibliothek des Prinzen Eugen
von Savoyen*. Graz 1986, fig.43
▶

628   1390–1400
Vienna, Österreichische Nationalbibliothek,
cod. 2759, Genesis, fol.10v
Wenceslas Bible
ILLUMINATION (Prague)
*Scaffolding, trowel, crane with treadwheel and
external lewis, ladder, mortar tub, hod, wheelbarrow*
Bi/Nu 216; Tyghem, fig.68; Minkowski, pic. 26; Brandt
I, p.251, fig.339; Hecht, p.256, fig.69,5 (outline of
level); Husa, fig.90; Martens, Peter, & Jankowski, Fritz:
'Meister Adams Hebekran', in *Brunswiek 1031
Braunschweig 1981*. Exhibition catalogue, Brunswick
1981, fig.3, p.138; Philippi, pl.54; *Wenzels Bibel.
Erläutert von Horst Appuhn*. Dortmund 1990 (= Die
bibliophilen Taschenbücher 1001), vol.5, fol. 10v
▼

628a   1390–1400

Vienna, Österreichische Nationalbibliothek,
cod. 2759, Judges (21), fol.28
Wenceslas Bible
ILLUMINATION (Prague)
Trowel, hod
Wenzels Bibel. Erläutert von Horst Appuhn. Dortmund
1990 (= Die bibliophilen Taschenbücher 1001), vol.4,
fol. 28

630   1390–1400

Vienna, Österreichische Nationalbibliothek,
cod. 2759, I Kings (16), fol.136v
Wenceslas Bible
ILLUMINATION (Prague)
Scaffolding, ramp, mortar-mixing pick, hod, pointed
stone hammer
Wenzels Bibel. Erläutert von Horst Appuhn. Dortmund
1990 (= Die bibliophilen Taschenbücher 1001), vol.5,
fol. 136v
▼

631   1390–1400

Vienna, Österreichische Nationalbibliothek,
cod. 2760, II Samuel (7), fol.82
Wenceslas Bible
ILLUMINATION (Prague)
Broad axe, hammer, wooden trestle with dog or
staple, crane
Bi/Nu 219; Husa, fig.89; *Wenzels Bibel. Erläutert von*
Horst Appuhn. Dortmund 1990 (= Die bibliophilen
Taschenbücher 1001), vol.5, fol. 82
▼

629   1390–1400

Vienna, Österreichische Nationalbibliothek,
cod. 2759, I Kings (12), fol.130
Wenceslas Bible
ILLUMINATION (Prague)
Tub, hammer, trowel, mortar-mixing pick, hod, nails
Bi/Nu 217; Husa, figs on pp.25, 27 (extract); *Wenzels*
Bibel. Erläutert von Horst Appuhn. Dortmund 1990 (=
Die bibliophilen Taschenbücher 1001), vol.5, fol. 130
▼

632   1390–1400

Vienna, Österreichische Nationalbibliothek,
cod. 2760, I Kings (6), fol.116
Wenceslas Bible
ILLUMINATION (Prague)
Crane with treadwheel and external lewis, ladder,
mortar-mixing pick, hod, wheelbarrow
Neuwirth, Josef: *Geschichte der bildenden Kunst in*
Böhmen. Prague 1893, vol.I, pl.II; *Wenzels Bibel.*
Erläutert von Horst Appuhn. Dortmund 1990 (= Die
bibliophilen Taschenbücher 1001), vol.5, fol. 116

▶

633   1390–1400

Vienna, Österreichische Nationalbibliothek,
cod. 2760, II Kings (6), fol.156
Wenceslas Bible
ILLUMINATION (Prague)
Broad axe, wooden trestle with dog or staple
Bi/Nu 220; Le Goff, p.562, fig.148; Husa, fig.86;
Wenzels Bibel. Erläutert von Horst Appuhn. Dortmund
1990 (= Die bibliophilen Taschenbücher 1001), vol.5,
fol. 156

▼

633a   1390–1400

Vienna, Österreichische Nationalbibliothek,
cod. 2760, I Chronicles (22), fol.27
Wenceslas Bible
ILLUMINATION (Prague)
Trowel, hod
Wenzels Bibel. Erläutert von Horst Appuhn. Dortmund
1990 (= Die bibliophilen Taschenbücher 1001), vol.6,
fol. 27

634   1390–1400

Vienna, Österreichische Nationalbibliothek,
cod. 2761, fol.38
Wenceslas Bible, third part
ILLUMINATION (Prague)
Broad axe, hammer
Bi/Nu 221; Husa, fig.97
(extract)

▶

634a   1390–1400

Vienna, Österreichische Nationalbibliothek,
cod. 2761, II Chronicles (8), fol.44v
Wenceslas Bible
ILLUMINATION (Prague)
Ramp, mortar-mixing pick, hod
Wenzels Bibel. Erläutert von Horst Appuhn. Dortmund
1990 (= Die bibliophilen Taschenbücher 1001), vol.7, fol. 44

▶

634b   1390–1400

Vienna, Österreichische Nationalbibliothek,
cod. 2761, I Ezra (5), fol.86
Wenceslas Bible
ILLUMINATION (Prague)
Scaffolding, hammer, ladder
Wenzels Bibel. Erläutert von Horst Appuhn. Dortmund
1990 (= Die bibliophilen Taschenbücher 1001), vol.7,
fol. 86

634c   c.1460

Vienna, Österreichische Nationalbibliothek,
cod. 2771, fol.49v
Bible stories of Evert van Sondenbalch
ILLUMINATION (Utrecht)
Work table, kiln, shoulder basket, brick mould
Pächt & Thoss, fig.83

▼

634d c.1460

Vienna, Österreichische Nationalbibliothek,
cod. 2771, fol.189v
Bible stories of Evert van Sondenbalch
ILLUMINATION (Utrecht)
Crane with treadwheel, mortar tub, mortar shovel,
hod, stand for hod, pointed stone hammer
Schöller, p.100, no.121; Pächt, Jenni, fig.100

▼

635 c.1445–50

Vienna, Österreichische Nationalbibliothek,
cod. 2773, fol.43
Guido de Columnis, The Trojan War
ILLUMINATION (Martinus Opifex, Vienna)
Scaffolding, crane, hod, one-legged stool, pointed
stone hammer
Kühnel, Harry (ed.): *Alltag im*
Spätmittelalter. Graz, Vienna &
Cologne 1984, fig.335

▶

634e c.1460

Vienna, Österreichische Nationalbibliothek,
cod. 2771, fol.257v
Bible stories of Evert van Sondenbalch
ILLUMINATION (Utrecht)
Scaffolding, hammer, mallet, basket, ladder,
plumbline, mortar-mixing pick, mortar shovel, hod,
stand for hod, chisel
Schöller, p.100, no.122 * p.88, fig.9; Pächt, Jenni,
fig.136

▶

636   1397–8
Vienna, Österreichische Nationalbibliothek,
cod. 2921, fol.38
Jansen Enenkel, *Weltchronik*
PEN-AND-INK DRAWING (Austria)
Crane with lewis, mortar tub, mortar-mixing pick,
one-legged stool
Bi/Nu 222; Miinkowski, pic. 33

▶

637   second half 14th century
Vienna, Österreichische Nationalbibliothek,
cod. series nova 2612, fol.36v
Speculum humanae salvationis
ILLUMINATION (upper Austria)
Scaffolding, hammer, trowel, ladder, mortar tub, hod
Bi/Nu 215; Minkowski, pic. 29; Schultz I, pl.1

▼

637a   1334–43
Vienna, Österreichische Nationalbibliothek,
cod. series nova 2639, fol.35v
Convenvola da Prato
ILLUMINATION
Square, compasses
Tezmen-Siegel, Jutta: *Die Darstellungen der septem*
artes liberales in der bildenden Kunst als Rezeption der
Lehrplangeschichte. Munich 1985 (= tuduv-Studie,
Reihe Kunstgeschichte 14), fig.37

▶

639   mid-15th century
Vienna, Österreichische Nationalbibliothek,
cod. series nova 12883, fol.110v
Speculum humanae salvationis
PEN-AND-INK DRAWING (southern Germany?)
Tub, scaffolding, trowel, crane, arch-shaped training
template
Kühnel, Harry: *Alltag im Spätmittelalter.* Graz, Vienna &
Cologne 1984, fig.15

▶

638   second quarter 12th century
Vienna, Österreichische Nationalbibliothek,
cod. series nova 2701, fol.249
Admont Great Bible
ILLUMINATION (Salzburg)
Broad axe
Bi/Nu 58; Binding (1972), fig.on
p.67 (outline); Baldass, Peter P.
von, Buchowiecki, Walther, &
Marzek, Wilhelm: *Romanische*
Kunst in Österreich. Vienna
1962, fig.43; Gutbrod, Jürgen:
Die Initiale in Handschriften des
8.–13. Jahrhunderts. Stuttgart
1965, p.151, fig.97

▶

640   second half 14th century

Vienna-Lainz, Bibliothek der Jesuitenresidenz,
MS 60, fol.1
Aegidius Columna, *De regimine principum*
ILLUMINATION
(France)
Trowel, ladder, hod, pointed stone hammer
Bi/Nu 224; Tietze,
p.37, fig.44   ▶

641   c.1340

Wolfenbüttel, Herzog-August-Bibliothek,
cod. Guelf. 8 Aug. 4°, fol.17
Rudolf von Ems, *Weltchronik*
ILLUMINATION (Bohemia)
Trowel, crane with treadwheel, crane with windlass, ladder, mortar tub, mortar-mixing pick, mortar shovel, hod, one-legged stool, pointed stone hammer, square
▼

642   end 14th century

Wolfenbüttel, Herzog-August-Bibliothek,
cod. Guelf. 1.5.2. Aug. 2°, fol.23v
Heinrich von München, Middle High German
Weltchronik
ILLUMINATION (Bavaria or Austria)
Scaffolding, crane, mortar tub, mortar shovel, pointed stone hammer
Milde, Wolfgang: *Mittelalterliche Handschriften der Herzog-August-Bibliothek*. Frankfurt am Main 1972, p.176, fig.87; Schöller (1987), p.100, no.124 * p.86, fig.7
▼

642a   end 13th century
Wolfenbüttel, Herzog-August-Bibliothek,
62. Gud. lat. 20, fol.60v
Martianus Capella, *De nuptiis Philologiae et Mercurii*
ILLUMINATION
Compasses
Schöller, p.100, no.125; Wirth, Karl-August: 'Eine illustrierte Martianus-Capella-Handschrift aus dem 13. Jahrhundert', in *Städel-Jahrbuch* NF 2, 1969, p.47, fig.6
▼

644   mid-15th century
Worcestershire, Great Malvern priory church
Window in south aisle of nave
STAINED GLASS
Compasses
Zahlten, Johannes: *Creatio mundi. Darstellungen der sechs Schöpfungstage und naturwissenschaftliches Weltbild im Mittelalter*. Stuttgart 1979 (= Stuttgarter Beiträge zur Geschichte und Politik, vol.13), fig.289
▼

646   c.1280–1300
Xanten, Cathedral of St Viktor
Console of a statue on pillar in choir
ARCHITECTURAL SCULPTURE
Mallet, chisel
Bi/Nu 275; Gerstenberg, fig.on p.166; Klapheck, Richard: *Der Dom zu Xanten und seine Kunstschätze*. Berlin 1941, p.49, fig.21
▼

643   12th century
Worcester, Cathedral
South transept
ARCHITECTURAL SCULPTURE
Compasses
Bi/Nu 59; Du Colombier, p.101, fig.60
▼

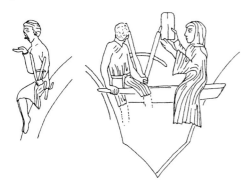

645   c.1300
Xanten, Cathedral of St Viktor
Door console, upper level
ARCHITECTURAL SCULPTURE
Chisel, pointed stone hammer
Bi/Nu 276; Gerstenberg, p.13, fig.e
▼

647   c.1220–30
York, Yorkshire Museum
Fragment of gravestone of St William (formerly in the Minster, central nave)
RELIEF
Mallet, chisel
Morris, Richard: *Cathedrals and Abbeys of England and Wales*. London, Toronto & Melbourne 1979, p.65
▼

648 c.1200
Zürich, Großmünster
Filling of a vault spandrel, west wing of the crossing
ARCHITECTURAL SCULPTURE
Mallet, chisel
Bi/Nu 61; Binding (1972), fig.on p.55 (outline);
Gerstenberg, fig.on p.164
▼

648a end 15th century
Zürich, Schweizerisches Landesmuseum
Diebold Schilling, *Luzerner Chronik*
ILLUMINATION
Scaffolding, trowel, ladder, mortar-mixing bin,
mortar-mixing pick, hod, stand for hod
Scheidegger, Fritz: *Aus der Geschichte der Bautechnik.*
Basle 1990, p.148, fig.91
▼

648b c.1500
Zürich, Schweizerisches Landesmuseum
Wall painting from the former Jakobskapelle of the
Augustinian church in Zürich
FRESCO
Mallet, crane with lewis, chisel
Wüthrich, Lucas: *Wandgemälde. Von Müstair bis*
Hodler. Katalog der Sammlung des Schweizerischen
Landesmuseums Zürich. Zürich 1980
▼

649 c.1470
Zürich, Zentralbibliothek,
MS A 120, fol.13
Bendicht Tschachtlan, *Berner Chronik*
ILLUMINATION
Scaffolding, crane with treadwheel and external
lewis, mortar tub
Tschachtlan, Berner Chronik 1470. Bearbeitet von H.
Bloesch, L. Forrer und P. Hiller. Geneva & Zürich 1933,
pl.2
▼

650 c.1470
Zürich, Zentralbibliothek,
MS A 120, fol.32
Bendicht Tschachtlan, *Berner Chronik*
ILLUMINATION
Broad axe, wooden pile-driving hammer
Tschachtlan, Berner Chronik 1470. Bearbeitet von H.
Bloesch, L. Forrer und P. Hiller. Geneva & Zürich 1933,
pl.8
◄

650a   15th century
Zürich, Zentralbibliothek,
MS C 5, fol.17
Bible stories
COLOURED PEN-AND-INK DRAWING
Crane with lewis, mortar tub, mortar-mixing bin,
mortar-mixing pick, square

▼

651   1340–50
Zürich, Zentralbibliothek,
Cod. Rh. 15, fol.6v
Rudolf von Ems, *Weltchronik*
ILLUMINATION (Upper Rhine, with French influence)
Scaffolding, trowel, crane with treadwheel and
hook, crane with treadwheel and external lewis,
mortar tub, mortar-mixing bin, mortar-mixing pick,
hod, one-legged stool, square, stone hammer
Bi/Nu 226; Tyghem, fig.64; Minkowski, pic. 22; Dürst,
Hans: *Rittertum. Schweizerische Dokumente –*
Hochadel im Aargau. Schloß Lenzburg im Aargau 1964,
p.81, fig.68 (= Dokumente zur Aargauischen
Kulurgeschichte 2)

▶

SUPPLEMENT

652   1476
Basle, Bernhard Richel, printer
Speculum humanae salvationis, fol.138v
WOODCUT
Beaker, scaffolding, trowel, ladder, hod
Bi/Nu 72; Schramm 21, no.185; Minkowski, pic. 79
▼

652a   1486
Germany
WOODCUT
Trowel, mallet, ladder, mortar tub, mortar-mixing
pick, mortar shovel, hod, chisel, pointed stone
hammer, water jug, square, compasses
Vetter, André, & Lamothe, Marie-José: *Das Buch vom*
Werkzeug. Geneva 1979, fig.on p.370
                                             ▶

652b   14th century
London, Courtauld Institute
Bible
Compasses
Gimpel, Jean: *Les bâtisseurs des Cathédrales*. Bourges
1976, fig.on p.32

653   1483

Lyon, Guillaume Le Roy, printer
Aeneid
WOODCUT
Trowel, crane, pointed stone hammer
Claudin, A.: *Histoire de l'imprimerie en France au XVe et XVIe siècle*. Paris 1901, vol.3, fig.on p.52
▼

654   1483

Lyon, Guillaume Le Roy, printer
Aeneid
WOODCUT
Ladder, pointed stone hammer
Claudin, A.: *Histoire de l'imprimerie en France au XVe et XVIe siècle*. Paris 1901, vol.3, fig.on p.53
▼

655   1491

Lyon, Jean du Pré, printer
La Mer des Hystoires
WOODCUT
Tub, trowel, mallet, crane, chisel
Claudin, A.: *Histoire de l'imprimerie en France au XVe et XVIe siècle*. Paris 1901, vol.3, fig.on p.499
Free copy of a woodcut from the workshop of Pierre Le Roy
▼

656   1491

Lyon, Jean du Pré, printer
La Mer des Hystoires
WOODCUT
Broad axe, crane, serrated stone hammer
Claudin, A.: *Histoire de l'imprimerie en France au XVe et XVIe siècle*. Paris 1901, vol.3, fig.on p.499
Free copy of a woodcut from the workshop of Pierre Le Roy
▼

657   1486

Paris, L'Image Saint-Christophe, printer
Livre des ruraulz prouffitz du labour des champs
WOODCUT
Pointed stone hammer
Claudin, A.: *Histoire de l'imprimerie en France au XVe
et XVIe siècle*. Paris 1901, vol.1, fig.on p.192

658   1468

Paris, Pierre Levet, printer
Pierre des Crescens, *Proufitz champestres et ruraulx*
WOODCUT
Ladder, pointed stone hammer, pointed pick
Claudin, A.: *Histoire de l'imprimerie en France au XVe
et XVIe siècle*. Paris 1901, vol.1, fig.on p.426

659   1488

Paris, Pierre Le Rouge, printer
La Mer des Hystoires, fol.176v
WOODCUT
Basket, crane with windlass, ladder, hod, pannier
Bi/Nu 285b; Kunze, Horst: *Geschichte der
Buchillustration in Deutschland. Das 15. Jahrhundert.*
Leipzig 1975, fig.on p.284 (text vol.)
The second French impression of this work appeared in
1491 at the works of Jean du Pré

660, 661   1488
Paris, Pierre Le Rouge, printer
La Mer des Hystoires, fol.176v
WOODCUT
Crane, crane with windlass, pointed stone hammer,
pointed pick, level
Claudin, A.: *Histoire de l'imprimerie en France au XVe*
et XVIe siècle. Paris 1901, vol.1, fig.on p.465
▼ ▼

662, 663   1488
Paris, Pierre Le Rouge, printer
La Mer des Hystoires, fol.176v
WOODCUT
Crane, hod, shovel, wheelbarrow, pointed stone
hammer
Claudin, A.: *Histoire de l'imprimerie en France au XVe*
et XVIe siècle. Paris 1901, vol.1, fig.on p.465
▼ ▼

664   1476
Paris, unknown printer
Valère Maxime
WOODCUT
Pointed stone hammer
Claudin, A.: Histoire de l'imprimerie en France au XVe
et XVIe siècle. Paris 1901, vol.2, figs on pp.200–01
▼

665   14th century

Toulouse, Bibliothèque,

MS 512, fol.96

French manuscript, *Grandes Chroniques de Saint-Denis*

ILLUMINATION

Bucket, scaffolding, mallet, crane, ladder, mortar tub, mortar-mixing pick, level, chisel, pointed stone hammer, pannier, hawk, square

Gimpel (1985), fig.on p.37

▶

665b   14th century

Paris, Bibliothèque Nationale

Bible stories

Trowel, ladder, pointed stone hammer, hawk

Gimpel, Jean: Les bâtisseurs des Cathédrales. Paris 1980, fig.on p.47

▼

665a   1337

Paris, Bibliothèque Nationale

Romance of Gottfried of Bouillon

ILLUMINATION

Trowel, ladder, hod

Erlande-Brandenburg, Alain: Triumph der Gotik. Munich 1988, fig.171

▼

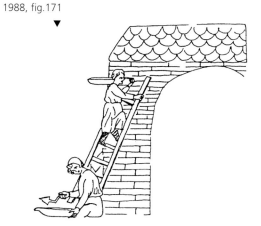

665c   c.1379

Paris, Bibliothèque Nationale

Grandes Chroniques de France

ILLUMINATION

Trowel, hod, pointed stone hammer

Gimpel (1980), fig.on p.36

▶

665d   mid-15th century

Paris, Bibliothèque de l'Arsenal

ILLUMINATION

Broad axe, roofing axe, bucket, trowel, ladder, mortar shovel, long-handled drill, hawk

Brochard, Philippe, & Pernod, Régine: So lebten sie in den Burgen des Mittelalters. Burgen und Festungen in Europa (no details)

▶

665f   1473

France

ILLUMINATION

Mallet, crane, ladder, frame saw, long-handled drill

Vetter, André, & Lamothe, Marie-José: Das Buch vom Werkzeug. Geneva 1979, fig.on p.133

666, 667   15th century

Radziwill Chronicle

ILLUMINATION

Axe

Donnert, Erich: Das Kiewer Rußland. Leipzig 1983, figs on pp.96, 137

The whereabouts of this manuscript are unknown

▼ ▼

665e   mid-15th century

Paris, Bibliothèque de l'Arsenal

ILLUMINATION

Broad axe, scaffolding, trowel, ramp, ladder, mortar shovel, hawk

Brochard, Philippe, & Pernod, Régine: So lebten sie in den Burgen des Mittelalters. Burgen und Festungen in Europa (no details), fig.on p.18

▶

668, 669   15th century
Radziwill Chronicle
ILLUMINATION
Hatchet, stone hammer
Donnert, Erich: Das Kiewer Rußland. Leipzig 1983, figs
on pp.159, 162
The whereabouts of this manuscript are unknown

▼   ▼

670   14th century
France
ILLUMINATION
Drill, broad axe, mallet, crane
Förster, Rolf Hellmut: Das Leben in der Gotik. Munich
1969, fig.on p.148

◀

671   15th century
France
ILLUMINATION
*Bucket, mallet, engraver's chisel, chisel, pointed
stone hammer*
Delort, Robert: Life in the Middle Ages. London 1974,
fig.on p.34

▶

672   15th century
France
ILLUMINATION
*Scaffolding, trowel, crane with windlass, ladder, hod,
drawing pins, level, pointed stone hammer*
Bi/Nu 287; Harvey, frontispiece

▼

672a   15th century
Flanders
ILLUMINATION
Scaffolding, ladder, hod, pointed stone hammer
Guiffrey, J.: 'La Guerre de Troie', in Revue de l'Art,
1899, p.206

673   15th century
Czech Republic
ILLUMINATION
*Scaffolding, trowel, crane, ramp, mortar tub,
wheelbarrow, pointed stone hammer, pannier*
Bi/Nu 281; Tyghem, fig.128; Chytil, Karel: Vyvoj
miniaturího malírství českého za dobý králu rodu
zagellonského. Prague 1896, p.17, fig.10

▼

LIST OF REFERENCE WORKS ABBREVIATED IN THE TEXT

Andrews, Francis B. *The Mediaeval Builder and his Methods*. Wakefield, Ottawa, 1974 (reprinted from original of 1925)

Aubert, Marcel. 'La construction au moyen âge' in *Bulletin monumental de la Société française d'archéologie*, 118, 119 (1960–1)

Binding, Günther, and Nußbaum, Norbert. *Der mittelalterliche Baubetrieb nördlich der Alpen in zeitgenössischen Darstellungen*, Darmstadt, 1978

Binding, Günther (ed.). *Romanischer Baubetrieb in zeitgenössischen Darstellungen*, Cologne, 1972 (2nd publication of the Architecture Department of the Institute for Art History of the University of Cologne)

Binding, Günther (ed.). Beiträge über Bauführung und Baufinanzierung im Mittelalter, Cologne, 1974 (6th publication of the Architecture Department of the Institute for Art History of the University of Cologne)

Binding, Günther. 'Der romanische Baubetrieb' in *Rhein und Maas. Kunst und Kultur 800–1400*, exhibition catalogue, Cologne, 1972 (vol.1, pp. 93–5)

Binding, Günther. 'Baumeister und Handwerker im Baubetrieb' in *Ornamenta Ecclesiae*, exhibition catalogue, Cologne, 1985 (vol.1, pp. 171–83)

Boesch, Paul (ed.). *Diebold Schilling, Spiezer Bilderchronik 1485. Nach dem Original der Stadt- und Hochschulbibliothek Bern, anläßlich der 6. Jahrhundertfeier der Schlacht bei Laupen*, Geneva, 1939

Brandt, Paul. *Schaffende Arbeit und bildende Kunst*, 2 vols, Leipzig, 1927–8

Coldstream, Nicola. *Masons and Sculptors*, London, 1991 (Medieval Craftsmen)

Du Colombier, Pierre. *Les chantiers des cathédrales*, Paris, 1973

Evans, Joan. *Das Leben in mittelalterlichen Frankreich*, Cologne, 1960

Friederich, Karl. *Die Steinarbeitung in ihrer Entwicklung vom 11. bis 18. Jahrhundert*, Augsburg, 1932

Gerstenberg, Kurt. *Die deutschen Baumeisterbildnisse des Mittelalters*, Berlin, 1966

Gimpel, Jean. *Les bâtisseures des cathédrales*, Paris, 1985

Grote, Andreas. *Der vollkommene Architechtus. Baumeister und Baubetrieb bis zum Anfang der Neuzeit*, Munich, 1959 (Grote, Ludwig (ed.). *Bibliothek des Germanischen National-Museums Nürnberg zur deutschen Kunst- und Kulturgeschichte*, vol.13)

Harvey, John. *The Mediaeval Architect*, London, 1972

Harvey, John. *The Mediaeval Craftsman*, London & Sydney, 1975

Hecht, Konrad. 'Maß und Zahl in der gotischen Baukunst 1–3' in *Abhandlungen der Braunschweigischen Wissenschaftlichen Gesellschaft* 21, 1969 (1970), pp. 215–326; 22, 1970 (1972), pp. 105–263; 23, 1971 (1973), pp. 25–236

Hermann, Hermann Julius. *Die westeuropäischen Handschriften*: 1. *Englische und Französische Handschriften des 13. Jahrhunderts*; 2. *Englische und Französische Handschriften des 14. Jahrhunderts*; 3. *Französische und Iberische Handschriften der 1. Hälfte des 15. Jahrhunderts*, Leipzig, 1938 (*Beschreibendes Verzeichnis der illuminierten Schriften in Österreich*, new series, ed. Julius Schlosser and Hermann Julius Hermann, vol.8, 7)

Husa, Václav. *Homo Faber. Der Mensch und seine Arbeit. Die Arbeitswelt in der bildenden Kunst des 11. bis 17. Jahrhunderts*, Prague, 1971

Jacobi, Franz. *Studium zur Geschichte der Bayerischen Miniaturen*, Strasbourg, 1908 (*Studien zur deutschen Kunstgeschichte* 102)

Kirchner, Joachim. *Die Philipps-Handschriften*, Leipzig, 1926 (*Beschreibende Verzeichnisse er Miniaturen-Handschriften der Preußischen Staatsbibliothek*, vol.1)

Klemm, Friedrich. *Handwerk und Technik vergangener Jahrhunderte*, Tübingen, 1958

Kühnel, Harry (ed.) *Alltag im Spätmittelalter*, Graz, Vienna and Cologne, 1984

Laborde, Alexandre Comte de. *La Bible moralisée conservée à Oxford, Paris et Londres*, Paris, 1911–27

Le Goff, Jacques. *Kultur des europäischen Mittelalters*, Frankfurt-am-Main, Vienna and Zürich, 1972

Leroqais, Victor. *Les livres d'heures. Manuscrits de la Bibliothèque Nationale*, 2 vols, Paris, 1927

Meiss, Millard, Lougnon, Jean, and Cazelle, Raymond. *Die 'Très Riches Heures' des Jean Duc de Berry im Musée Condé Chantilly*, Munich, 1973

Meiss, Millard. *French Painting in the Time of Jean de Barry. The Limbourgs and their contemporaries*, vol.3, New York, 1974

Minkowski, Helmut. *Aus dem Nebel der Vergangenheit steigt der Turm zu Babel*, Berlin, 1960

Muschg, Walter, and Gessler, E.A. *Die Schweizer Bilderchroniken des 15. und 16. Jahrhunderts*, Zürich, 1941

Oechselhäuser, Adolf von. *Die Miniaturen der Universitätsbibliothek zu Heidelberg*, vol.2, Heidelberg, 1895

Pächt, Otto, Jenni, U., and Thoss, Dagmar. *Die illuminierten Handschriften und Inkunabeln der Österreichischen Nationalbibliothek VI, Flämische Schule I*, Vienna, 1983 (Österreichische Akademie der Wissenschaften, Phil.-Hist. Klasse, Denkschriften, vol.160)

Pächt, Otto, and Thoss, Dagmar. *Die illuminierten Handschriften und Inkunabeln der Österreichischen Nationalbibliothek I, Französische Schule*, Vienna, 1974 (Österreichische Akademie der Wissenschaften, Phil.-Hist. Klasse, Denkschriften, vol.188)

Pächt, Otto, und Jenni, U. *Die illuminierten Handschriften und Inkunabeln der Österreichischen Nationalbibliothek III, Holländische Schule*, Vienna, 1975 (Österreichische Akademie der Wissenschaften, Phil.-Hist. Klasse, Denkschriften, vol.124)

Philippi, F. *Atlas zur weltlichen Altertumskunde des deutschen Mittelalters*, Bonn and Leipzig, 1924

Randall, Lilian M.C. *Images in the Margins of Gothic Manuscripts*, Berkeley, Los Angeles, 1966

Recht, Roland (ed.). *Les bâtisseurs des cathédrales gothiques*, catalogue, Strasbourg, 1989

Scheidig, Walter. *Der Miniaturenzyklus zur Weltchronik Ottos von Freising im Codex Jenensis Bose*, q.6, Strasbourg, 1928

Schöller, Wolfgang. 'Ein Katalog mittelalterlicher Baubetriebsdarstellungen' in *Technikgeschichte* 54, 1987 (2), pp. 77–100

Schramm, A. *Der Bilderschmuck der Frühdrucke*, 23 vols, Leipzig, 1922–43

Schultz, Alwin. *Deutsches Leben im 14. und 15. Jahrhundert*, 2 vols., Prague, Vienna and Leipzig, 1892

Smidt, Firmin de. *Enkele XIIIde-Eeuwse Steenhouwersmerken in de Sint-Niklaaskerk te Gent*, Brussels, 1974 (*Medelingen van de Koninglijke Vlaamse Academie voor Wetenschappen, Letteren en Schone Kunsten van België. Klasse de Schone Kunsten*, vol.36 (1974), no. 4

Thoss, Dagmar. *Das Epos des Burgunderreiches. Girat de Roussillon. Codex 2549 der Österreichischen Nationalbibliothek in Wien*, Graz, 1989

Tietze, Hans. *Die illuminierten Handschriften der Rossiana in Wien-Lainz*, Leipzig, 1911 (*Beschreibendes Verzeichnis der illustrierten Handschriften in Österreich*, ed. Franz Wickhoff, continued by Max Dvořák, vol.V)

Treue, Wilhelm. *Das Hausbuch der Mendelschen Zwölfbrüderstiftung zu Nürnberg*, Munich, 1965

Tyghem, Frieda van. *Op en om de Middelewse Bouwerf*, Brussels, 1966 (*Verhandelingen van de Koninglijke Vlaamse Academie voor Wetenschappen, Letteren en Schone Kunsten van België. Klasse de Schone Kunsten*, vol.28, no. 19)

INDEX

ACKNOWLEDGEMENTS

Most of the drawings were prepared by Angelika Steinmetz-Oppelland and Martina Schönenborn, either from illustrations in the works cited in the text or from photographs kindly supplied by libraries or museums. We would like to thank the following institutions in particular:

Antwerp, Koninklijke Museum voor Schone Kunsten (no.7)
Antwerp, Museum van den Bergh (no.8)
Berlin, Staatlichen Museen, Preußischer Kulturbesitz (no.72)
Brussels, Bibliothèque Royale (nos 101, 103, 104, 105, 109)
The Hague, Mauritshuis (no.152)
The Hague, Rijksmuseum Meermanno-Westreenianum (no.154)
Geneva, Bibliothèque de Genève (no.184)
London, British Museum (nos 250, 276a)
Macon, Bibliothèque de la Ville (no.298)
Manchester, John Rylands Library (no.315b)
New York, Pierpont Morgan Library (no.404c)
Paris, Bibliothèque de l'Arsenal (no.420)
Paris, Bibliothèque Nationale (nos 440, 462, 466, 470)
Waddesdon Manor, Rothschild Collection (nos 601a, 601b)

If you are interested in purchasing
other books published by Tempus, or in case you have
difficulty finding any Tempus books in your local bookshop,
you can also place orders directly through our website

www.tempus-publishing.com

or from

BOOKPOST
Freepost, PO Box 29,
Douglas, Isle of Man
IM99 1BQ
Tel 01624 836000
email bookshop@enterprise.net